CHURCH AND ~~STATE~~

245

Essays in Political Philosophy

First published in 1984 by
Cork University Press, University College, Cork

Second impression 1985

Copyright © Cork University Press 1984

British Library Cataloguing in Publication Data
Clarke, Desmond M.
  Church and State: essays in political philosophy.
  1. Church and state — Ireland
  I. Title
  332'.1'09417   BR796.3

  ISBN 0-902561-29-4
  ISBN 0-902561-30-8 Pbk

Printed in the Republic of Ireland by Tower Books,
86 South Main St., Cork

Church and State
Essays in Political Philosophy

For Ann,
who asks good questions

Contents

Acknowledgements

Some of the initial work on various parts of this project was supported by a grant from the Arts Faculty, University College, Cork, in 1980. During the academic year 1982-83, I enjoyed the hospitality of the Philosophy Department at the University of Notre Dame, Indiana, where the final draft was completed. My travel to the U.S. was partly financed by a grant from the Scholarship Exchange Board, Dublin. Finally, publication of the manuscript was supported by a grant from the National University of Ireland. I gratefully acknowledge the support and financial assistance of these institutions.

Earlier versions of some of the arguments used here appeared in the following publications: 'Emergency Legislation, Fundamental Rights, and Article 28.3.3 of the Irish Constitution', *The Irish Jurist,* XII (1977), 217-233; 'The Concept of the Common Good in Irish Constitutional Law', *Northern Ireland Legal Quarterly*, (Winter, 1979), 319-342; 'Equality of Opportunity and Public Financing of Higher Education', *Studies,* Autumn/Winter (1980), 226-238; and 'The Role of Natural Law in Irish Constitutional Law', *The Irish Jurist*, XVII (1982), 187-200. I am grateful to the editors concerned who gave these arguments their first public appearance.

My thanks also to the Committee and staff of Cork University Press, and to their anonymous referee for helpful comments in preparing the manuscript for publication; and to the Catholic Press and Information Office, Dublin, who generously supplied copies of various public statements of the Roman Catholic Hierarchy during recent years.

Desmond M. Clarke
May 1, 1984

Introduction

'We know, and what is better, we feel inwardly, that religion is the basis of civil society and the source of all good and of all comfort.'

Edmund Burke, *Reflections on the Revolution in France*[1]

Burke gives the impression of someone who is absolutely certain of his views, and he seems to base them on his feelings of moral outrage towards opponents. This is a fair reflection of one tradition in Irish political and religious thinking which is still accepted, if only implicitly, by many politicians and their supporters in the electorate. It also coincides with the spirit of many interventions of the Roman Catholic Church in Irish politics in the twentieth century. The essays in this book explain and defend a position which is the exact opposite to that of Burke. They rely on reason, rather than inner feeling or faith; and they argue for the separation of civil government from religious institutions.

All the essays depend, in one way or another, on some concept of the *autonomy* of the individual — in relation to others, to institutions of the state, and to the churches.[2] The explanation of autonomy and the definition of its limits may seem like a purely academic exercise, if we cannot deliver the kind of certainty which Burke claimed for his project. Nevertheless, philosophy does not claim to compete with the certainty, and in some cases the arrogance, of religious teachers and political ideologies. It can only offer to examine alternative theories and to point out their practical and theoretical implications. Besides, the admission of fallibility may persuade those who suffer from a surfeit of certainties to reflect on the political situation in Ireland from a different perspective which has not been adequately explored.

The autonomy of the individual is a basic assumption in contemporary moral and political theory. It is partly inspired by traditional theories of

11

free will, but it can be described and defended even by those who are shy of such metaphysical speculation. Without some assumption like this, it is impossible to maintain our usual understanding of moral responsibility and moral actions at all.

To speak of an individual as autonomous is to claim that he acts without being subject to external control. We say that one person or institution 'controls' another, when the preferences or desires of one causally determine the decisions and actions of the other. Autonomy, then, is a form of independence or self-determination. The autonomous individual is one who is motivated by his own beliefs, desires or values; he is one who rationally formulaes his own life-plan and implements it without external constraints from others. In other words, to be autonomous is to be free from external controlling influences, and to decide one's actions in the light of one's own values and beliefs. In this sense, autonomy is not a simple fact about someone which remains unchanged; rather, it is a capacity which needs to be cultivated. An individual may be said to be more or less autonomous.

One might be tempted to re-define autonomy in such a way that what remains is only a metaphysical shadow of a real flesh and blood individual. The standard way of doing this is to say that a person is 'controlled' by his own desires or appetites, and not only by those of others; these desires are said to encroach on his freedom of action, so that even when he seems to be acting freely he is not 'truly free'. True freedom, on this analysis, is only realized when the 'inner self' completely dominates wayward desires. The implicit distinction between legitimate and illegitimate desires, which is assumed in this version of autonomy, presupposes that we already have a moral theory in order to make this kind of distinction. Thus, those who claim to be privileged seers in moral debate would prefer to insert their theory of the good life into the very definition of autonomy, so that those who act contrary to some moral theory are, by definition, not acting autonomously.[3]

One notorious example of the manipulation of the concept of autonomy in favour of a controlled form of human behaviour is the theological account of Original Sin. According to this theory, human faculties are so weakened that they cannot function properly without the help of a power or force, called grace, which the Church makes available to believers. It follows that truly autonomous action is impossible for those who reject the help of the Church; what may appear to be autonomous behaviour is merely the control of duped individuals by their own passions. A more secular version of the same theory is to understand human behaviour as ultimately caused by a great variety of disparate factors, both internal and external to the agent, and to dissipate the concept of autonomy in the complexity of those determining influences.

Both the theological and secular re-definitions of autonomy are capable of cynical manipulation in the hands of those who exercise power over people. However, those who are motivated by benevolence are not beyond controlling people with an equal disregard for autonomy. For this reason, the churches are often perceived by those who suffer from their ministry as benignly motivated dictatorships. They specify for individuals how they ought to behave, and they justify their choice of values by reference to a central praesidium which authoritatively interprets the demands of a religious tradition. In exactly the same way, the secular equivalent of the churches identifies a political ideal or social programme which it believes, in its wisdom, to be 'in the best interests of the people'. In both cases the exercise of power, in the form of threats (e.g. of eternal damnation), manipulation (e.g. by indoctrination), and perhaps even physical coercion (e.g. by imprisoning political or theological dissidents), is the principal means by which even the benevolent oppressor hopes to control people. Whether or not an institution recognizes the value of individual autonomy, therefore, is much better seen by the way in which it treats individuals than by examining any philosophical or ideological tracts which it issues in defence of its behaviour. In fact, the more likely situation is that the awkward questions about autonomy are ignored, or at least they are given second place while pursuing the more important task of getting people to act as some institution would like them to act (whatever the implications for autonomy).

The basic assumption in the essays collected here is that the scope of individual autonomy should be as wide as possible while maintaining a similar degree of autonomy for others, and that the definition of autonomy should not determine in advance which moral rules we should accept. The reason for this is very simple: without the autonomous choices of individuals, we have no way of discovering what the moral law requires. In other words, there are two very different strategies or traditions available for constructing a moral/political theory. One is to claim that we already know the truth about these matters, and to define the individual's scope for free action in relation to the already accepted rules. This is the strategy which is common to most churches and totalitarian regimes. The alternative strategy is to concede as much freedom as possible to individuals, and then allow them to construct moral/political rules which are understood as conventions for facilitating their realization of basic human objectives. The two strategies may often issue in common rules, such as the rule against murder; however, the difference between the two approaches is still very important. The second approach is fundamentally characterized by the high value it puts on individual autonomy. The first approach, by contrast, is notorious for its compromise of autonomy in the interests of conformity to rules. There is a very wide ideological gap between the two approaches which is apparently impossible to reconcile. It is equally impossible to rationally choose between the two unless the options available are made sufficiently explicit.

Much of the difficulty in coming to grips with ideological differences derives from what might initially look like esoteric problems in theory of knowledge. Those who are honest enough to make their ideology explicit, however, cannot avoid the problem of explaining how they are so sure of the values they hold, and why they think they are justified in coaxing or forcing others to endorse the same values. Some of the issues which arise in this context are examined in Chapter I. I argue that there are no objective values available for inspection in some metaphysical space. Instead I suggest that one plausible way of understanding moral values, by analogy with Locke's contract in the *Second Treatise of Government*, is to think of moral rules as implicitly agreed conventions which autonomous agents are willing to endorse. In this approach to morality, there can be no moral rules without first assuming the autonomy of consenting individuals.

The same conclusion is defended in a complementary argument in Chapter 2. Irish political thought and Irish jurisprudence have been significantly influenced by the claim that there is a Natural Law available to any rational person who is willing to impartially examine moral questions, and that this natural law provides objective norms which are binding on all, irrespective of their religious affiliation.[4] This theory has also been preached by the Catholic Church as a solution to problems in sexual ethics. I argue for the opposite conclusion. The particular version of natural law theory which has been defended in Ireland is seriously defective. In fact, the Roman Catholic Church does not seem to accept that human reason, when left to its own resources, can discover the natural law at all. For that reason, religious faith — interpreted by a central authority — claims to provide the only reliable basis for deciding what the natural law demands. This combination of an unreliable reason, supported by religious faith, is hardly acceptable to those who depend on human reason for moral guidance.

The understanding of moral and political norms suggested in the first two chapters implies that fundamental disagreements are often unavoidable, even among people who share a common cultural and religious tradition. This gives rise to a serious problem of tolerance. How can one give principled support to some moral or religious tradition, and at the same time tolerate those who completely reject that tradition? In discussing the concepts of tolerance and pluralism, I argue that tolerance does not imply moral relativism. The question of tolerance only arises in any serious way for those who genuinely endorse a set of values, and then find themselves faced with defenders of alternative values. Chapter 3 examines the possibility of holding one set of values with conviction, and at the same time tolerating those who hold the opposite view. One of the main stumbling blocks to any progress on this question is the assumption of infallibility, whether implicitly assumed by stubborn supporters of some tradition, or explicitly claimed for theological reasons by a church.

The question of infallibility is directly addressed in the subsequent chapter, in which the theological thinking of one church is analysed to clarify its stance on religious liberty. I argue in Chapter 4 that the Roman Church is not committed to religious freedom, as this is normally understood in Western democracies. Religious freedom, as a basic right, is closely related to the concept of autonomy. Religious liberty is a right of individuals to non-interference, by any external power or institution, in the choice of religious beliefs or affiliation. It includes the right to reject all religions, including that proposed by the Catholic Church. The documents of the Second Vatican Council only appear to defend this right; in fact, they directly defend the right of the Church to preach and teach, and only by implication argue that civil authorities should not interfere in the individual's efforts to fulfil those religious duties which the Church imposes on him. The key to this interpretation is the Church's assumption that it has the power to compel individuals to perform those internal acts of belief and submission which civil powers are incompetent to deal with; and secondly, that civil authorities should foster religion by facilitating the work of the Catholic Church. It is abundantly clear that civil authorities cannot foster religion and at the same time mind their own business with respect to religious belief. The denial of religious freedom by the majority church, despite its rhetoric to the contrary, together with the assumption of infallibility in moral teaching, undermine one of the main supports for tolerance and pluralism in Ireland.

It should be clear from recent statements of the Catholic Hierarchy that they are not opposed to pluralism in principle, as long as pluralism is understood in a way which favours the majority church. Part of the difficulty in getting a clear picture of the Bishops' views on pluralism and religious liberty derives from their penchant for insinuating, rather than clearly stating, what they support and what they reject. For example, they reject pluralism if it is understood in terms of a caricature: 'The mere fact that some members of a society want or do not disapprove of something is not, of itself, sufficient reason for framing or changing the laws of that society to allow or not forbid it. Examples like "fraternities of friendly rapists or bigamists" within the society caricature this point, but make it nonetheless.'[5] There have been no serious calls for this nonsensical form of pluralism in Ireland in recent years, but the mere mention of it has the effect of suggesting that one's opponents defend something like that. However, even the caricature helps make an important point, but against the claims of the churches.

The mere fact that a religious group believes something or disapproves of something has no bearing at all on the desirability of corresponding legislation. This remains true even if a majority of the people in a given region share the same religious belief. The content of legislation has to be decided by reference to criteria or standards which prescind from the insoluble controversies about the truth of different religious traditions. The Catholic bishops appear to agree with this conclusion in their written submission to the New Ireland Forum; they agree that the legislature should not pass laws just because the Catholic Church approves or disapproves of something.[6] However, it is clear from the context that this is a comment on the *motivation* of the legislators, rather than on the content of the laws they should pass. For the bishops go on to say that the demands of the moral law are '*largely* accessible to human reason whose conclusions may well coincide with the teaching of the Catholic Church'.[7] In other words, since human reason is weak and unreliable, the truth about the moral law can be simply and easily learned from the Catholic Church. So we should not be surprised if the laws of a largely

Catholic community reflect Catholic values; nor should we apologize for this.

> A Catholic country or its government, where there is a very substantial Catholic ethos and consensus, should not feel it necessary to apologise that its legal system, Constitutional or Statute, reflects Catholic values. Such a legal system may sometimes be represented as offensive to minorities. But the rights of a minority are not more sacred than the rights of the majority.[8]

This is a classic example of confusing facts with values. No one who knows anything about the history of Europe is 'surprised' if the laws of different states reflect the religious values of the voting majority in each state. No one would be surprised if a society of religious believers, who believed that blood transfusions are seriously immoral, were to criminalize blood transfusions. Our degree of surprise, however, is hardly a criterion for constitutional legislation. The fundamental inspiration of pluralistic legal systems is that the rights of minorities are valued just as highly as the rights of majorities, and that the legal system should refrain, as much as possible, from enforcing values which are patently religious. Apparently, the Catholic Hierarchy in Ireland does not believe that most of the values they support are purely religious; they think that these values are supported by 'reason'. But this is usually the case with any religious group. Religious believers often assume that 'reason' supports their beliefs, even in the face of obvious dissent from rational people who share different religious views. The test of whether a belief is religious or not, is not what its supporters say about it. Rather, if accepting some belief systematically coincides with being a member of a church, then such a belief ultimately rests on religious faith. The Catholic Church's teaching about the morality of contraception is a clear example of this.

The rejection of religious liberty and of pluralism, as usually understood, makes for especially difficult problems in Chapter 5. This concerns enforcing moral and religious views by legislation. The overruling of the free choice of those who disagree with us, by legislation, is often justified by paternalism. I argue in Chapter 5 that, except in special circumstances, paternalism cannot be morally justified because it undermines the essential presupposition for any moral system, which is the autonomy of individuals. Those who wish to paternalistically control others' behaviour are assuming in themselves precisely what they deny in the case of others, namely, that we are autonomous agents who must freely, if at all, cooperate in the formulation and implementation of moral conventions. Legal coercion is usually justified to protect people from the ill-effects of others' behaviour. I argue that the actions which detrimentally affect others in the community do not coincide with those which traditional morality classified as immoral. The most obvious example of this in Ireland is population control. The privacy of human conception is irrelevant to answering the question: is this a *public* act, in Mill's sense of an action which directly affects the interests of others? Quite clearly, the decision to have children significantly affects other members of any community which has endorsed social policies to support the education and welfare of children. Therefore in drafting legislation to protect the interests of citizens, the state may be primarily concerned with population control rather than with the 'morality' of the behaviour by which children are conceived.[9]

The first five chapters argue that human conventions can successfully specify the most basic norms according to which individuals and societies ought to regulate their mutual interactions. The basic requirements of justice are often called human rights. In Chapter 6, I try to identify the procedures by which human rights are specified, and I examine the extent to which human rights, in this sense, are honoured in Irish constitutional law. The discussion is presented in the form of the standard conflict between individual rights and the 'common good'. The central contention of this chapter is that Irish political and legal traditions in the last sixty years are not agreed on any one concept of the common good, and that the phrase has been used in a variety of contexts to justify repressive legislation. In particular, I argue that the provisions of the Constitution which grant immunity to emergency legislation effectively undermine all the guarantees of individual rights which are mentioned in Articles 40-44 of the Constitution.

The next two chapters are concerned with education, both as a good in itself and as a formative influence on the beliefs of young people. As a good in its own right and, more obviously, as a means to realize other goods such as employment and its financial rewards, education is a limited commodity to which many unsuccessfully seek access. A question of justice arises, therefore, in evaluating the procedures used to determine access to education in Ireland. This is discussed under the heading of 'equality of opportunity'. Despite appearances to the contrary, those who demand equality of opportunity may be opposing a number of distinct features of our educational system which require independent analysis. Some of the issues in this debate are analysed in Chapter 7. I argue that, from the point of view of justice alone, those who are involved in primary education should be favoured over others in a context of limited financial resources. There may be good economic reasons for financing easier access to training and research at third level institutions, but these reasons are independent of considerations of equal opportunity. Likewise, there may be good reasons for eliminating the enormous disparities in income between those involved in equally demanding types of work, but again this issue is separate from equal opportunity requirements. Paradoxically, perhaps, I argue that the case for highly subsidized third-level education has not been established by arguments based on equality of opportunity.

The thesis of Chapter 8 is that the rights of children, in Ireland, to be educated without indoctrination are ignored by the collusion between the churches and the Department of Education in only making available exclusively religious schools in most parts of the country. The issues broached here hinge on such controversial problems as the separation of church and state, the non-endowment of religion, and the rights of young children to freedom of thought and expression. The only obvious explanation of why the churches have so strenuously opposed the rights of children to be free of religious indoctrination is that they are convinced that most adults will not join a church if the decision on joining is deferred until adulthood, when most other serious decisions are made. By contrast, if the young are sufficiently indoctrinated at an early age, then there is reason to hope that the non-rational assent of early years will survive into adulthood, at least under the guise of formal membership of a church. If the rights of children and parents were recognized, however, then non-denominational schools, with significant managerial input from parents, would be made available to all children, without prejudice to the obvious rights of any religious or non-religious group to own, operate and fund private schools.

The final chapter, on ideology, introduces some of the issues which have been encountered but deferred in earlier chapters. The extent to which our moral/political views are theories, and the extreme flexibility involved in bringing evidence to bear on justifying such theories, is discussed in the concluding chapter. This underlines the precarious status of many of the views expressed in the earlier chapters. One cannot remind those who disagree with one's views that they are treading on thin ice, without acknowledging the fact that we all share the same unsure footing. This admission has the advantage of involving disputing parties in a discussion which is acknowledged to be ideological. There is clearly no room here, at least according to earlier chapters, for anyone to take a stand and say: 'I have the truth and you better accept it whether you agree or not.' One of the reasons for using the term ideology, rather than the slightly more neutral term theory, to describe moral and political disputes, is that an ideology usually involves such a commitment to certain values that the ability of its proponents to see the validity of opposing positions is often seriously impaired. The theologically comprehensive worldview of Roman Catholics is an ideology in this sense, and it typically relies on indoctrination for its propagation. There is no transcendent perspective available to mere mortals from which we might impartially adjudicate the relative merits of alternative ideologies; and philosophy provides none either. Therefore all the discussions of basic, controversial issues about rights, justice, and the autonomy of individuals, can only be reasonably held in a context in which no one comes to the investigation with a prior assumption of infallibly certified truth. The most fundamental issues of justice, the autonomy of the individual, and the role of religious institutions in society are questions which can only be sensibly addressed by those who are conscious both of the limitations of any one theory and of the ideological context in which alternative options are endorsed.

1

Moral Conventions

It is characteristic of our use of simple and familiar words that we assume we understand them well as long as we have a fair amount of agreement in their use. Once disagreement arises, however, we need to look more carefully at our previous assumptions and to examine our ideas more self-consciously. The word 'moral' is familiar enough to give rise to exactly this illusion of clear understanding. For when people disagree in the moral opinions they hold, they often disagree also in what they mean by the idea of morality. There is ample room in this kind of situation for both disagreement and confusion.

Many of the issues which arise in later chapters presuppose agreement about what is meant by a 'moral' belief or conviction. It is no longer enough to be able to give examples of moral beliefs and to signal one's conviction with enthusiasm. One needs to look more critically at the concept of a 'moral' belief; to comment on the connection between moral beliefs and religious beliefs; and to take some stand on the so-called objectivity of moral or political claims, together with the implication that objective standards can be invoked to resolve disagreements. The results which are defended here will be put to use in subsequent chapters, where the tedium of the initial discussion might be eventually justified in retrospect.

The first question that needs to be broached is the claim that moral or political claims are, in some sense to be determined, objective.

Objectivity

In the case of serious disagreement about moral or political issues, the parties in dispute often appeal to 'objective' standards to settle the disagreement.[1] It is even more likely that each side will label its own view as objective as an alternative way of claiming that it is true or correct. And if they fail to reach agreement on whatever is at issue, they will often at least agree that what they disagree about can be objectively settled. Since the term 'objective' is so casually used by both sides, it would clarify the status of moral disagreements and, by implication, the status of moral claims generally if the meaning of 'objective' were less ambiguous.

In its standard usage, 'objective' is contrasted with 'subjective', and neither one of the terms is clear. 'Subjective' often means: whatever pertains exclusively to an individual human subject. Thus, expressions of likes or dislikes, impressions, feelings, attitudes, etc. are all subjective, insofar as they are conditions of an individual subject and do not exist apart from the subject in question. In another sense these are all objective, in that they are real conditions of an existing subject; but this only helps underline the fluidity of the distinction being made. We standardly use the term 'objective' in connection with things, events or states of affairs which are believed to exist independently of a conscious subject. In its paradigm use, a physical thing and its real properties are objective; and any claims one might make about these are objective claims.

'Objective' is not the same as 'true'. If I see a green bus parked outside my house and then report: 'there's a yellow taxi outside', my claim is both objective and false. It is because it purports to describe an objective state of affairs — and does so incorrectly — that we would say that the report is false. If two conflicting reports purport to describe the same objective state of affairs, then at least one of them is usually false. Whatever it is that is parked outside my door, it cannot both be and not be a bus at the same time.

'Subjective' reports may also be false; I can misdescribe or misreport how I feel about something, and everyone is familiar with the experience of simulating interest, enthusiasm or joy in a situation in which the opposite is genuinely felt. The mere fact that a claim or report is subjective does not preclude the possibility of its being true or false. Thus objective claims are not necessarily true, and subjective claims are not prevented from being true or false.

However, in the standard account of 'objective' and 'subjective', the interesting difference for ethics and politics is that two conflicting subjective reports may both be true. If I say: 'I love coffee' and if my neighbour says: 'I hate coffee', we may both truly report our respective likes and dislikes. Since both reports are true, there is no issue to be resolved between us. We disagree about drinking coffee, but our disagreement does not require any resolution, nor would it make any sense to try to determine which of us is 'right'. That question does not arise.

Many people approach moral and political disagreement on the assumption that it should be classified as either 'objective' or 'subjective' in the sense just described. If it is objective, then at least one of two incompatible views must be wrong, and the issue can be resolved (at least in principle) by consulting some objective criteria which are definitive.[2] If moral disagreement is subjective, then conflicting moral opinions are like expressions of like or dislike, approval or disapproval; in that case, there is no issue to be resolved between the two parties, and it makes no sense to even try to determine which side is right. The question of correct or right moral opinions does not arise.

It is generally accepted that moral beliefs cannot be described as subjective in this sense. If we had no other option available, we would have to conclude, therefore, that they are objective. I will argue, however, that moral beliefs are neither subjective nor objective in the sense just explained and that it is a mistake to force moral and political discourse into either side of this dichotomy.

Moral disagreement cannot be understood as purely subjective. If 'x is immoral' only means something like: 'I disapprove of x', then conflicting moral views are like conflicting expressions of like or dislike for coffee. If one person says: 'I disapprove of x' and another says, 'I approve of x', there is nothing further to be resolved between them. Each may guide his actions in accordance with his likes and dislikes, but neither one will make demands on the other that he modify his attitudes or change his approval or disapproval. However, in typical cases of moral belief, we expect that the reasons we have for disapproving of something should convince others to disapprove. We do not shrug our shoulders, rest our case and say simply: 'I don't favour torture too much and you do; we seem to disagree on this. Let's have another tea or coffee, whichever we prefer!' The subjective account fails to explain our anticipation, and in some cases our demand, that the moral opinions of others should coincide with our own. Therefore, when confronted by significant disagreement about important moral issues, we assume that one side or the other (or both) should change its moral beliefs.

There are equally strong objections to any objectivist account of moral discourse. If we imagine that there exist, independently of individual subjects, a whole complex of things and events — such as planets and their motions, buses, cabbages, the cycle of the seasons, etc. — and that among this series of objectively existing entities and events there are moral values, norms or principles, then we equally fail to account for moral discourse. On this assumption we could explain how incompatible moral views could not both be 'true'; we would just consult the objective principles and either one or both of the conflicting moral views would fail to reflect it accurately. And that would settle the issue for good, it seems.

There is a number of standard objections to this naive objectivist account. Firstly, what kind of things, events or properties would 'objective moral principles' be? Would they be the etherial myths of Plato's imagination? Where, or in what medium, would they exist? Are they things, or more like properties of things? Or are they events? There is no satisfactory answer available along these lines.

Secondly, how would we get to know these objective norms? It seems as if there is no point in positing the existence of objective norms as a way of resolving moral disagreements unless we also have some reliable way of knowing them. Otherwise we are buying a theoretical pig-in-a-poke. In fact, the evidence here is exactly in the opposite direction. If such objective norms existed and if we had some way of knowing them, then we might have hoped to have resolved many more fundamental disagreements in ethics and politics than we have to date. The objectivist thesis looks like this: 'there really are objective standards there, and if we could only know them we would resolve our disputes. But we unfortunately can't have access to them at present.' But not being able to know, with reasonable certainty, what these norms are is no better than having none there in the first place.

Finally, even if we did assume their existence, and even if we could know what they were, why should we ever accept them? How could the mere existence of moral norms impose obligations on free human agents? The picture in the background here is, possibly, of a king or ruler who forces his subjects to comply with the law. So that once the law is known one understands that one had better comply with it or else! Could the requirements of the moral law be explained by this analogy? Hardly. This would reduce moral obligation to the fear of failing to comply with an objective norm which, from the point of view of the individual agent, is arbitrarily imposed.

The assumption of an objective moral law in this sense is so implausible a theory that no one would be reasonably tempted to endorse it, except for its one saving feature: it would explain how incompatible moral beliefs are not equally valid and it would therefore explain our common assumption that, of two conflicting moral beliefs, at least one of them must be mistaken. But the theoretical price to be paid for this explanatory outcome is too high. Some other way must be found for giving an intelligible account of moral/political discourse, which would not reduce it to merely subjective expressions of approval, and at the same time would not encumber it with mythical metaphysical entities which are dubiously identified by what is often called ethical intuition. The following account is one way out of the impasse.

Facts and Values

One of the most obvious features of moral opinions is that they allow great latitude for disagreement. Even in western Europe one finds significant differences between reasonable people about the morality of various kinds of conduct, including examples such as abortion or capital punishment which are evidently not trivial. Side by side with this kind of disagreement one finds that people from the most diverse cultures can usually succeed, in a relatively short time, in reaching agreement on what we normally call scientific problems. And in situations where scientific agreement is not reached we tend to think that it is only a matter of time before it will be, and that experimental results will have a decisive effect on the outcome of discussions among those in disagreement.

The contrast between moral beliefs and factual or scientific claims was first made prominent by David Hume in the 18th century.[3] The distinction hinges on the reasons we can give for holding one moral belief rather than another. The reasons which support our beliefs are usually different from the causes which explain how we acquired them initially. Thus, if someone had strong convictions about the immorality of war, we might inquire into the cause of their conviction along these lines: was he involved in a war? Were his parents pacifists? Did he lose members of his family or some of his best friends in war? And so on. Whatever account we get in response to these queries is irrelevant to deciding whether the belief about war is plausible. In fact, the more implausible an opinion seems, the more likely we are to look for a causal explanation of why someone would endorse it. In other words, the cause which explains why a person believes something is independent of whether the belief in question is a plausible or credible one.

Reasons, on the other hand, are not concerned with how a person came to believe what he does, but with why he should continue to believe it. They are not concerned with the conditions which brought it about that someone believes this or that, but with what justification he might offer for continuing to endorse such a belief in the future. In this sense, reasons are relevant to whether or not one's opinions are true or are plausible. Therefore it would be confusing reasons and causes if someone were asked: 'Why do you believe in God?', and answered: 'Because I was brought up a Christian.' In one sense, i.e. in the causal sense, that is why he believes in God; it explains how he came to be in his present condition of belief. In another sense, of course, one is not justified in believing anything because one was brought up to believe it. Reasons are those considerations which are relevant to deciding the credibility of an opinion, whereas causes only indicate how one came to hold a given opinion no matter how incredible it is in the light of the available evidence.

Once we acknowledge the difference between these two ways of explaining why someone holds the opinions he does, the distinction between factual and moral opinions can be made by reference to the reasons for belief that a person can give. No matter what one believes or what opinions one holds, we can legitimately ask why one continues to hold such an opinion, where the question is now understood as a request for a reason (or reasons) for such a belief. Answering such why-questions is usually called the justification of one's belief. Hume's distinction between factual and moral opinions relies on the kind of justification one can offer for one's beliefs. If I can justify my opinions by reference to empirical evidence, then my opinion is a factual one; if my belief is moral or political, then I cannot justify it in this way.[4] This point can be seen by reference to an example.

If one person A, says: 'I think that abortion is wrong', someone else, B, might ask: 'Why do you think abortion is immoral?' A answers: 'because it is taking an innocent life'. B responds: 'Why is taking life wrong?' and A tries again: 'Because it is one of God's commandments, and I believe the commandments.' Again B asks: 'Why do you believe the commandments?' and A is still patient: 'I believe the commandments because God told Moses to obey them'. B is still not lost for a further question: 'Why should you believe God and do what he commands?' and A tries again to reply: 'Because *it is right* to obey God'. B's questioning and A's responding must come to a stop somewhere. The point of Hume's distinction is that their eventual resting place in the discussion cannot be simply a factual claim about how the world and God are, but must involve some reference to values, or what ought to be done. In the case just examined, the final reason was: 'It is right . . .'

Since moral judgments are specifically concerned with how we ought to behave, it is evident that no amount of evidence about how things are in the world can finally decide how things ought to be; in fact, it is very often the case that we are more inclined to spell out our beliefs about how we ought to behave when confronted with the contrary in fact. In other words, we cannot finally decide how men ought to behave by simply listing factual information about man, the world or God's commands to man. In the final stages of our discussion, those who disagree as *A* and *B* above may find themselves still at odds abut more basic and more general moral principles or beliefs. And one of the main problems in moral discussions is concerned with trying to reconcile such fundamental differences in value judgment between individuals and cultures.

Once we recognize that moral opinions are not reducible to factual claims, there is a tendency to down-grade them and to lapse into a position of holding that all moral opinions are equally valid. This is a mistake. It is precisely because they are not factual claims at all that moral opinions cannot be evaluated by the same criteria as factual claims. Indeed, it is only be stretching the meaning of the word 'true' that we can talk about moral opinions as being true or false. In a literal sense they are neither true nor false, and the fact that they cannot be evaluated in this way is no indication of their relative importance. Of course there is also a sense in which moral opinions may be said to be true or false — when they are evaluated relative to a common or agreed standard.

When people agree on standards they may agree or disagree in applying the standards to particular cases. For example, if a community agrees on what a 'good house' is, they can then proceed to apply this standard of good housing to various showhouses around the country. In Ireland, a good house would usually have a well-insulated roof and walls, some way of heating the house in cold weather, some ventilation system (such as windows which can be opened), etc. Once we agree on a standard like this one, there is still room for disagreement in applying the standard to different houses. For example, if a builder says that he has a good house for sale, we might dispute his claim by saying: the roof leaks, the walls are damp, there is no fireplace or central heating. And we might summarize our position by saying that his claim is false. What is significant about this case for the discussion of moral opinions is that we can only reasonably dispute the truth of his claim about the house by reference to an agreed standard for good housing in Ireland. To say that the builder's claim is true is equivalent to saying that it passes the standard criteria for good houses; to say that his claim is false likewise presupposes an agreed standard which his house-building fails to satisfy.

If the standard itself is disputed, we can only reach agreement by looking to a more general standard on which the disputants can agree. And it is evident in the case of houses that the standard or criteria for what constitutes a good house are very much dependent on what we use houses for, the kind of climate we enjoy, etc. In the case of disagreements about moral opinions, however, we cannot as easily agree on general standards or principles because we fail to agree on a general end or objective for man's life. And in the absence of an agreed standard of behaviour, we cannot legitimately talk of true or false moral opinions (by comparison with true or false claims about good houses). Thus when people agree on general standards of behaviour, they can express their more specific agreement or disagreement in terms of the truth or falsehood of opinions; but if they fail to agree on common standards, then those who talk about the truth or otherwise of their moral opinions are using the English language prejudicially in their own favour.

In summary, moral opinions are not equivalent to factual claims at all; empirical evidence is not decisive or adequate to resolve moral disagreements; when people disagree about the morality of specific actions they may legitimately talk about their opinions as true or false only in relation to a common or agreed standard. But if people disagree on the more general standards of human behaviour, then it is misdescribing the situation to talk about their opinions as true or false. Disagreement about moral standards must be approached from a different perspective.

Choosing between Standards

Moral or political standards are best understood as belonging to communities of people rather than to individual moral agents. This makes it easier to explain how individuals can cheat on the community by failing to observe the moral standards and still enjoy whatever benefits result from such moral standards being observed generally in the community. Besides, if we predicate moral standards of communities we can also more easily explain how most people, at least initially, adopt the moral standards of the community in which they are reared. For being reared in a given community is the *cause* of one's accepting the moral norms which that particular community exemplifies.

So far, this way of approaching the problem of moral justification says nothing about why one should continue to accept any set of moral standards once one begins to question them. To resolve this problem one must first inquire into the relative merits of alternative moral standards.

In general, explicit moral standards result from reflection on forms of life or life-styles. This means that we usually evolve a certain life-style first and then make explicit what standards of human behaviour are implicit in the life-style in question. Evidently, the relative variety of life-styles available will result in a corresponding variety of moral standards. These moral standards or norms often take the form of a convention, i.e. a more or less implicitly accepted arrangement between different individuals in which the success of the arrangement (for achieving certain objectives) depends on each partner in the convention understanding what is involved, and recognizing that he must play his part and rely on others doing theirs to realize success for all involved. A simple example of a convention in this sense would be the example of travel companions. Imagine a situation where *A* regularly gives *B* a lift to work, and that *A* meets *B* at the railway station. Whenever *B* is sick or does not arrive for whatever reason, *A* waits for five minutes and then drives on to work without him. Whenever *A* is sick, etc., *B* waits for five minutes and then takes the next available train to work. This arrangement is such that if *A* waits on any given morning for *B*, he knows what to do after five minutes. He believes that *B* understands the arrangement, and believes that *B* is in fact using the arrangement to let him know what to do. Their convention only works as long as both are aware of the arrangement and more or less consistently abide by it. And the result is that they do not unnecessarily delay each other getting to work while they wait for half an hour or wonder what to do in the situation of one member of the pair not showing on time.

Moral conventions are much more complex than the simple case just given, and they are also less easily related to clearly definable objectives. However, they are related to some more or less fundamental human needs or aspirations, and to the extent that they are, moral norms are subject to critical evaluation. In the example of the travel companions, *A* and *B* might have delayed each other rather frequently before they agreed on the arrangement of waiting for five minutes. Had they got together and discussed alternative arrangements with a view to avoiding delay, they might have looked at arrangements made by other people in similar situations and examined how well or how badly they worked. Thus, two other fellow travellers, *C* and *D* might have had a similar problem and arranged to phone the absent partner after ten minutes. Looking for a phone which was in order usually took another ten minutes, and they often found that they did not have the exact change required for telephone calls. The eventual result was often a long delay before finding out whether or not the other party was going to work that day. Given that the reason for making some arrangement in the first place was to avoid delay, this looks like a poor plan. In a somewhat similar way, to the exent that we can specify the objectives of moral conventions we can also hope to evaluate the relative merits of different moral standards.

Basic moral standards reflect complex arrangements which are thought to facilitate the satisfaction of fundamental human needs. Such basic needs evidently include survival, the satisfaction of hunger and thirst, but they also frequently include such things as respect, the experience of autonomy and freedom, the power to control one's life within reasonable limits. One need not be a hedonist to look to fundamental human needs or aspirations as a source of many of our moral conventions. To the extent that basic needs such as these are more widespread among men, the correlative moral conventions are correspondingly universal. Of course the fact that most people agree on their basic needs or aspirations does not imply that they must automatically agree on the appropriate convention to facilitate the satisfaction of such needs. However, even the first level of agreement — that is, agreement on human needs or objectives — is a start in the direction of evaluating the relative merits of different moral standards.

Moral standards are also complicated by community beliefs, especially religious beliefs. In the case of religious belief, we are on especially delicate ground because the significance of religious belief for the life of the believer is often in inverse proportion to the evidence which would warrant the belief. In other words, the variety of different religious beliefs and the level of personal commitment involved in many of them is embarrassingly out of proportion to the credibility of such beliefs. Evidently conflicting beliefs about God, the soul, the after-life, and such topics cannot all be true in a factual sense. Religious belief is relevant in this context because religious belief tends to result in a definite kind of life-style. We live the way we do, not only to satisfy our basic needs or aspirations, but also because of what we believe about God, the soul, immortality, and the relative importance of various human goods; and precisely because these are articles of faith we have no objective tests to discriminate between those which are credible and those which are not. One of the immediate results of this is that many of our moral standards or conventions are automatically beyond critical or rational evaluation because they derive initially from religious faith.

Moral standards are also determined, to a certain extent, by individuals' decisions, but this is not central to our usual understanding of intersubjectively valid moral norms. There is a tradition in ethics, especially represented by the German philosopher Immanuel Kant, which suggests that the basis of all moral norms is the individual conscience or, as he calls it, pure practical reason. However, Kant's moral philosophy is itself a good example of the point already made above — that moral norms are explicit versions of standards of behaviour which are central to a given way of life. Kant made explicit what was implicit in his own religious tradition and then identified the result with morality in general. So while moral standards may indeed derive from the decisions or beliefs of an individual agent, such standards only hold for the individual who constructs them, unless they come to be accepted as in some sense conducive to human development in a more general way. And at that stage they are subject to the same type of evaluation as community conventions.

Moral standards, then, may be understood as conventions for human behaviour which have developed as part of a given style of life and which have been made explicit by reflection. These conventions are not arbitrary since they have evolved partly as a means of facilitating the achievement of basic human goals or aspirations. They are also influenced by religious faith, among other things. To the extent that basic moral norms are means to achieving fundamental human goals, they may be critically evaluated and compared; to the extent that they derive almost completely from a religious point of view which does not overlap with basic human needs and aspirations, they escape the possibility of being critically evaluated.

Justifying Moral Standards

The problem of justifying one's moral views can now be tackled again in the light of the discussion of moral standards as social conventions which are more or less suitable for realizing basic human objectives or aspirations. As was pointed out above, the problem of justifying one's moral views is the same as the problem of giving reasons for holding such views or of showing why it is reasonable to believe or adopt them. For the reasons outlined above, there is no question of trying to show that one's moral views are true or false in the usual sense of these words. It is rather a question of showing that one's moral views are reasonable or credible, and this indicates the possibility of alternative moral views being equally reasonable.

Giving reasons for a certain moral view — for example, that divorce or political assassination is immoral — may be a relatively easy thing to do depending on how specific the moral view in question is, and how much agreement may be assumed on matters of principle. There is no sharp line of demarcation here between matters of principle and the application of principles to specific moral decisions. However, it might be useful for the sake of discussion to introduce a rough distinction between the two and to give names to the kinds of disagreement which arise in each area.

The source of moral disagreements may be located, in a broad sense, at three different levels; (i) in the description of man's basic needs and aspirations; (ii) in the general standards of conduct which are conducive to realizing these; (iii) in the application of these standards to more specific moral problems.

(i) At the most fundamental level, people may dispute about man's basic needs and aspirations. To some extent this is a factual, empirical question which can be answered by scientific investigation. However, as was mentioned above, it is possible to add on a religious description of man's nature to what can be empirically discovered, and this complicates the whole discussion because the ultimate basis of such theological claims is faith. Insofar as they derive from faith, such claims cannot be rationally evaluated. This does not imply, of course, that theological descriptions of man's place in nature are irrational — though they may be that too. It simply means that for those who hold different beliefs about man which are ultimately based on religious faith, there is no rational way of deciding the plausibility of competing opinions. And if the real source of such disagreements is not acknowledged, it is impossible at a later stage of the discussion to make any progress in resolving moral disagreement.

(ii) Assuming some level of agreement at least in the empirically based description of man's nature, his needs and his fundamental aspirations, there is room for alternative arrangements or conventions as means to realize basic human objectives. Just as it is possible to get from Dublin to Cork by walking, cycling, flying, etc., so it is possible to satisfy basic human needs by a variety of different strategies. However, it is also possible to comment on the relative merits of different means to the same end; if one is in a hurry or is not trained to walk long distances, it is normally unreasonable to walk from Dublin to Cork. Likewise, the relative merits of alternative moral norms or conventions may be evaluated vis-à-vis the agreed objectives for which these conventions are adopted in the first place. Disagreement at this level of discussion can be called *disagreement in principle*. It may be explained by reference to disagreement at the first level (in describing man's nature), or it may result from adopting different strategies to achieve a relatively common objective for man.

There is a further complication which should be acknowledged at this point, before introducing step (iii) sources of disagreement. The general description of 'human needs and aspirations' on which step (ii) strategies depend, is not a simple, ordered list. It includes a variety of rather basic, incommensurable human values, and we have no easy way of comparing the relative importance of different items on the list. For example, how much individual liberty ought we surrender in order to cultivate order in community living? How much autonomy might we surrender in order to increase our 'standard of living' (and by what percentage)? It would seem to be naive in the extreme to imagine that there are simple answers to such questions; and it would be both naive and presumptuous to imagine that one's own intuitions or hunches about them are true or valid for all. One can only hope to make plausible claims at this basic level by refusing to be too specific and by keeping one's eye on the lessons of human history. Since this issue re-emerges in the discussion of human rights in Chapter 6, it might be deferred until then for more detailed discussion.

(iii) Even if agreement is reached at the first two levels, reasonable people may continue to disagree about the application of their general moral norms to specific cases. For example, two people may agree that respect for human life is a fundamental value and still disagree about the merits of abortion legislation. What is significant about this level of disagreement — which might be called *disagreement in application* — is that it follows roughly the same pattern as disagreement in principle, except that the possibilities for disagreement have increased enormously. It is very much an oversimplification of the problem to imagine that agreement in principle can logically force agreement in application, even in those cases where the disputants agree on all the factual information which is relevant to the specific moral cases in question. And it is both arrogant and self-deluding to think that those who disagree with us at this level are therefore less enlightened or less rational. For this implies that we neither understand the source of our disagreement nor are willing to recognize our own fallibility. If basic human needs and aspirations can be realized by a relative variety of fundamental moral norms, it is all the more evident that these basic norms or values can be implemented in an even greater variety of specific applications.

Justice: Ends and Means

The discussion so far suggests that to justify one's moral views one should refer to agreed norms of conduct in a society and to justify these, in turn, one should refer to their function as means to realizing fundamental human objectives. This interpretation of moral views and their justification seems to rely on the principle that 'the end justifies the means'. In one important sense this is true; without any reference to human needs or aspirations moral norms become so detached from reality that it is impossible to give any reasonable or critical account of why one ought to accept or reject any given moral system. In another sense which is closer to the usual connotations of the slogan, this interpretation of moral norms is not committed to the principle that 'the end justifies the means'. To explain the second sense of the principle it is necessary to say something about utilitarian moral theories and the problems they characteristically have with the idea of justice.

Ethical theories can be divided broadly into two types, utilitarian and non-utilitarian theories. The distinction is based on how they define what it means to say that something if morally good (or evil). While this kind of distinction might seem initially to be a mere question of semantics, the implications of adopting one theory rather than another can be disastrous for those who must suffer the consequences of the choice. For example, the utilitarian may justify the torture of innocent people on the principle that such inhuman practices provide evidence which helps avert greater evils. Before elaborating on the morality of torture and its discussion by different moralists, the distinction between the two kinds of ethical theory needs to be clarified.

The utilitarian first distinguishes between the morality of an action and the consequences of an action, where consequences are understood as all those things which can be reasonably anticipated to follow from a given action. He needs some non-moral way of evaluating the consequences of an action which indicates how welcome or unwelcome these consequences are. For example, if giving pleasure is his criterion, he can say that those effects of actions which are pleasurable are welcome, and those which are not pleasurable are unwelcome. Obviously the utilitarian does not have to be a gross hedonist; he may just as easily be a self-sacrificing political activist whose primary objective is the establishment of an 'ideal' political system. In the latter case, any action which is conducive to establishing such a political structure is welcome, and those which hinder its establishment are unwelcome. Nor must the utilitarian be so single-minded about what he considers welcome that he must fall into any simple classification like either of the two suggested above. The main point is that, however he does it and however lengthy or complex the list, the utilitarian must first characterize what consequences of human actions he considers to be welcome and which ones he considers to be unwelcome.

Once this is done, the utilitarian then defines what it means to say that something is morally good: a human action is *morally good* if the welcome effects of the action outweigh the unwelcome effects. This basic principle is subject to many and obvious qualifications. For example, welcome effects for whom? How does one measure or balance the relative significance of the welcome and unwelcome effects? How many of the effects, especially those which are indirect and difficult to foresee, must one take into account in judging the morality of an action in advance? However these and similar standard problems are resolved, the fundamental principle of utilitarianism is that the morality of an action is decided *only* in terms of the effects of the action, and that the welcome or unwelcome nature of such effects is evaluated independently of any reference to *moral* criteria.

It is important to recognize the implications of this last remark because there is a danger here of confusing the utilitarian theory with others which are quite different. Most moralists take the effects of an action into account in trying to decide its morality, and doing that is not sufficient to make them utilitarians. The utilitarian is special in that he cannot take *anything else* into account except the effects of an action, and he cannot use any moral criteria (apart from his utilitarian one) to weigh the merits or otherwise of the effects of an action. Thus, in looking at the likely effects of an action, he cannot consider that some of them are immoral or unjust, because he is attempting to define what it means to say that an act is moral or immoral by reference to the effects of the action. If he uses the concept of 'morality' to characterize the effects of an action, and then uses the utilitarian principle to decide the morality of the action, he is arguing in a circle by assuming exactly what he is trying to clarify, viz. what it means to say that something is moral! It is for this reason that the utilitarian must distinguish between saying, on the one hand, that an act is morally good and, on the other hand, that its consequences are good, or evil, in a non-moral sense of 'good'. To avoid confusing the issue, I have referred to the non-moral evaluation of the consequences of actions as being welcome or unwelcome. This point can be highlighted by taking a second look at the example of torture.

If the utilitarian is asked: is torturing a suspect in a criminal investigation immoral?, he may only decide the issue by looking at the consequences of torturing a given suspect. Thus he will consider that one of the unwelcome consequences will be that the individual concerned will undergo inhuman and degrading suffering. Despite this, if the torture is sophisticated, the individual will at least probably survive. Besides, there might be unwelcome consequences if the media make an issue of the torture and embarrass the public officials who condoned it. On the plus side, the torturing of the individual might result in very useful information being made available to the police which would help stop future crimes by acquaintances of the tortured person. The utilitarian then simply calculates — in a rather rough and ready fashion — whether the welcome effects of torturing someone outweigh (or are likely to outweigh) the unwelcome effects. And if they do, then the act of torturing the criminal suspect is *a morally good act*. In this calculation of welcome and unwelcome consequences, the question cannot be raised as to whether torture is an immoral act no matter what the consequences, without abandoning the utilitarian position. For to introduce such further questions is to concede that something other than the consequences of the action may be taken into account in deciding its morality. And to do this is to cease being a utilitarian.

Evidently, the principle that 'the end justifies the means' applies in a significantly unqualified sense to the utilitarian theory. But this is not the case in the theory of moral conventions.

Non-utilitarian theories leave open the possibility of evaluating the morality of human actions by reference to something other than the non-moral consequences of an act. What the other factors are and how they are integrated into a theory determine a variety of alternatives to utilitarianism. The alternative theories are also in agreement, therefore, in rejecting the seductive simplicity of 'the end justifies the means' because an action may be judged to be immoral no matter how beneficial the consequences may be. Among the considerations which alternative moral theories consider is the justice or injustice of actions which, on purely utilitarian grounds, are considered to be moral.

The concept of justice is closely linked with the moral equality of members of a community. Obviously the equality in question here does not presuppose equality in size, in natural abilities, or in the significance of one's contribution to the society. What is at issue is that, as members of a community, the members are to be treated with equal respect and to be guaranteed equal rights relative to the other members of the community. The justification of the claim to equality of treatment hinges on the contractual nature of a political community and on the decision involved in agreeing on moral norms or moral principles.[5]

Moral principles become established and accepted when a community evolves an agreed convention for realizing fundamental human objectives. The fact that alternative conventions are possible and appear to be equally conducive to realizing the common ends of the society indicates that there is a 'decision' involved in the adoption of one convention rather than another. Whatever decision is made can be shown to be reasonable or unreasonable by reference to the ends to be achieved; but no decision can be logically forced on the community by its intrinsic reasonableness. Once accepted and established, the convention is then normative for the behaviour of members of the community.

Considerations of justice are relevant at the 'moment of decision'. This does not imply that the members of any given community sit down together at a certain point in time to make this kind of decision, nor that they explicitly consider the various alternatives which are available before settling on one of them. Rather, the community may be considered to have adopted their moral standards by a series of more or less implicit, and very gradual, historical decisions and to constantly reaffirm such decisions by their willingness to uphold their traditional moral values. What is at stake in considerations of justice is whether the members of the community would be willing to give their active co-operation to a system of moral norms if they were not guaranteed equal status, as citizens, with others in the community. In other words, the reasonableness of their consenting to a code of moral conventions depends on whether the conventions will be equitably applied to all members of the society. In the example of torture just mentioned, it is unlikely that members of a community will agree in advance to a system of moral conventions which would allow a real possibility of their being tortured by those who happen to have the power to enforce their convictions, moral or otherwise, on others. Although this may be conceded in a flippant way by ideologues of the utilitarian variety, it is invariably the case that they do not envisage any real likelihood of being tortured themselves. Consequently, their apparent willingness to have the same utilitarian principles applied to themselves is merely a theoretical concession to consistency, based on commitment to an ideology, rather than a real willingness to be tortured for *other* people's reasons.

This seems to be the point in Kant's suggestion that a moral principle must be capable of being universally applied to qualify as a moral principle.[6] Kant's point is not simply to convict his opponents of being inconsistent in holding one moral principle for themselves and a different (less favourable) one for others. Kant can be understood as saying: any principle which will not be applied equally to all members of a given community will not be accepted by the community. And if it is not acceptable to the members (because it would be unreasonable for them to accept it) then it is not a moral principle. It would be a relevant matter to this discussion if anyone could locate a reasonable community of people who were (even reluctantly) willing to accept the convention that others might torture them, without moral qualms, whenever it seemed that it was in the best interests of the community, in the estimation of the torturers, to do so.

This amounts to saying that, in the sense which is normally implied by the principle, the end does *not* justify the means. In other words, the justice and therefore the morality of an action such as torturing a suspect, is dependent on the conventions which a community is willing to accept in order to realize basic human objectives, and no community is likely to accept such a principle because of its disastrous consequences. The equality of the citizens in the sense outlined above implies that members of any community would be unwilling to give their consent to conventions for moral behaviour which could have the consequence that their own fundamental needs and aspirations would be put in jeopardy by force.

Moral Obligation

One of the characteristic features of moral norms which is difficult to explain is their peculiar obligatory force, or the fact that we think of them as demanding that we *ought* to do one thing or avoid doing something else. This difficulty is rather different from the earlier questions about moral disagreement; for, although people tend to have different opinions about what moral norms they accept, they also tend to think that whatever norms are accepted are only *moral* to the extent that they bind or oblige those who accept them to behave in certain specifiable ways. And the sense in which people are obliged to behave or not to misbehave is thought to be common to a variety of different moral beliefs.

Despite initial appearances to the contrary, however, moralists also disagree about what moral obligation is, and their disagreement on this point coincides with differences of opinion about the justification of moral views. Some examples of how this occurs make the point more clearly than an abstract discussion of the problem.

Moral obligation is often thought of by analogy with a command from someone in authority. The obligatory character of commands is associated with the power of whoever gives the command to enforce it; and for the person who is commanded and who knows about the authority and power of the commander to enforce compliance, the awareness of his situation produces a feeling of compulsion which motivates him to co-operate. This approach to the problem of moral obligation is unsatisfactory. We need only think of the situation of being threatened with a gun by someone who has no legitimate authority over us to see why the theory does not work.[7] In the situation of being threatened, we would experience a similar motivation to comply with whatever demands are made by the gunman; but we would not regard his requests as having any moral obligation, nor would we be willing to admit that the threatening gunman has any authority to make the demands he does. Consequently, we cannot understand moral obligation by comparison with the feeling of being compelled by another's exercise of power over us, unless we first explain the difference between someone who has authority and someone else who has no authority over us.

Indeed, even if the question about authority could be satisfactorily dealt with, it would help very little in understanding moral obligation. The reason for this is that people exercise various kinds of authority over others. The most readily understood example of this is where the person in authority exercises a definite function in a community which is established by law or by a quasi-legal agreement. Whenever someone legitimately exercises their function according to the rules of the community which determine the function in question — e.g. an abbot in a monastery or a judge in a legal tribunal — then there is a presumption that whoever is subject to his authority should obey his command. In spite of such an assumption, it is still possible to ask whether it is morally right to obey even the legitimate commands of people in authority. So that unless the authority of the one in charge is qualified as a moral authority, rather than any of the other kinds of authority he might have, the model of commands is of little help in understanding moral obligation. However, if the person in command is acknowledged to have moral authority we make no progress either, because we are assuming exactly what we are trying to explain, namely, what is meant by saying that someone has *moral* authority.

One of the most prevalent examples of this approach is where people think of God as the person in authority and then imagine that God issues commands to his subjects; the biblical story of God giving the moral law to Moses in the form of commands is a mythical version of this theory. If morality is understood as doing what God tells us to do, then moral obligation can be apparently understood as a result of God's authority and his power to enforce compliance with his law. Clearly, the power to enforce compliance here is usually understood, by comparison with the civil law, as the power to threaten and punish the disobedient rather than the power to change the disobedient into obedient observers of the law. All the problems raised above occur just as readily in the case of God commanding as in the example of a human commander issuing orders. It is in no way irreverent even for Christians to ask: but why should we obey God? Another way of asking the same question which makes its implications more obvious is: have we any moral obligation to obey God and, if we have, what is the source of this moral obligation? It is plainly begging the question to claim that we ought to obey God because he commands us to obey him, for the question can be asked again: why ought we obey his command to obey him? This can only be answered by some theory of God's moral authority, and this in turn presupposes what we are trying to explain!

This question is a well-known one in the history of philosophy and theology. It was traditionally formulated as follows: is something moral because God commands it, or does he command things because they are moral? In other words, is there something intrinsic to some kinds of human behaviour which makes them moral or immoral independently of God's commands, so that we could understand God's commands as a revelation of what is moral and immoral, rather than a creation of the distinction between the two? Without some intrinsic difference between the moral and the immoral, God's commands would be arbitrary.

The distinction between reasons and causes which was discussed above can be put to work again to make progress at this stage. In asking for the source of moral obligation we may be inquiring either into the causes of an individual's feeling obliged, or into the reason why he should feel obliged. In some obvious sense, the causes of our feeling obliged about certain kinds of behaviour, and feeling guilty about others, are tied in with our early training and moral education. Once we have come to accept moral views, however reasonably or unreasonably we did this, then those moral views will act as a private watchdog or conscience for each of us, and the extent to which they influence our behaviour will depend, among other things, on the kind of personality we have. As in the previous use of this distinction the problem which confronts us at the moment is not a question about causes, but a problem about giving reasons or providing a justification; in the present case, it is the problem of giving reasons for being obliged by moral values. In other words, what is it about moral values which makes those who accept them obliged to act in certain ways or to refrain from acting in other ways?

The idea that moral norms have some kind of intrinsic value which is independent of their being commanded by God or enforced by some other moral authority, and independent of the subjective and differing views of individuals, provides a clue to the obligatory character of moral norms. If one accepts the suggestion that moral norms are conditional arrangements for satisfying basic human aspirations, and that they operate as conventions in a community which are more or less explicitly accepted by the members, then the obligatory character of moral principles can be explained in two ways: (a) in terms of the objectives to be achieved by observing such moral norms, and (b) in terms of the conventions already endorsed by members of a given community.

(a) Once moral norms are understood as means to achieving human objectives, then they are obligatory to the extent that we think they are the most suitable (or the only) means available for achieving these objectives. This implies that we could rewrite our moral norms as follows: if you wish to achieve such-and-such objectives, then you ought to do this and avoid that.[8] Since the kinds of objectives which are relevant to the first part of the sentence are assumed to be relatively universal and uncontentious, the first part of the principle is often left out and we are told, instead: you ought to do this and avoid that. This way of understanding moral obligation also helps explain the various degrees of obligation we associate with different norms. To the extent that the objectives sought are very basic human objectives, then the (moral) obligation to make use of the appropriate means to realize them is correspondingly serious. On the other hand, to the extent that the objectives one aspires to are not universal but result from one's own personal preferences or religious convictions, then the obligation to use the recommended means to realize them is personal or subjective rather than something which can apply to others who do not share one's objectives.

(b) The fact that moral norms are primarily social conventions, rather than private plans for achieving one's own objectives, implies a second source of obligation which results from the community's expectations. The travel companions example used earlier helps explain how this comes about. Once such an arrangement for travelling together is made, each party to the arrangement expects the other to comply with it. There is no mention of anything like moral obligation here; rather, the success of the arrangement depends on its being complied with on a regular basis. If one party often takes advantage of the other or enjoys the benefits of the arrangement without sharing its burdens, the second party will presumably feel cheated and will not be willing to continue with it. Likewise, in the case of community conventions for acceptable behaviour, there are obvious benefits to all the members of the community in the shared arrangements for protecting the members' interests and for establishing standards of behaviour which make community life possible at all. The conventional character of moral norms, therefore, adds an extra degree of obligation in that the community expects its members who have at least implicitly accepted its norms to comply with them. And, as in the example of the travelling arrangement, each member realizes that the demands of the community are not arbitrary, for each member shares the benefits as well as the burdens of the common norms.

Once these two kinds of obliging factors are learned and internalized by a member of the community, he will most likely experience a sense of obligation and will be able to use the language of conscience. This very brief analysis suggests two problems which can hardly be left without mention.

In the sense of community membership which is relevant here, a person can belong to more than one community at the same time. This is especially the case, for example, with a religious person in a secular society. If someone is a Christian, then he or she belongs to a community with shared values and a reasonably common lifestyle. At the same time, he or she may belong to a secular society in which Christians are a minority. This situation can rather easily give rise to a serious problem of principle when the values of the two communities come into conflict. If his religious convictions also imply that he must give priority to Christian values when they conflict with alternative moral values, then he must have recourse to some critical norms to decide how he should act. Before saying something about this problem, the other type of conflict should be introduced.

For a person who belongs to a given community with reasonably entrenched moral values, a conflict may arise between the obligation which derives from his membership of the community and the obligation which derives from the more basic considerations of human objectives and the means to achieve them. This kind of difficulty is inevitable; otherwise there could be no change in the moral values of a community unless everyone changed overnight from one set of values to another. Assuming this does not happen, the more usual situation is where some members of a community fail to accept some of its moral norms and reject the claim of the community that they are obliged to observe these values until everyone else changes too. As in the first type of conflict, the person in this quandary needs some critical criteria to help resolve his difficulties.

How can someone reasonably choose between the demands of alternative moral communities, or between the demands of the community and his own estimation of what is likely to be conducive to achieving fundamental human objectives? There is no easy way out of this difficulty, because whatever suggestion is made will itself be a moral principle, and will therefore need to be justified just as much as the conflicting moral principles between which it is meant to adjudicate. This is not often appreciated, especially when loyalty to one's moral principles is established as an unquestionable moral principle. How could a person ever justify the claim that, no matter what conflicts may arise, he should hold on firmly to the set of moral values which he had initially adopted? To do this is to commit oneself indefinitely to moral stagnation.

In the discussion of community conventions for realizing basic human objectives there was no indication of the size of the community in question, nor of the historical experience of the community. Both are relevant to decisions in conflict situations. We can query the apparent certainties of one relatively small or isolated human community by reference to a wider human community; and we can question the wisdom of our current insights by reference to the history of similar social strategies in the past. This is not a suggestion that we might decide moral issues by voting, and that we get closer to the 'truth' by increasing the size of the electorate. However, as long as we are limited to rational procedures for deciding moral or political issues, we have nothing else to turn to except the common wisdom of a variety of different communities in different historical conditions.

This kind of result is only unsatisfactory for those who imagine that some exact decision procedure should be available for resolving conflicts between community-based moral conventions. The facts almost speak for themselves in this connection. We have no such decision procedures available, and those who think otherwise are suffering from metaphysical delusions. Here again the theory of moral and political obligation fits the available evidence; it allows for ambiguity at exactly those points at which one cannot avoid ambiguity in one's moral or political life.

Objectivity again

This account of moral/political norms, and of the kind of obligations which they impose, is neither subjective nor objective. Morality is not explained exclusively by reference to the personal feelings, attitudes or wishes of any one individual and, in that sense, it is not subjective. On the other hand, it is not objective in the sense that moral principles exist independently of human history or culture, and of man's creativity in devising strategies for facilitating his realization of fundamental human objectives. Morality is a human creation — like law, language and culture; asking whether it is subjective or objective is a little like asking whether current traffic legislation is pink or blue. The question does not properly arise.

One of the implications of dropping the objectivity claim and the two-valued logic usually associated with it in ordinary language,[9] is that conflicting moral judgments may be equally valid or reasonable. The reason for this is obvious. Within one general strategy for realizing basic human objectives, it may be accepted that 'x may be done' (or x is not immoral). Within another moral tradition, equally dedicated to realizing basic human values, it may be accepted that 'x is immoral'. There is no progress made here by assigning one claim to a list of true statements and therefore the other to a list of false statements. Each may be reported as a 'true' statement within a given tradition; but since we usually do not use the word 'true' in such a relativized sense, it is preferable not to speak of true moral beliefs at all. They might be classified instead as valid, plausible, or reasonable. Thus conflicting moral beliefs, from conflicting moral traditions, may both be equally valid or reasonable.

This is surely not the suggestion that all moral views are equally valid; it is merely an explicit acknowledgment of the fact that unresolvable moral and political disagreements are part of our historical experience. The most obvious explanation of such disagreement is the one just given, where the disagreement derives from different moral traditions or conventions. However, it is also possible to have moral dilemmas even within a single moral tradition, especially in those cases where one's set of moral values and consequent duties have not been streamlined into a coherent, hierarchically arranged structure.

One objection made to this kind of account is that it is too loose, too vague and too imprecise to be of any use in making moral decisions; one does not live one's life guided by fuzzy platitudes about basic human values! However, this objection misses the whole point of a *theory* — which is, generally, to account for relevant facts. The principal objection against many traditional ethical or political theories was that they merely reflected the values of a very narrowly defined community, and therefore that they failed to apply to other moral/political traditions. For this reason they precluded the possibility of genuine moral disagreement, choosing to explain such disagreements in terms of the moral insensitivity or irrationality of dissenters. The merits of this general account are, by contrast, that it both explains the real hold of moral obligation as something which is not purely subjective or psychological; and at the same time that it recognizes the possibility of genuine differences in the historically conditioned general strategies which different societies have developed for realizing basic human objectives.

It is also important to realize that one does not become moral by discussing the relative merits of moral theories. This theory suggests that one becomes a moral agent by being trained in the moral conventions of one's community, by acquiring relatively permanent dispositions to act in certain ways and to refrain from acting in others. These dispositions to act morally were traditionally called virtues. So that this account of moral values changes little in our traditional understanding of moral education. In this sense the objection is conceded. One does not guide one's behaviour by general considerations about basic human values; one guides one's behaviour by reference to the relatively permanent dispositions which are acquired in the course of moral education in a given set of moral conventions. However, the moral conventions of any one community are subject to rational or critical review in the light of historical experience and of an understanding of basic values which is not limited to our local community.

2

Natural Law

Natural law, or the law of nature, is often appealed to as an objective, moral norm to which one may turn for guidance by general principles and for detailed solutions to specific moral or political dilemmas. It is also considered, by many, to be the only remaining bulwark against relativism, our only protection against the theory that all moral or political norms are equally valid, and the implication that one can only discover what is right or just by consulting local custom or law. Thus Leo Strauss wrote:

> To reject natural right is tantamount to saying that all right is positive right, and this means that what is right is determined exclusively by the legislators and the courts of the various countries . . . . The contemporary rejection of natural right leads to nihilism — nay, it is identical with nihilism.[1]

The limited choice suggested by Strauss is characteristic of many proponents of natural law: either one endorses a natural law theory, or else one must concede that there are no moral standards by which the customs or laws of different societies may be evaluated.

The stark options which are available in this type of argument might suggest that there is one, clearly identifiable and reasonably agreed theory which is named by the term 'natural law'. However, on closer inspection, one is bewildered by the multiplicity of views which have been defended — in moral philosophy, political theory, jurisprudence or Roman Catholic theology — as *the* natural law. The sheer variety of natural law theories might tempt the sceptically minded to reject a priori any attempt to provide a coherent account of natural law. Such a move, however, would make it impossible to initiate a meaningful dialogue with political and moral thought in Ireland in the twentieth century. For that reason alone, therefore, it may be worthwhile once again to attempt to understand what is meant by natural law.

Natural Law as a Theory

It is important to recognize at the outset that any account of natural law will be a theory.[2] This may seem like a redundant remark to those who reject it out of hand, and it may appear to be patently incorrect to those who believe that natural law — or their own version of natural law theory — is 'the truth' which is sufficiently clear and well known that it should not be burdened with the uncertainties associated with theories. Despite the reluctance on both sides, however, natural law is a theory. And this immediately raises the question: what is it a theory of? What kind of evidence could we introduce to decide in favour of this theory as opposed to other alternatives?

One way of appreciating the theoretical role of natural law is by distinguishing between the moral convictions of individuals — which are usually the result of their religious and moral education, among other things — and the reasons they might give to support their convictions if they are challenged to defend them against objections. We find ourselves with many moral convictions which are sufficiently firm that we would only modify them with the greatest reluctance. These views may range over a great diversity of issues, such as: torture; war; truth-telling; sexual morality; human rights; divorce; and so on. There is nothing surprising in the fact that we might hold definite views on these and many other issues, and yet not be able to give a coherent, general account of them. In such an account, the apparent diversity of issues involved is subsumed under general principles or norms which explain, in each case, why we hold the particular views we do. It is in this loose sense that natural law is a theory. What it purports to offer is a coherent explanation and justification for the moral/political views we hold on a great diversity of particular issues.

If natural law is a theory, then it is quite possible that two people would share the same moral views on all or almost all important issues and, despite that, that they might endorse different theories. It is also possible, of course, that they would continue to hold their moral views and have no theory at all to explain them. The distinction between, on the one hand, one's moral views and, on the other, the theory used to explain or defend them leaves enough latitude to the moral agent to have no moral theory at all, or to change his theory without necessarily modifying either his morality or his behaviour.

Once the theoretical character of natural law is recognized, one is less surprised at the diversity of theories which have been called 'natural law' theories.³ Alternative versions of natural law are not only distinguished by slight historical or accidental features, depending on the author or era in which they were written; the theories are sufficiently different, even in basic assumptions and in the very meanings of their fundamental concepts, that it is close to meaningless to talk about 'the natural law'. There is a long historical tradition in the West which could be called the natural law tradition; but there is nothing which is named, without an unacceptable level of ambiguity, by the term 'natural law'. This is not to imply that any theory one might examine is unreasonably vague or ambiguous; rather, the term 'natural law' is ambiguous insofar as it fails to identify which of the many incompatible theories of natural law it claims to denote. Aquinas' theory is not equivalent to that of Suarez, and Locke's theory is not equivalent to Rousseau's; in contemporary philosophy, Nozick's theory is not equivalent to that of Finnis.

If anyone wishes to defend a natural law theory, therefore, he must first specify which natural law theory he means. The theory most often invoked in moral and political discussion in Ireland in the twentieth century, and likewise in politics and jurisprudence, is a version of the natural law theory developed by St. Thomas Aquinas in the thirteenth century. The remainder of this chapter is confined to that theory or, at least, to one interpretation of it. I argue that, as a theory, it fails to realize its objectives and should be rejected.

It follows from what has been said so far that the rejection of the theory does not imply that one must reject the moral values which it was meant to explain; likewise, in rejecting one version of natural law theory, it does not follow that all other versions of the theory are equally unsuccessful. However, without surveying in detail the full range of natural law theories which are available, one might reasonably claim that the objections traditionally raised against natural law theories have not been satisfactorily answered. And for this reason, with few exceptions, natural law theories have been abandoned by contemporary philosophy.

Before examining the Thomistic natural law theory in some detail, it is necessary to underline the fact that a rejection of this one theory is neither more nor less than precisely that; the rejection of one theory. It is a standard fallacy of rhetorical overstatement — the fallacy of a false dilemma — to assume that there are only two options available in a complex issue. One is the position being defended as the truth, and the other option is usually so implausible that one's opponent could hardly wish to defend it. In discussions of natural law one tends to be offered two options only: either to endorse natural law theory, or to accept an extreme version of moral relativism.[4] There are many plausible moral theories available — such as those of Kant or Mill and, more recently, those of Mackie or Rawls — which reject both natural law and relativism. Each theory must be examined on its own merits, and the work involved in this cannot legitimately be short-circuited by the fallacious argument: those who reject natural law (or a particular version of it) must be moral relativists!

The Thomistic theory is based on two major assumptions: one is concerned with what kind of knowledge would count as a moral theory; the second assumption is concerned with the use of 'nature' talk as a basis from which to justify one's moral views. Both assumptions deserve a closer analysis.

Aristotelian Science

Aristotle proposed an ideal or model for human knowledge — a model which would apply to any knowledge which is reliable enough to merit the name 'science' — and this model dominated Western thinking about valid knowledge until the seventeenth century. The model was originally derived from axiomatic geometry, and was generalized by Aristotle to apply to all disciplines. Even in Aristotle's own work on biology and physics it proved impossible to adapt scientific knowledge to the imposed standard; in fact, for nearly twenty centuries the history of science is a history of the discrepancy between an artificially contrived model which failed to fit science, and the real progress in human knowledge which was judged, by this model, to be less than scientific. It was only in the seventeenth century that, for the first time, the obvious success of scientific work provided the impetus to emancipate scientific knowledge from the arbitrary restrictions of Aristotelian methodology. Then, for the first time, it was possible to say publicly: my knowledge of optics or physiology is scientific, but it does not fit the Aristotelian model. So much the worse for Aristotle!

Aquinas, in the thirteenth century, endorsed the Aristotelian model as an ideal for human knowledge and he applied it, with some qualifications, to moral philosophy. If this model failed so dramatically in physical science, it had even less hope of success in ethics and politics.

Briefly, the Aristotelian model for human knowledge involved distinguishing, in any discipline, between basic axioms or principles and the rest of the knowledge-claims which in some sense are dependent on the basic axioms. In geometry, the axioms were said to be self-evident, or true by definition; and all the theorems of geometry are logically derived from the axioms by a series of discrete, logical steps.[5] Since the axioms are (assumed to be) true, and the theorems are logically derived from them, then the theorems must also be true.

By analogy with this account of geometry, Aristotle demanded that in any human knowledge which was reliable — i.e. not just a series of inter-connected, possibly false, opinions or beliefs — one must establish first principles (or axioms) which are guaranteed to be true, since they are self-evident; and then one must be able to argue, by valid logical steps, from the first principles to a whole series of other more detailed claims. The truth of the latter is established by logical derivation from the first principles. In other words, the reason why we think our other claims are true is that we are able to deduce them by logically reliable steps from first principles of which we are independently certain.

When this model is applied to moral or political philosophy, as it is by Aquinas, the result is catastrophic. It requires that we identify some first principles of ethics which are self-evident, and then that we deduce, from these principles, all the specific or detailed moral claims which we wish to make. The certainty or reliability of our moral claims about, for exam-ple, divorce or war, must derive — logically — from the certainty or self-evidence of our first principles.

Aquinas discusses the natural law in precisely these terms. The first principle of natural law is: that good should be pursued and done and evil avoided.[6] Aquinas claims that this principle is self-evidently true, just as the basic laws of logic are self-evident.[7] Most critics have challenged this first principle for the same reason. If one wishes to make it self-evident, this can only be done at the expense of making it trivially true. In other words, if by the word 'good' one means whatever one ought to do, and by the word 'evil' one means whatever should be avoided, then it is true, by definition, that one should do good and avoid evil. But this gives us no idea at all as to which things are good and which are evil. The first principle becomes true simply in virtue of the way we speak English (or Latin); and therefore it could be accepted by anyone, no matter what his views on the morality of particular actions.

If on the contrary we allow the words 'good' and 'evil' to have some independent content and to mean something more specific — for exam-ple, if 'evil' includes torture, and 'good' includes honesty — then of course the first principle is no longer self-evident in any sense which is remotely like Aristotle's understanding of the axioms of geometry.

The problem about the triviality of the first principles of natural law is not the only one which is inherited from the Aristotelian ideal of science; the analogy of logical inference also creates problems. One cannot derive any conclusions from the first principles of natural law without making many other assumptions. Most of these will be factual assumptions about human behaviour, economics, the likely consequences of different human actions, psychology, etc., so that any 'conclusion' one might hope to draw about the morality of some specific issue, such as the use of nuclear weapons in war, will so depend on all the assumptions made in the course of explaining one's moral opinions that it is no longer even plausible to speak about *deducing* one's moral views from first principles.[8]

If Aquinas' theory of natural law were reducible to the analogy with axiomatic systems, it would scarcely deserve the notoriety it has earned, and it would be difficult to explain why it should be called a *natural* law theory at all. The other major assumption of his theory which needs to be discussed is the idea that 'nature' could supply a basis for moral norms. However, before doing so it is important to emphasize the significance of the scientific model for Thomistic natural law theory. It is beyond the scope of this essay to even attempt to explain how the Aristotelian model took such a firm hold in the West that Ptolemy, Copernicus and Galileo were thought not to have produced scientific knowledge but mere hypotheses which seemed to fit the available evidence.[9] A true science of astronomy must begin with self-evident first principles! This model of science is now recognized to be a mistaken ideal. It never fitted moral/political science either; and yet three centuries after the emancipation of physical science from the shackles of Aristotelian methodology, there are still many who demand — without being able to implement the 'ideal' themselves — that ethics and politics must be founded on first principles which are self-evident. No one has ever achieved this impossible objective; one can only speculate as to why it is still proposed as a necessary condition for a viable moral theory. The answer may lie in a dogmatic assumption of infallibility on the part of its main proponents.

Nature Talk

The word 'nature' has so many different meanings that any attempt to distinguish them seems doomed to failure from the outset. The following suggestions are meant to isolate some of the more obvious contrasts which are implicitly assumed in talking about what is 'natural'.

(a) Nature as metaphysical: one of the tenets of Aristotelian and Thomistic metaphysics was that one could successfully distinguish between what is essential to something — such as a tree, a planet or a human being — and what is merely accidental or non-essential. For Aristotle, a planet has not only characteristic properties, but also characteristic motions; likewise, a person has both essential properties and characteristic kinds of actions. Once this distinction was made, then a second step involved postulating the existence of some principle, or cause, in each thing as the intrinsic explanation of its characteristic properties and actions. This principle was called the substance or the nature of the thing. It was something in each thing which explained *why* it had the essential properties it had.

The nature or substance of something was not just a term to refer to its various essential properties, a kind of synoptic term which could be used to denote these properties even if we had not discovered what they were. Rather, 'nature' was assumed to denote a real, objective something or other which was not reducible to the sum total of those properties which we regard as essential or characteristic of something. It follows that if we could ever discover the nature of something, we would thereby have the key to understanding its characteristic properties/actions. This is one of the senses in which Aquinas' theory is a natural law theory.

(b) Laws of nature: the characteristic properties/actions of things are not random; the patterns according to which they are found, or occur, were therefore called laws of nature (in the metaphysical sense of that term). The laws of nature are the regular patterns through which the nature of something is revealed. With the development of science, the metaphysical connotations of the original language were lost and 'laws of nature' came to mean simply 'scientific laws'. In this sense, anything is 'natural' if it happens according to scientific laws.

This understanding of 'natural' is fundamental to two of the distinctions on which natural law theory relies: the distinction between natural and artificial, and the distinction between natural and supernatural.

(c) If something happens as a result of an intentional, human act, then it is said to be artificial as contrasted with natural. This is not an easy distinction to draw, since everything which happens[10] is determined by the laws of nature and is therefore 'natural' in sense (b). Among these 'natural' events or occurrences, some are such that they would not have happened without the intervention of human agency. In this sense, if I water my flowers and they flourish, their flourishing is both natural and artificial; it is natural because the flowers only grow according to the laws of nature. At the same time the flourishing of my flowers is artificial because it would not have happened (they would have 'naturally' died) had I not intervened to water them.

Given a distinction such as this, one might say that those events which occur without any intentional, human agency are 'natural' in a narrower sense than that defined in (b); and those which occur only with the help of an intentional intervention by human agency are *artificial*.

It should be clear, however, that all human actions and their consequences are artificial according to this distinction. Since morality and the law are exclusively concerned with intentional human actions — as opposed to either unintentional acts, or naturally occurring physical events — it follows that all morally good or evil human actions are artificial. The mere fact that some action is artificial could never decide its morality since, by definition, all intentional human actions are artificial.

(d) Natural versus supernatural: if God directly intervenes in human history and suspends the usual pattern of events, his intervention is said to be supernatural. The Christian tradition assumed that God's creation and conservation of the universe is causally at work in every occurrence; so that even 'naturally' occurring events are caused by God. However, if God were to suspend the usual or normal causality of scientific laws and intervene directly to change the natural course of events, such an occurrence would be said to be supernatural.

What is 'natural' — in one or more of the four senses just indicated — is appealed to in natural law theory as a basis for justifying moral values. Such an appeal is nearly always fallacious. It would be impracticable to attempt to examine a list of natural law theories in order to show, in each case, where the fallacy is committed. However, it is relatively easy to show how the mistake is made in one or two cases, and to leave the task of checking different versions of the natural law to their respective defenders. Besides, the use of natural law arguments by the Roman Catholic Church in its official teaching will provide a paradigm of the kinds of fallacies which should be avoided in moral theory, and some of these are discussed below.

From Nature to Norms

It is almost an axiom of moral and political philosophy since the time of David Hume that it is impossible to deduce, logically, moral norms from any set of propositions which does not already include (at least implicitly) a moral principle. This thesis is often described in terms of the logical discrepancy between factual and evaluative statements. This is not the best way of explaining Hume's thesis because it implies that so-called factual claims are value-free. The irreducibility of value judgments can best be explained by staying close to Hume's own version of the thesis: if one wishes to defend or justify a moral norm or principle, and if one hopes to do so by logically deriving it from some other beliefs, then these other beliefs must include moral values on pain of committing a logical fallacy.[11] Hume is not claiming that factual beliefs are irrelevant to making moral judgments; that would be absurd. His point is simply that one cannot hope to logically derive a moral belief from a non-moral belief.

It is a major problem in natural law theory to explain how one might proceed from a discussion of human nature (or any other nature) to a defence of one's moral principles. At least three different strategies seem to have been tried, and none of them is successful.

The first strategy is to argue from a metaphysical account of man's nature to the kind of moral norms which ought to be obeyed. This falls foul of the charge that it commits Hume's fallacy. There is no metaphysical description of man which will imply any set of moral norms, unless one smuggles the relevant moral norms into the initial metaphysical description. In that case, the problem of justifying one's moral views is only deferred to the next step of the discussion, rather than being resolved in the way in which natural law theorists might have hoped.

As an example of this kind of reasoning, one might consider this passage from Jacques Maritain's *The Rights of Man and Natural Law*:

I am taking it for granted that you admit that there is a [metaphysical] human nature, and that this human nature is the same for all men. I am also taking it for granted that you also admit that man is a being gifted with intelligence, and who, as such, acts with an understanding of what he is doing, and therefore with the power to determine for himself the ends which he pursues. On the other hand, possessed of a nature, being constituted in a given determinate fashion, man obviously possesses ends which correspond to his natural constitution and which are the same for all — as all pianos, for instance, whatever their particular type and in whatever spot they may be, have as their end the production of certain attuned sounds. If they don't produce these sounds they must be tuned, or discarded as worthless. But since man is endowed with intelligence and determines his own ends, it is up to him to put himself in tune with the ends necessarily demanded by his nature. This means that there is, by virtue of human nature, *an order or a disposition which human reason can discover and according to which the human will must act in order to attune itself to the necessary ends of the human being. The unwritten law, or natural law, is nothing more than that.*[12]

The suggestions about the role of human reason in discovering the demands of natural law will be discussed under the third strategy below. Maritain's point here is, simply, that whereas non-rational creatures automatically 'act' according to scientific laws, human agents must discover the natural law by reason and then voluntarily direct their actions according to the norms which they discover. However, the relevant consideration at this point is the idea that the moral norms one ought to follow can be simply 'read off' from an inspection of our natures. Maritain talks about 'the ends necessarily demanded' by human nature; he claims that 'there is, by virtue of human nature, *an order or a disposition . . . according to which the human will must act in order to attune itself to the necessary ends of the human being.*' If we translate the necessity of the 'must' and the necessity of the 'necessary ends' into plainer English, we get the following: unavoidable or unchangeable facts about human beings determine how they ought to behave morally. This is a paradigm of Hume's fallacy.

It is not simply that Maritain argues fallaciously in suggesting that we should derive moral conclusions from a factual description of human nature and its dispositions. It is almost a defining feature of this tradition — exactly analogous to its corresponding theory of how science ought to be constructed — that it consistently urges how something should be done, without ever successfully doing it. This might be tolerable as a promissory note for a research programme which is incomplete. But after seven centuries it is challenging the reader's patience to keep saying: 'one should derive moral values from natural descriptions', when no one has successfully done so. This is a case where the failure of a project might indicate that it has been somehow misconceived; and Hume's fallacy explains the kind of misconception involved.

The proposal that one might derive moral values from a description of natural dispositions could only be salvaged by explicitly adding another premise which Maritain wished to exclude; i.e. a premise to the effect that one can discern God's intentions in nature, and that man ought to obey God. This proposal will be taken up in more detail below.

The second strategy for moving from nature talk to objective moral values is to rely on the distinction between natural and artificial occurrences. As already indicated above, all intentional human actions and their consequences are artificial, and therefore any action which is open to moral evaluation is, by definition, artificial. Therefore no one could reasonably argue that an action is immoral simply because it is artificial. There is evidently more here than meets the eye, and the real source of the objection to so-called 'artifical' actions must still be unearthed.

It is patently clear that we consistently interfere in the 'natural' occurrence of events and that we often regard our interventions as morally good. This is surely our appraisal of interventions such as the cultivation of food crops, the prevention of natural disasters (when possible), and so on. So that our actions are not immoral because they are artificial; rather, only some artificial actions are said to be immoral. To distinguish between those which are immoral and those which are not, an *independent* moral criterion must be introduced into the discussion. And if that criterion could be identified, we would know why some people regard a number of artificial actions as immoral. However, this proves to be a very difficult assignment.

There are no plausible explanations available, in the literature, as to why actions which are unnatural — in the sense of artificial — are immoral, except theological reasons or considerations. In other words, on closer analysis this strategy turns out to be not a version of natural law but a disguised, theological criterion of morality. Since the best examples of this strategy are found in the Church's discussion of 'artificial' contraception, it may be preferable to await until the Church's attitude to birth control is discussed below before giving examples of this second strategy.

The final strategy available to natural law theorists — to bridge the gap between nature talk and claims about objective moral values — is to focus on *human reason* as the defining feature of human nature and the means by which we discover moral principles. In general terms, since what is most charactristic of human nature is its rationality, 'to act according to nature' for man is equivalent to 'acting according to reason'. Therefore, to discover the natural law one need only discover what is reasonable or rational. This is the strategy which is preferred by those who recognize the more obvious pitfalls of the first two strategies — notably by John Finnis; it is also less easy to clearly identify and discuss since so many different moral theories may be based on 'rational' human behaviour.

Two comments are in order before trying to focus on this approach to
natural law more accurately. Many natural law theorists in the Thomistic
tradition — from Aquinas to Maritain — put reason to work in discovering the natural law in such a way that it relies on one or other of the first
two strategies already discussed. For example, when reason reflects on
the nature of man it is said to discover certain innate, natural dispositions which are indicators of how one ought to behave, and so on. Insofar as such rational investigations also rely on the first two strategies,
they are subject to all the objections already introduced.

Secondly, it would be a misuse of standard philosophical usage to include all rational moral systems as natural law theories solely in virtue of
the fact that they depend on human reason for their justification. If one
wished to classify all rationally developed moral theories — from Plato
and Aristotle, Mill and Kant, to Rawls, Gewirth, Nozick or Locke — as
natural law theories, this semantic manoeuvre would have the effect of
disguising the obvious differences between such theories which, in many
cases, are related as almost exact contraries. It is for this reason that
those who reject what are traditionally called natural law theories are not
necessarily moral relativists; one can defend a reasonable moral theory
which is not a natural law theory.

If one distinguishes between the many rational moral theories which
are usually not classified as natural law theories and those which are, the
one feature which seems to characterize the latter group is its commitment to the Aristotelian model of knowledge and its associated belief in
the self-evidence of basic moral principles. The most recent defenders of
this approach are Germain Grisez and John Finnis.[13] Finnis argues that
the reasonableness of pursuing basic human values — such as
knowledge, friendship, etc. — is self-evident. He claims that 'knowledge
is good' is self-evident, in the sense that it cannot be justified by
reference to some more basic or fundamental claim; that it is a correct
judgment; and that any attempt to deny this claim is self-defeating
because the very claim which is being denied must be assumed in its attempted denial. This argument fails. Those who wish to deny the intrinsic value of knowledge may do so by either assuming that only one claim
has an intrinsic value, namely: the claim that knowledge is not good; or
by assuming that all knowledge-claims, including the denial that
knowledge is good, have only some extrinsic value. In other words,
knowledge might be classified as a value which is secondary to other
human values, and therefore it has no intrinsic value or value in its own
right.

There is another objection to this approach which is similar to the one already made against the 'first principle' of natural law. One might be willing to concede that human knowledge is a basic human good as long as the claims being made on its behalf are so general and vague that they commit no one to specific moral behaviour. As with Aquinas' first principle, the attempt to achieve certainty in basic moral values can only be realized by trivialising one's claims. Endorsing truisms commits no one to any particular kind of behaviour.

An alternative version of the third strategy — which is sometimes combined with Finnis' approach — is to use the concept of rationality as the controlling concept of a moral theory. What is rational or reasonable then determines what is moral. The history of discussions of what is meant by 'reasonable', however, is as disputed as the parallel history of moral theories. To focus attention on what is reasonable, rather than on what is moral, only changes the language in which our standard disputes about moral theory are conducted. There is no ready solution in this direction. Only those who have not seriously taken up the challenge can simplistically say: objective moral standards can be readily established by rational argument.

To summarize the argument in this section: one of the characteristic features of natural law theories is the idea that one can justify one's moral beliefs by deriving them from a theory of human nature. Man's nature, as an objective reality, determines our objective moral values. It is one thing to claim that this can be done; it is quite another thing to actually do it. No one has so far successfully derived objective moral norms from a description of human nature. If they had done so, some of the most difficult problems in the justification of moral principles would have been resolved.

Three different approaches have been tried in the attempt to derive norms from nature, and in some theories more than one of the three strategies have been combined together. In the first approach, the attempt to derive moral values from a metaphysical theory of human nature is frustrated by Hume's fallacy. This objection applies even if one is sympathetic to the particular metaphysical theory of nature which is assumed. The second approach, which involves classifying some behaviour as immoral because it is artificial and therefore unnatural, also fails, because it fails to provide a plausible reason for believing that some artificial actions are morally good and some morally evil. In many cases in which one can guess at the hidden criterion on which this distinction is made, the only basis for describing unnatural actions as immoral is a theological one. Finally, the third strategy — of attempting to define moral behaviour in terms of what is rational — only succeeds in replacing disagreements about what is moral with corresponding disagreements about what is rational.

The many problems which confront natural law theories emerge as soon as we put them to work to help resolve any disputed issue. This holds true in political theory, in familiar questions about sexual ethics, and even in jurisprudence. For example, senior members of the Irish judiciary have often appealed to 'the natural law' to reach a decision on fundamental issues of rights or in adjudicating conflicting interpretations of constitutional law. It is not surprising that these judgments have stumbled into the quicksands of natural law controversies, and that what might have promised to provide guidance has lead instead to the exact opposite. One need look no further than the Supreme Court decision in *G. v. An Bord Uchtála* (1980) for a variety of conflicting interpretations of what 'natural law' means, and for a corresponding range of decisions by each of the five justices involved.[14]

The detailed issues which are involved in any particular decision by the Courts may not be of immediate interest to the general reader. The same can hardly be said, however, of the Roman Catholic Church's reliance on natural law theory in expounding its views on marriage and a great variety of different questions. These have been so much a feature of Irish experience in the twentieth century, not just for members of the Church, but for many others who are affected by the Church's influence on the medical services and, more generally, on legislation, that they deserve explicit discussion and analysis.

Natural Law and the Church

The Roman Catholic Church, as recently as the Second Vatican Council, has continued to endorse the natural law as a moral law which is universally binding.[15] At the same time it has not given any clear or consistent explanation of what it understands by 'the natural law'. It is almost as if Church authorities believe that there are objective moral values which can be discovered by reason, independently of religious faith, and that whatever those values are, they are what the Church means by natural law. Natural law, in other words, refers to the moral values rather than to any particular theory or coherent account of these values.

This would be an unobjectionable way of talking if it only involved a slightly archaic way of denoting moral values. However, the Church has also given some indications of what account or theory of natural law it endorses, and in sketching arguments for its teaching on contraception it has made it clear that it is relying on a version of natural law theory which is subject to many of the objections discussed above.

Before examining some of these arguments in more detail, it is necessary to clarify the status of the Church's claims about natural law. Does the Church accept that the natural law can be discovered by reason alone? If not, should one conclude that the teaching of the Church about natural law is part of its *theological* tradition and hence, to a great extent, falls outside the scope of rational criticism?

The Church sometimes teaches that the natural law may be discovered by reason alone. Thus Pope Pius XII, in the encyclical *Humani Generis* (1950), says that 'absolutely speaking, human reason by its own natural force and light can arrive at a true and certain knowledge . . . of the natural law.'[16] However, there is an equally strong tradition in the Church to the effect that reason is not very reliable in accomplishing what, absolutely speaking, it might be able to achieve. Pope Pius XI was a strong proponent of this thesis. In his encyclical on marriage, *Casti Connubii* (1930), he warned Christians against relying on human reason to discover the moral law:

For Christ Himself made the Church the teacher of truth in those things also which concern the right regulation of moral conduct, even though some knowledge of the same is not beyond human reason. . . .

Wherefore, let the faithful also be on their guard against the overrated independence of private judgment and that false autonomy of human reason. For it is quite foreign to everyone bearing the name of a Christian to trust his own mental powers with such pride as to agree only with those things which he can examine from their inner nature, . . . a characteristic of all true followers of Christ, lettered or unlettered, is to suffer themselves to be guided and led in all things that touch upon faith or morals by the Holy Church of God through its Supreme Pastor the Roman Pontiff, who is himself guided by Jesus Christ Our Lord.[17]

A similar sentiment is repeated in the encyclical, *Mit brennender Sorge* (1937):

The moral conduct of mankind is grounded on faith in God kept true and pure. Every attempt to dislodge moral teaching and moral conduct from the rock of faith, and to build them on the unstable sands of human norms, sooner or later leads the individual and the community to moral destruction. The fool, who hath said in his heart, there is no God, will walk the ways of corruption. The number of such fools, who today attempt to separate morality and religion, has become legion.[18]

For this reason one finds repeated claims in the teaching of the Church to the effect that the Roman Catholic Church is the exclusive, authentic 'teacher of the whole moral law'.[19] For example, Pope Paul VI wrote in *Humanae Vitae* that the teaching of the Church was 'founded on the natural law, illuminated and enriched by divine revelation'. He continued:

No believer will wish to deny that the teaching authority of the Church is competent to interpret even the natural moral law. It is indisputable . . . that Jesus Christ . . . constituted them [i.e. Peter and the apostles] as guardians and authentic interpreters of all the moral law, not only, that is, of the law of the Gospel, but also of the natural law, which is also an expression of the will of God . . .[20]

The following gloss might capture the ambivalence of these statements about the capacities of human reason. Theoretically speaking, it is possible for reason, independently of religious faith, to discover some of the first principles of natural law. However, reason is fallible and is very often misguided. The Church, by contrast, is infallible. Hence to the extent to which philosophers might reach conclusions which disagree with Roman Catholic Church teaching, the philosophers are mistaken. The Church, therefore, provides an infallible guide to the demands of the natural law. Because it is claiming to provide an infallible guide, its teaching cannot be based on the fallible reasons of philosophy but must be based, ultimately, on religious faith.

Since the Church approaches its teaching on natural law in this way, it is not surprising that by the term 'natural law' it means the moral law ordained by God. Thus Pius XI, in the encyclical *Quadragesimo Anno* (1931) speaks about 'nature, or rather God the author of nature,' as establishing purposes in various kinds of activity. And when he claims, in the same encyclical, that the right to private ownership is a natural right, he says that 'nature, rather the Creator himself, has given man the right to private ownership'.[21] The 'law of nature' is merely a part of a more comprehensive 'law of God'; thus, 'the law of nature, or rather God's will promulgated by it, demands that right order be observed' in the application of natural resources to human use.[22] Pope Paul VI likewise wrote of the 'creative intention of God, expressed in the very nature of marriage and its acts,'[23] and claimed that any intentional efforts at birth-control must be realized 'with respect for the order established by God'.[24]

What is presented here is evidently a *theological interpretation* of natural phenomena. One is asked to read various natural patterns of events as, in some sense, indications of God's will for man. And since it is a theological interpretation, it is no longer surprising that reason is not adequate to the task. The suggestion that reason could, in principle, discover the natural law amounts to saying: if reason were to adopt a teleological interpretation of nature and to interpret patterns of events as if they were indications of a divine intention, then reason could thereby discover the natural law. However, if human reason were to propose such an interpretation of nature, it could hardly be proposed as something which is reasonably established; it would be nothing more than a guess or an unconfirmable hypothesis. Therefore faith alone can provide such guidance in natural law thinking, because what is being taught is a religious interpretation of nature.

One might react to this conclusion by saying: if the Church's natural law thinking is so fundamentally theological, why not make its status clear for everyone to see? Why not simply say: our natural law beliefs about the immorality of artificial contraception are just like our beliefs about the Immaculate Conception or the Trinity; they are part of our religious faith which cannot be appreciated except by those who accept the faith. This is too simple a solution to the problem, however, because the Church is committed to the view that man must be able, by reason alone, to recognize moral distinctions. Otherwise he could never rationally evaluate the moral teaching of any proposed revelation and therefore he would have no way of choosing between the invitations to faith of conflicting religious traditions. The Church needs both options at once. It needs to maintain the possibility of rationally discovering the natural moral law in order to make the choice of the Church's teaching rational; and at the same time it needs to be able to say that those who disagree with its moral teaching have made a mistake, for the Church is the ultimate guide to all moral teaching. It is the attempt to juggle both of these options at the same time that has led many sympathetic readers, who try to understand the Church's reasoning on moral matters, to give up the effort in frustration. One or two examples of such reasoning may highlight the ambiguity in question.

The alleged immorality of artificial contraception is based on the assumption that it frustrates the 'intrinsic nature' of sexual intercourse between married persons. Thus Pope Pius XI, in *Casti Connubii*:

But no reason, however grave, may be put forward by which anything intrinsically against *nature* may become conformable to *nature* and morally good. Since, therefore, the conjugal act is destined primarily by *nature* for the begetting of children, those who in exercising it deliberately frustrate its *natural* power and purpose sin against *nature* and commit a deed which is shameful and intrinsically vicious. . . . any use whatsoever of matrimony exercised in such a way that the act is deliberately frustrated in its *natural* power to generate life is an offence against the law of God and of *nature*. . . . the cultivating of mutual love, and the quieting of concupiscence . . . are not forbidden . . . so long as they are subordinated to the primary end and so long as the intrinsic *nature* of the act is preserved.[25] (Italics added).

The language in which this teaching is expressed is softened in later Church teaching, but the teaching itself remains essentially unchanged. Thus Pope Paul VI, in *Humanae Vitae*:

In the task of transmitting life, [parents] . . . must conform their activity to the creative intention of God, which is expressed in the very *nature* of marriage and its acts, and manifested by the constant teaching of the Church. . . . God has wisely disposed *natural* laws and rhythms of fecundity which, of themselves, cause a separation in the succession of births. Nonetheless the Church, calling men back to the observance of the norms of the *natural* law, as interpreted by her constant doctrine, teaches that each and every marriage act must remain open to the transmission of life. . . . an act of love which jeopardises the disponibility to transmit life which God the Creator, according to particular laws, inserted therein, is in contradiction with the design constitutive of marriage, and with the will of the author of life . . . [man's control over conception must be determined] by the respect due to the integrity of the human organism and its functions . . .[26] (Italics added)

These attempts to explain the Church's stand on the immorality of contraception may initially appear to argue from biological laws to moral principles. If that were the case, the Church's teaching would be patently fallacious in attempting to derive moral values from a consideration of the natural rhythms of the human cycle of fertility. A closer reading of the texts, however, shows that there is an extra assumption introduced which bears the full force of the moral conclusions. And the extra assumption is a *religious belief*.

The Pope's teaching could be translated as follows. God is the cause of nature and of everything in nature. In creating nature as He does, He has a definite plan with which human agents may or may not co-operate. One can discover God's intentions — at least the Church can infallibly discern God's plan — by properly interpreting the hidden meanings in apparently secular events. Conception is one such event. In discerning the intentions of God, the Church is guided by biological laws. So, when it talks about the 'intrinsic nature' of the marriage act, it is really talking about the biological laws which control fertility in human beings.

The Church does not argue that every act of marital intercourse must have the possibility of causing a conception; that is absurd. Nor is it immoral to engage in sexual relations when one is certain that conception is impossible. The characteristic of an immoral act (in this context) is precisely any attempt to interfere in or to modify the natural cycles of human fertility. Such attempts to frustrate nature are fully in keeping with the laws of nature, and therefore they are natural in sense (b) above. On the other hand, they are only artificial in the same sense in which all rational exploitation of scientific laws is artificial; they cause effects which, without human intervention, would not have occurred. But this alone could never make them immoral.

The immorality of artificial contraception, on the Church's view, depends exclusively on *one* consideration: that such methods of birth-control contravene *the Church's interpretation of God's intentions,* insofar as these intentions are revealed in the unmodified course of natural cycles of fertility and infertility. This is a natural law theory only in the weakest sense possible. There is no reasoning in this theory which philosophers can dispute because it is not based on reasons. It is exclusively based on the religious faith of the Church.

A similar conclusion is required in relation to the Church's ban on voluntary, human sterilization. Pope Pius XI taught:

Christian doctrine establishes, and the light of human reason makes it more clear, that private individuals have no other power over the members of their bodies than that which pertains to their natural ends; and they are not free to destroy or mutilate their members, or in any other way render themselves unfit for their natural functions, except when no other provision can be made for the good of the whole body.[27]

The same teaching is repeated by Pope Paul VI:

Equally to be excluded, as the teaching authority of the Church has frequently declared, is direct sterilisation, whether perpetual or temporary, whether of the man or of the woman.[28]

The moral objections to sterilization depend exclusively on the contraceptive purpose of the procedure. Mutilation of the human body is not intrinsically evil — otherwise no operation could ever be condoned, because what is intrinsically evil is never permissible in Catholic morality. Nor is sterilization immoral because it renders someone incapable of conceiving; there are various medical therapies, some surgical and some involving radiation, which render the patient sterile, but they are not *intrinsically* evil on that account. The reason why voluntary sterilization is said to be intrinsically immoral is not because of the physical characteristics of the operation or its consequences; it is exclusively because the subject of a sterilization intends the medical intervention as a contraceptive procedure. Therefore, even if such a procedure were unsuccessful and the patient's potential for procreation were unaffected, the procedure would still be immoral. The only natural law consideration which could support this position is the theological theory of God's intentions. One ought not to interfere in nature because God does not wish to be frustrated in controlling the procreative contingencies of married sexual life!

While it is clear from these two examples that the Church's teaching on sexual morality is often expressed in the language of the natural law, it should not be implied that natural law thinking is only used in such contexts. For example, Pope Pius XI based his teaching on social reform on the natural law, and likewise his condemnation of Nazism; Pope John XXIII appealed to the natural law to support claims about human rights. However, although the specific issue may change from one occasion to another, one feature is constant in the Church's natural law thinking, namely: the lack of appeal to any rational arguments in support of its teaching and, in their place, the claim that the Church can infallibly interpret the objective moral law or the natural law. The Church's teaching, therefore, is ultimately an expression of its own religious faith; it is part of its theology, and not amenable to rational evaluation.

Conclusion

The term 'natural law' is used to denote a wide variety of very different theories and even, in Roman Catholic moral teaching, those moral values which the Church endorses as objective and rationally established. Any discussion which tries to come to terms with the natural law tradition must take cognizance of this semantic variation, at the risk of compounding our present lack of understanding with further obscurities.

If 'natural law' means simply those moral and political values which are endorsed by the Church and which are believed by the Church to be rationally established, then the term is doing double duty for two different roles. It both identifies certain values or principles, and implicitly takes a stand on the question of their justification. There is no serious objection to the first of these, except its propensity to cause confusion. The second role, however — concerned with justification — needs to be clarified and defended by reference to some theory or other. This is the area in which most uses of 'natural law' occur.

If 'natural law' refers to some theory — some general account which explains why one holds the moral views one does or why such views are plausible — then the term ambiguously denotes a whole series of alternative theories. Anyone wishing to defend his moral views is only dodging the problem of justification by failing to specify which of the many natural law theories he covertly defends. Rather than examine a sample of different theories, I have confined the discussion in this chapter to Aquinas' natural law theory.

The Thomistic tradition of natural law theorizing suffers from a number of fatal flaws. It mistakenly attempts to construct ethics by analogy with a disreputable model of scientific knowledge; it can only claim that its first principles are self-evident by trivializing them; it is permanently open to Hume's objection, that it attempts to derive moral standards from non-moral (metaphysical) descriptions of man's nature; and it attempts to deduce specific moral guidance from vague, general principles by ignoring the complexity of the argument which connects the two. If all these objections are constantly made by critics of this particular natural law tradition, one might wonder at the apparent enthusiasm of the Roman Catholic Church to embrace such a theory.

The answer to this question is clear enough. Church teaching on such matters as contraception and sterilization is only apparently built on a natural law base. In fact, the Church's teaching rests, ultimately, on a theological interpretation of nature which is not open to rational evaluation. The Church needs to assume that some basic moral principles can be rationally discovered; hence the use of the 'natural law' rhetoric. At the same time, it is deeply committed to the belief that its own theological sources, inspired by faith, are the ultimate arbiters of all moral questions. The muddle which results from this combination of theology and natural law rhetoric is not a philosophically defensible theory at all. It is one part of the Church's more comprehensive ideology which purports to explain why those who are believers have no need to look beyond the limits of their faith for the principles which resolve all their moral and political dilemmas. 'Natural law', in this context, is merely the pseudo-reasonable mask of a religious belief.

3

Tolerance and Pluralism

The virtue of tolerance is often confused with a complete lack of moral principle, in such a way that the most unprincipled people are also, by definition, the most tolerant. If one combines this mistake with a penchant for false dilemmas, one is too easily offered the option between being principled, being 'willing to stand up and be counted', and being tolerant. Whatever one might do in practice, at least in theory this approach almost forces people into admitting that they cannot afford to be tolerant. If one is a person of principle one cannot at the same time be tolerant!

To avoid this conclusion it is necessary to explain how moral convictions and the virtue of tolerance are compatible. Obviously such a theoretical discussion will not automatically make people more tolerant, no more than a philosophical discussion of truth-telling will make them honest. However, to the extent that intolerance is taught as an integral part of our common ideology, any successful challenge to that ideology may help undermine at least one source of intolerance.

Since the term 'tolerance' may mean quite different things to different people, there is no point in defending tolerance without first explaining what it means. In its paradigm use, a number of conditions must be satisfied before one can properly speak of tolerance.[1] The first condition is that two people or two traditions disagree about the moral/political merits of some significant course of human action. This only happens if both sides sincerely hold their moral/political beliefs with conviction. Thus, one normally does not speak of tolerance if those who disagree on a course of action share the same views about its ill-merits, and one side is expected to condone behaviour which the other side equally condemns. Tolerance presupposes a genuine difference in the moral evaluation of some type of behaviour. Likewise there is no question of tolerance — in the sense to be discussed here — if the issue at stake is relatively insignificant (when judged by the standards of both sides). We often speak of a tolerant person in the context of those who are very patient with the foibles of their fellowman, or of those who are willing to ignore a great variety of more or less annoying eccentricities in others. However this wider usage will be ignored here in order to focus attention on major differences in value judgements about important instances of human behaviour or public policy.

It should also be noted that, even by this first condition, it would be impossible to be tolerant if one had no reasonably firm moral/political convictions which could conflict with those of others.

The second condition presupposed for tolerance is that the disputed behaviour falls within what might be called the 'sphere of competence' of both parties. This condition needs to be expanded in some detail. An Irish citizen is normally not said to tolerate the purely personal or private immorality of a citizen of Sydney, Australia. Whether he likes it or not, and whether he approves of it or not, we tend to think that there is nothing he can do about it and, besides, that it is none of his business. This introduces two new factors which are relevant to deciding whether there is any issue of tolerance at all: (a) the *responsibility* of one agent to interfere in the behaviour of others; and (b) the *ability* of one agent to intervene in frustrating what he considers to be the immoral behaviour of others. Since the second factor is less contentious, it might be discussed first before dealing with the issue of responsibility.

If someone behaves in a manner of which I strongly disapprove, and if I believe (even mistakenly) that I can do nothing to stop him or at least to inhibit his actions, then my failure to intervene is not an example of tolerance. My failure to act on my own moral principles is explained simply by my belief that I am unable to prevent or impede the behaviour of which I so strongly disapprove. This set of circumstances is often covered by a condemnation of the behaviour in question, partly to indicate publicly that one's inaction is not to be interpreted as condoning, and partly to alleviate the frustration of not being able to do anything else in response to the demands of one's own moral principles. Even here, however, the act of condemning some behaviour may be a fruitless exercise if it has absolutely no effect on the behaviour which is opposed.

The other factor involved — one's degree of responsibility for another's action — is both more complex and more disputed. What is at stake here is one's responsibility for failing to intervene in the immoral behaviour of another and to that extent sharing responsibility for the action which results. To clarify this point it is necessary to rely on two distinctions; one is the distinction between causing something and failing to prevent its occurrence. The other is the distinction between private and public actions. Both of these are sufficiently complex to demand a lengthy discussion in its own right; something short of that, with supporting footnotes, will have to suffice here.

The first distinction tends to coincide with the distinction between utilitarian and non-utilitarian moral theories. For the classic utilitarian, the moral worth of an action is decided exclusively by reference to its consequences. Thus any actions or inactions on my part which have exactly the same consequences, or even comparable effects on a utilitarian scale, have exactly the same moral worth. If I cause the death of a child by intentionally drowning it, or by failing to save the child from drowning in circumstances which make it easy for me to do so, both my action and inaction are equally reprehensible.[2] In each case the resulting consequences involve the death of the child; and therefore both action and inaction merit the same moral evaluation. It is irrelevant to the morality of the issue that in one case I took positive steps to drown the child, whereas in the other case I merely failed to do something which I could have done without much inconvenience.

If the utilitarian is committed to this kind of moral evaluation, then the mere occurrence of non-moral evils anywhere in the world — such as famine, curable disease, avoidable consequences of natural disasters — is a challenge to his moral conscience. To the extent to which he can effectively diminish the ill-effects of such natural occurrences — minimally by donating a percentage of his salary to alleviate the suffering of victims — he is morally responsible for their occurrence. There is a question, for the utilitarian, of comparing the unwelcome consequences for the agent with the unwelcome consequences, for example, for those starving in the Third World. However, the suffering of starving people is hardly comparable to the slight inconvenience or lower standard of living experienced by those who donate part of their salary to alleviate others' suffering. By a judicious choice of examples therefore, and the inevitable occurrence of enough natural disasters to challenge the utilitarian's conscience, it is permanently true that the classic utilitarian is expected to forego all luxuries to alleviate the suffering of others, for he is responsible for such suffering in others to the extent to which he intentionally fails to alleviate it.

There is another tradition in moral philosophy which contrasts an agent's responsibility for what he intentionally does with his responsibility for what he intentionally fails to do. It is not easy to explain why merely failing to prevent something evil is any less immoral than intentionally causing the same evil. One line of explanation is the following. Those evils which naturally occur, such as famine, ill-health, etc., are neither moral nor immoral. Morality is only a feature of human actions insofar as they are intentional and voluntary. Hence, moral norms are primarily directed towards influencing the intentional behaviour of human agents. If we compare the intentional perspective of two moral agents — one of whom directly causes some evil while the other merely fails to prevent some evil — the action of the first agent can only be described in terms of his decision to cause evil. It is the very paradigm of a morally evil act. The intention of the other agent (who fails to prevent the occurrence of evil) may be described in a number of ways; to that extent what he meant to do is not unambiguously evil. He may plausibly describe his inaction as not interfering, as being slow to respond to the moral demands of the situation, as being lazy, etc. In other words, there is often available a variety of excusing, plausible descriptions of his behaviour which would diminish the degree of his responsibility involved in the occurrence of the evil event.

Like most distinctions in ethics and politics, this is not a very clear line of demarcation. One could easily think of examples of action and inaction where it is extremely implausible to distinguish the moral evil of a contrasting pair of events. For example, to disconnect the life-support system of a patient in a medical centre is hardly much worse than the intentional failure of a member of the medical staff to reconnect such a machine if it accidently became disconnected. In this case the difference between acting and failing to act is of minimal moral significance. However, in many less bizarre cases, especially those which tend to happen in real life situations, the moral responsibility of those who fail to prevent evil is usually diminished by a variety of other factors apart from their moral weakness. By contrast, the intentional commission of a voluntary evil action is the paradigm of moral evil.

The possibility of tolerance partly depends on a distinction, such as this, between an agent's responsibility for what he intentionally does, and the agent's moral responsibility for what he fails to prevent. This kind of distinction is combined with other considerations in a rather rough-and-ready calculation before one decides to tolerate some form of moral evil. Anticipating the discussion to some extent, it is hardly a commendable stance to tolerate behaviour which is so reprehensible that it almost announces its own immorality. Torture is such a case.

The other factor involved in gauging an agent's responsibility depends on a distinction between private and public actions. Since this is discussed in some detail in Chapter 5, the results of that discussion will be assumed here. Briefly, an action is 'private', not in proportion to the relative secrecy with which it is performed, but in proportion to the limitation of its likely consequences to the agent who performs the action. As in the previous case, this provides no sharp line of demarcation between private and public acts. However, it does provide a kind of continuum between extremely public acts, such as planning for nuclear warfare, and extremely private acts, such as breaking a promise one makes to oneself to improve one's behaviour. What is at stake for questions of tolerance is not the isolation of a set of completely private acts, but a consideration of the relative privacy of an act compared with others which might be differently evaluated.

The various factors discussed so far can now be put to use in describing tolerance. Tolerance, as a moral virtue, only arises when: (i) one is confronted with a significant instance of human behaviour in another which one considers to be morally evil, while the agent considers it to be morally good or at least morally acceptable; and (ii) the circumstances are such that it is at least possible for the dissenter to either prevent or inhibit the behaviour in question. In considering the second condition, there are two factors which need to be considered and the distinctions introduced here make room for the possibility of tolerance. One is the distinction between doing something and failing to prevent its occurrence, together with the assumption that one is more responsible for the former than the latter. The other distinction hinges on the difference between private and public actions; one has more responsibility for the prevention of public actions than one has for the prevention of private actions and their consequences.

The consideration of the action-inaction distinction makes explicit another consideration which is unavoidable in making room for tolerance; that is a consideration of the relative moral importance of different actions. The addition of too many qualifications and distinctions to any moral stance may cause it to degenerate into an effete casuistry; on the other hand, the lack of fairly obvious distinctions is the mark of the fanatic. The intolerant are more likely to suffer from fanaticism rather than over-qualification. So they might bear with one more distinction in trying to identify the source of their particular malady. This is, as already mentioned, the distinction between more or less grave moral responsibilities.

In training children or in cultivaitng a moral sense in adults, it is a dangerous gamble to consistently overstate the importance of too many guidelines, whether moral or otherwise. If almost every rule is of the greatest importance — like every vaguely confidential document being classified as 'top secret' — the most likely outcome is that the evaluative guidelines will eventually be ignored. There is a strong tradition in Roman Catholic moral theology of exaggerating the moral significance of human failings. Slight sexual indiscretions were traditionally classified as deserving eternal damnation, as were minor deviations from the proprieties of diet associated with Fridays or fast days.[3] Failure to be physically present for most of the Sunday liturgy was similarly considered to be in the same category as murdering one's neighbour. It is irrelevant that some instances of gravely immoral behaviour were such that they required a special procedure for absolving the guilt of the sinner; when one is sentenced to eternal damnation the finer points of ecclesiastical absolution pale into insignificance.

In such a moral framework as this, in which so many disparate and obviously incommensurable actions are all classified together as meriting eternal damnation, it is not surprising if the official belief of Christians is undermined by a reserve of scepticism about the whole scale of values which is taught by the churches. When one no longer believes the 'mortal sin' account of sexual indiscretions, one may likewise abandon one's evaluation of the moral evil of politically motivated murder or torture. In fact, the extreme penalties promised for all serious moral lapses were such that creative theologians had to invent a great variety of 'pastorally motivated' excuses in order to explain away the magnitude of sins being committed by pious, God-fearing members of the faithful. Many of these 'excusing factors' could then be exploited to eventually undermine the apparent moral evil of heinous crimes.

To avoid the double-thinking of official and unofficial classifications of morality, where the official list includes too much and the unofficial list excuses too much, it would be preferable from the outset to have a clearer picture of rather fewer seriously immoral actions. This kind of classification might be patterned after a theory of rights. If a satisfactory level of agreement could be reached in identifying human rights, not only as vaguely expressed political ideas but also as specific, minimal safeguards for the well-being of individual citizens, then the most serious of one's negative moral obligations could be defined by reference to the rights of others.

This adds a third factor to the two already listed in defining tolerance. It would be easier to be tolerant of behaviour which is only moderately or slightly immoral than of blatant cases of seriously infringing the human rights of others. As in the two previous distinctions, we again fail to find a sharp distinction here between two classes of actions: those which are seriously immoral and those which are not. However there is sufficiently broad agreement on the distinction between very seriously immoral acts and trivially immoral acts, that even a relatively unclear distinction like this can throw some light on decisions about what kind of behaviour we ought to tolerate.

The difficulties which emerge in trying to make the distinctions introduced so far make it obvious that we are operating in a field in which knowledge and certainty are not easily achieved, if at all. Since human fallibility was one of the main arguments of John Stuart Mill in favour of tolerance,[4] it is essential to consider fallibility, at some length, as a fourth condition which should determine one's attitude towards tolerance.

Fallibility and Moral Norms

The logic of intolerance is so seductive in its simplicity that the burden of making room for tolerance falls inevitably on those who dissent from the simpler theory. This is especially true in trying to explain how someone can endorse moral values with great conviction and at the same time recognize the possibility that he may be mistaken; more accurately, that those who disagree with his moral evaluation of some course of action may not be mistaken. Recognizing one's fallibility in moral matters does not imply moral relativism. In fact those who defend the classic relativist position would find it impossible to justify the kind of tolerance which is being advocated here. Classic relativism precludes the possibility of disagreeing with the moral beliefs of others; and it also undermines the kind of conviction about moral beliefs which is necessary to sustain tolerance itself as a moral virtue. Tolerance or intolerance are equally acceptable for the relativist.

Chapter 1 above argued for the possibility of equally moral, though incompatible, courses of action which are directed towards achieving the same or comparable ends. This implies that two competing proposals might both be equally moral despite their obvious differences. To speak about one or other being necessarily immoral is a mistake.

It was also argued that it is inappropriate to speak of moral claims being true or false. And yet there is no difficulty in describing a course of action as moral or immoral. To say that a moral value is 'true' is to endorse it. It does not necessarily imply that there are objective criteria available, by analogy with physical science, which could provide evidence to decide among competing moral claims. There are right ways of doing things, and wrong ways; there are morally good actions and grossly immoral ones. There are politically viable social policies and those which ruin or corrupt the body politic. All these distinctions can and must be made, without naively relying on a correspondence theory of truth for value-judgments. This understanding of the status of value-judgments implies that it is logically possible for two contrasting moral evaluations to be both equally valid. The classic principle of logic — that of two contrary opinions at least one of them must be false — does not apply in moral or political philosophy. This loosening of logical restrictions on moral discourse provides the first step in the argument in favour of a less inflexible style of moral evaluation. From the assumed validity of my own moral/political views I can no longer draw any immediate inference about the validity of contrasting views. The validity or otherwise of different views has to be decided by some independent criteria.

In attempting to provide an independent evaluation of someone else's view, I cannot avoid Mill's argument about my own fallibility; and this supplies a well-founded reason for tolerance.

There is a caricature of Mill's argument available which is so implausible that it provides his opponents with a convenient 'straw man' to discredit the merits of his suggestions. The caricature runs as follows: I can never be absolutely certain of my own beliefs, whether in science or politics, because I am fallible. The mere possibility of being mistaken undermines whatever conviction I might have about anything. Therefore no matter what situation I might encounter in which the most immoral behaviour — that is, according to my fallible standard — is condoned, I am not justified in intervening because I may be mistaken, and the contrary opinion may be more valid. Thus, for example, if I know of cases of sadistic torture of innocent children, I am not morally justified in objecting because it is at least logically possible that my moral opinions about torture are mistaken and those of the torturers valid. If Mill's argument supports this position it effectively undermines all possibility of moral conviction, because it intervenes at precisely that point at which principles are implemented in practice, to frustrate their application to any real life situation.

Mill's argument is directed, not at reasonable moral conviction, but at the gratuitous assumption of infallibility which excuses us from the need to re-evaluate our convictions in the light of competing moral/political claims. Mill, in brief, objects to infallibility as one of the theoretical foundations of fanaticism. Once the assumption of infallibility is removed, then the burden of justification is placed squarely on the shoulders of those who would hope to impose their own moral standards on others.

To understand either Mill's thesis or the contrasting stance of the Roman Catholic Church, it is necessary to explain what is meant by 'infallibility'. To say that a person or institution is infallible is to claim that it is impossible for it to be mistaken (in some respect or other which is specified). This is not equivalent to claiming that one is not, in fact, mistaken on a given occasion or issue. It would be odd to describe anyone as having moral convictions (or any other kind of convictions) if they did not think of themselves as not mistaken about those beliefs. Infallibility is the much stranger claim that, not only is one not mistaken, but it is not even possible for one to be mistaken. What kind of reasons might one give, or what kind of evidence might one invoke, for believing, about oneself: 'I am infallible'?

There is no rational basis whatever for this belief. No matter what reasons I might introduce to support it, and no matter what evidence I might produce in its favour, the evidence or reasons may themselves be mistaken unless I argue in a vicious circle and beg the very question at issue. Thus my belief in my own infallibility is only as reliable as the fallible reasons or evidence I can introduce to support it. And to the extent that such reasons are fallible, so is my belief in my own infallibility.

There is nothing new in this conclusion for the one institution on earth which publicly claims to be infallible, namely, the Roman Catholic Church. The teaching of the Church makes it abundantly clear that no Christian can reasonably claim to *know* that the Church is infallible. To make such a claim would be to fall into the fallacy just mentioned. Roman Catholics claim to believe, for religious reasons, that the teaching of the Church is infallibly guided by God. If their belief is misplaced, the Church is fallible. There is no rational procedure available for deciding the issue one way or the other, since no evidence could possibly count, no matter how damaging on rational grounds, against a religious belief.

It follows that no one can rationally support the belief in his or her own infallibility, and this is the first premise of Mill's argument. However it is hardly necessary to believe in one's own infallibility in order to have a high degree of certainty and conviction about any claim, whether moral, political or empirical. A qualified certainty in empirical matters and a high degree of conviction in both moral and political claims are both consistent with acknowledging the possibility of being mistaken. On the contrary, the assumption of infallibility precludes the very possibility of ever being mistaken. When combined with a fairly primitive logic of moral discourse, one could argue from the guaranteed 'truth' of one's own beliefs to the necessary 'falsehood' of opposing views. If this kind of conclusion is further combined with an un-discriminating attitude towards lesser and greater moral evils, the implications are obvious. Almost all opposing views are not only guaranteed to be wrong; but they are also so serious that it is indeed difficult to find any reason why one should tolerate them.

This is anticipating the conclusion; it must still be shown how, even without an assumption of infallibility, one might plausibly combine a strong conviction about one's own beliefs with a recognition that they may be false or misguided.

There is an obvious appearance of contradiction in saying: 'I promise to meet you at noon tomorrow, but I may not turn up.' It is similar to the apparent inconsistency in saying: 'I believe with great conviction that this is immoral, but then again I may be wrong.' One tends to think that promises are frustrated by riders which undermine them, and that moral convictions are similarly undermined by the concession of fallibility. And yet that is precisely what is needed to make room for tolerance.

When I say: 'I promise to meet you at noon, but I may not turn up', the qualification on my promise may be understood in either of two ways. On one reading it means: 'I have reasons to believe that I will not be able to keep my promise.' This kind of qualification does indeed frustrate a promise, because part of the convention of making promises involves not making a promise when one has a specific reason to believe that it cannot be honoured. However, if the qualification meant something like this: 'we all know that it's possible that some un-foreseeable circumstance might arise (such as death!) in which I would not be able to keep my promise.' On that interpretation, the qualification does not frustrate the promise because it is understood as merely making explicit one of the background, general assumptions which is implicit in all promise-making.

In a similar way, I cannot claim to believe something with great conviction if I have any good reason at present to think that my belief is not true, valid or plausible. In other words, I am overstepping the support of the evidence at my disposal if I claim to believe something with great conviction and, at the same time, to have a specific reason for doubting it. However if my qualification means: there is a general conditon which is only implicitly acknowledged in most knowledge-claims, i.e. the fallibility of those who make such claims, then there is no longer any inconsistency in both believing something with conviction and recognizing the possibility of being mistaken. To recognize such a general possibility is very different from having some specific reason to doubt a particular belief or knowledge-claim.

The condition of those with strong moral convictions needs to be described in terms which are similar to the case of the mortal promise-maker. Mill's argument is an attempt to make explicit the general qualification to the effect that one might be mistaken or misguided, and to work out the implications of this general qualification for questions of tolerance and pluralism. The moral agent who has strong moral convictions should be described as follows: he believes that certain kinds of behaviour are seriously immoral. To say that he believes this with conviction implies that he is willing to act on the basis of his beliefs. His conviction about moral values and the implementation of those values in action are subject to the general qualification that he may be mistaken or misguided. Therefore his level of conviction is open to challenge to the extent that he is confronted with equally convinced, honest and reasonable claims in favour of an alternative view. It is the presence of such an alternative which challenges the otherwise convinced fallible moral agent.

The Challenge of Others' Beliefs

The argument thus far is not meant to convert moral convictions into pusillanimous moral scepticism. However, once we are confronted by another moral agent or moral tradition which differs from our own and we are challenged to justify our imposing our values on the behaviour of others, the question of tolerance arises for the first time. In other words, the reasonably defended honest moral convictions of another provide me, perhaps for the first time, with a reason for doubting the apparent certainty with which I hold my own views. It should be noted that, even at this point, I am not expected to believe inconsistently that something is both moral and immoral. Nor am I invited to merely condone the behaviour of others which all are agreed is clearly immoral. The situation is rather more complex.

If one could focus, somewhat artificially, on the morality or otherwise of a single action *x*, then the convictions of two moral agents, *A* and *B*, might be described as follows:

(i) *A* is convinced that *x* is immoral.

Therefore, in the normal course of events *A* will avoid *x* and will try to prevent the occurrence of *x*. Especially if *x* is not trivial and if it in any significant way affects the interests of *A*, *A* will not only avoid *x* but he will also tend to intervene in others' behaviour to prevent *x*'s occurrence.

(ii) *B* sincerely believes that *x* is morally good, or at least is not morally evil.

The sincerity of *B*'s belief about *x* is a necessary condition for taking it seriously into account. However, sincerity is not enough. One could sincerely believe almost anything. If *B*'s belief about *x* is based primarily on his religious beliefs — which *A* does not share — *A* has no common criterion by which to examine the plausibility of *B*'s belief. If however *B*'s beliefs can also be defended as reasonable beliefs, then whether or not they are also religious is irrelevant. If *B* has a plausible case in favour of his belief, this fact alone provides *A* with a reason for qualifying his own conviction about *x*. Evidently, the criteria by which *A* and *B* reach their respective conclusions about *x* may themselves be a matter of dispute between them, so that it is clearly begging the question at issue for either side to arbitrarily endorse his own criteria only — especially if it is done implicitly — for resolving the disagreement. If *A* examines *B*'s belief and both continue to defend their own beliefs, there is still no question of tolerance on *A*'s part. This issue only arises when *B* does *x*, and *A*, knowing of *B*'s action, has both an interest in, and a real possibility of, intervening to block *B*'s doing *x*. At this point *A* must take into consideration the various factors which have been introduced above. These can be summarized as follows:

(a) A is aware of his own fallibility, and since moral/political issues are not subject to proof, he must concede a real possibility of being mistaken.

(b) It is logically possible that both *A*'s and *B*'s beliefs are equally valid or equally mistaken. Therefore *A*'s conviction, even if well placed, need not imply the error or implausibility of *B*'s opposing view.

(c) *A* would most likely continue to believe and act on his own beliefs about the morality of x, but how could he justify imposing his evaluation of x on B by interfering in the latter's actions? His justification for thus interfering will be decided by considering three factors: the relative importance of x for A; the extent to which B's action, in doing x, is directly and immediately detrimental to A; and the contrasting levels of responsibility, between A and B, for x's occurrence.

This kind of analysis does not provide A with a calculus for deciding when to interfere with B's actions and when not to interfere. No such calculus is available in moral/political issues.[6] However it does provide A with a reason for not interfering in B's actions, and in many cases it provides him with reasonably clear guidance. Without some way out like this, A is faced with even less palatable options. He can endorse inconsistent beliefs; he can apparently retain his moral convictions but not implement them in practice; or he can be intolerant.

By contrast with this analysis, the paradigm of intolerance is explicable in the following terms:

(a) A believes that he is infallible in moral matters. Since he cannot be mistaken he hardly needs a plausible justification for his views; they just cannot be wrong.

(b) Incompatible moral views cannot both be valid and, since he cannot be mistaken, those who disagree with him are necessarily mistaken. B must therefore be mistaken.

(c) x is numbered among the many values which are of the greatest importance — there are many such — and therefore there is a serious moral obligation on A to prevent the occurrence of x. Whether or not x directly affects A is irrelevant, and it is also a minor consideration that x occurs directly as a result of B's decision rather than A's. The very occurrence of x is so repugnant to A's moral sensitivities and besides, the toleration of x may encourage other people to change their moral evaluation of x where they should be guided by the infallible teacher, A, that A perceives the prevention of x as a serious moral obligation. It is something he must do.

Tolerance and Pluralism

Pluralism is the political equivalent of tolerance at the level of individual agents; similar arguments, with appropriate modifications, can be introduced to defend it.

The issue of pluralism in Ireland is not an abstract philosophical question but a concrete political problem. Any progress in coping with the political repercussions of conflicting traditions must depend, to a large extent, on the skill and sound judgment of politicians. And this is not learned in philosophy. However, there are also issues of principle involved in accepting any pluralist thesis. Philosophical analysis may help explain how one can be a principled participant of one tradition and still endorse pluralism without inconsistency.

By pluralism here is meant the political recognition of competing claims on the resources and power of the state, and the recognized validity of alternative political and religious ideologies in any given society. Since this formula is too vague to exclude almost anything, it needs to be developed by illustration from specific examples. Religious pluralism is an appropriate case study.

Religious pluralism is sometimes understood as a political arrangement which can be worked out, in practice, *after* the main churches have been identified and granted the status of a recognized religious tradition. Thus, in Ireland, one might list those religious traditions with a significant percentage of the population as official members — such as Roman Catholic, Church of Ireland, Methodist, Presbyterian, Jewish, etc. — and then take care that the political and social arrangements of the State do not unduly favour one of these at the expense of another. The school subsidy policy of the Department of Education would be an example of this form of pluralism; any of the main religious traditions is entitled to comparable financial subsidies in building and operating a religious school.

Robert Paul Wolff has articulated the principal objections to this way of understanding pluralism.[7] The main objection is that it systematically favours those interest groups or institutions which are sufficiently powerful to be identified as such, against all those who either belong to none of the relevant groups or else belong to a group which is not definable in terms of the categories available within a given classification. It is also the case, in most western democracies, that representatives of the various interest groups help determine the ground rules within which any 'pluralist' policy is likely to be implemented. In the case of religious pluralism, the major churches (in Ireland) help define what counts as a religion, which groups fall within their concept of religion, and what kind of favours are appropriate to those on the list. There are two reasonably large groups who are 'left out' in this arrangement. The first includes all those who do not formally belong to one of the main churches; religious toleration does not apply to them since, in practice, they are not recognizable as a religious group. Secondly, there at least seems to be a rather significant number of citizens who are officially members of a church and who have not had any democratic opportunity of selecting those who claim to speak on their behalf in religious matters. This includes both dissident members of religious traditions, and also those who are content with their theological tradition but dissatisfied with the political choices of their unelected religious 'leaders'. In short, this understanding of religious pluralism amounts to the establishment of the relatively concurring political views of unrepresentative leaders of the most powerful religious traditions in the State.

A more open policy of religious pluralism, based on tolerance, would make efforts to undercut the political privileges of membership of one of the major churches. Those who belong to minority religious traditions, those who belong to no religion, and those who repudiate, usually not in public, the political machinations of their undemocratically selected leaders — all of these should be protected from the political, social or legal ill-effects of not endorsing the policies of a major local church.

This argument might be answered by a response like this: the elected representatives of the people in the *Oireachtas* make the laws, and these in turn are directly elected by the people at large, all of whom have an equal vote independently of their religious affiliation. Therefore, political power is shared equally by all citizens, and religious groups are not differentially treated. While this is true, it misses the point both of Wolff's objection, and of the role of organized interest groups in a modern democracy. It is naive on the part of non-participants to imagine that government works this way; and it would be grossly dishonest on the part of religious 'leaders' to claim that they do not attempt, and often succeed, in wielding political influence in favour of their own religious traditions. This is sometimes done by public statements issued by religious leaders. It is more often and more discreetly accomplished in recent times by less public influence in determining the composition of advisory committees, in making appointments to sensitive public offices, including university posts; it is most notoriously done in Ireland by controlling the educational sector and significantly influencing a number of government appointed and financed Boards.[8]

It is obviously not implied in this argument that citizens should be disqualified or discriminated against in any way, in public life, because of their religious beliefs. The point at issue is between two forms of religious pluralism. One involves a systematic bias in favour of organized religions, and tries to strike a balance (which is acceptable to those favourably affected) between the interests of the official leaders of major religious groups in the State. The other, which is the sense of pluralism being proposed here, involves widening the scope of 'religious tolerance' to include many more positions on the religious continuum than those which are represented by the leaders of the main churches. It involves by-passing the well articulated and politically motivated interests of religious leaders in favour of the autonomy and freedom of individual citizens.

Religious tolerance implies neither favouring nor discriminating against individual citizens of a democracy solely because of their personal choice with respect to religious belief. It applies to non-religious citizens as much as to those who support a religious tradition.

Religious pluralism is not the only example in which the concept of tolerance is mistakenly prejudiced in favour of established interest groups. The same holds true in the professions, especially those which are self-regulating; in labour unions and employers' organisations; in competing political traditions; and in the pseudo-cultural manifestations of such political traditions. The coincidence of citizens' membership of a number of these groups leads to the polarization of a society in which everyone takes refuge, out of necessity, in the interest groups which he finds least unacceptable. The history of Northern Ireland provides a vivid case of such polarization. Where a society stops short of such extreme cases of polarization, the state may succeed in arbitrating, referee-style, between established interest groups, but its success in such arbitration or its good luck in avoiding social polarization could hardly be explained in terms of a biased form of pluralism. Besides, such a pluralism is often sponsored merely by pragmatic political considerations which have more to do with the next election than with any long range considerations of justice or the well-being of citizens.

The Justification of Tolerance

The early part of this chapter indicated how it is at least logically possible to find some space between our personal convictions and their apparent implications for action, in which to locate the possibility of tolerant non-interference.[9] This purely personal stance can be embodied in political structures which restrain the state from interfering, favourably or unfavourably, in the affairs of citizens which, by analogy, fall outside the scope of the state's competence. Both at the personal level and at the social or political level, the logical space in which non-interference is morally or politically possible does not in itself explain or justify the kinds of decisions which are made in favour of tolerance. At least some remarks in this direction are necessary.

Mill's justification for tolerance is, ultimately, a utilitarian one. Roughly, one ought to tolerate (within limits) the 'immoral' behaviour of others because this will more likely lead to human happiness than its alternative, interference or repression. If it could be shown, on empirical grounds, that tolerance does not in fact lead to the kinds of consequences which Mill envisages, his justification of tolerance would collapse. Herbert Marcuse, as a critic of Mill, claims that 'tolerance is an end in itself,' and not just a means to an end. However, he also argues that 'the telos of tolerance is truth.'[10] Therefore to the extent that what masquerades as true tolerance is more like intentional collusion in subverting 'the truth', tolerance should be substituted by intolerance in order to restrict the influence of those who corrupt the people and also to balance the natural inertia in favour of falsehood by a compensating injection of propaganda for the other side. Whatever one thinks of these reasons, of Mill or Marcuse, they both clearly base their defence of tolerance (or 'true tolerance') on a moral/political principle. There is no escaping the need to provide such a justification because, as already indicated, relativism alone will not help decide between tolerance and intolerance.

The justification of tolerance at the individual level involves a value judgment about the merits of freedom and autonomy. The justification of pluralism as a political policy, while relying on similar arguments, also involves a consideration of the role of government in a democracy and the limits of its competence.[11]

At the individual level, tolerance is a moral stance in favour of the autonomy of individuals as against other reasons one might have for overriding their autonomy. Those who perceive other human agents as merely instruments in the realization of some extrinsic objective will hardly be disposed to tolerance. However, even those who presume to decide for others what is ultimately in their best interests may also rate autonomy as less important than some other value. For example, if I think that reaching 'the truth' (Marcuse) is of ultimate significance, and if I believe I know what 'the truth' is, then I have reason to devalue the autonomy of others in favour of leading them, freely or otherwise, to the truth. Likewise, if I believe that their salvation, in the religious sense, is more important than their autonomy, then I may similarly rate autonomy as less important than salvation.

An alternative way of describing these value-judgments is by saying that people disagree on what constitutes 'the good', in a comprehensive sense, for human beings. Those ideologies which identify one (human) value as preeminent are likely to subjugate most other values to the realization of this one value. Those theories which recognize the relative incommensurability of competing human values will tend to have more complex accounts of human flourishing and, correspondingly, a more nuanced position on tolerance.

The most basic objection to the steam-roll approach — this or that is *the* basic value and everything else must be realigned — once bereft of the assumption of infallibility, is that it involves denying or rejecting in another human agent precisely that assumption on which the possibility of moral judgment and moral action depends. There are situations in which benign paternalism has a role, and some of these are mentioned in Chapter 5. Apart from these exceptional cases, however, the exercise of 'superior moral judgment' is a crude exercise of power rather than of moral authority. It denies for another agent, without independent justification, the very basis of moral judgment on which the action of overriding the other's autonomy depends. At the level of public policy, pluralism is also justified by similar considerations.

The same conclusion is reached by a consideration of the 'common good'. To the extent that state institutions perceive the individual citizen as subservient to some 'national goal' which might also be called the common good, toleration is a less important value than whatever is thought necessary to achieve such a national goal or objective.[12] The articulation of such a goal need not always derive from the malice of unbalanced dictators; we can equally be duped by a national or nationalist ideal of an 'Irish-speaking nation with its own cultural identity'. The argument here is not against having such an ideal and publicly supporting it. The argument only supports the independent value of individual autonomy and the kind of tolerance which this implies. The autonomy of individuals can be undermined as much by religious or nationalist ideals which are otherwise commendable, as it can by the corrupting control of totalitarian regimes.

Limits of Tolerance

I argued above that tolerance is not the same as being unprincipled and that tolerance does not imply moral relativism. Nor is tolerance equivalent to an unprincipled appeasement of every conceivable evil. There are limits to what should be tolerated, and although the limits are subject to reasonable dispute, it is not difficult to identify some clear examples where tolerance is self-defeating.

The reasonable limits of tolerance are explained by the proposed rationale for tolerance. Insofar as a policy of non-interference is not justified by the concept of tolerance, there is no longer any moral reason for accepting such a policy. For example, religious pluralism or tolerance is sometimes characterized as if it implied the necessity of tolerating whatever is taught or done in the name of religion.[13] This is clearly an absurd suggestion. If someone sincerely believes, for religious reasons, that other citizens should be sacrificed to the gods, the state would hardly change its legal definition of murder in order to accommodate such aberrant behaviour. Likewise, if parents sincerely believed, for religious reasons, that their children should not be educated at all; that they should not avail of essential medical services when seriously ill; or that their children should be deprived of their minimal needs in food or drink in order to punish them for their sins, the state would be expected to intervene on behalf of the children in question. Religious tolerance does not means a hands-off attitude to everything which is sincerely inspired by religious belief.

However it also follows that, since none of these is required by tolerance, the state can both interfere in these or similar cases and still defend a principle of tolerance or of religious pluralism.

The state, as an institutional expression of basic values in a society, is committed to defending those values against all serious, imminent threats to them, and it is irrelevant to the state that such threats might be inspired by religious or political fanaticism. Thus the state is committed, through its agencies, to defending the basic rights of individual citizens, including those of children. It is not committed to tolerating everything done in the name of religion, especially if what is done directly affects the interests of others apart from those who have the strong religious convictions.

Likewise, the state is not necessarily committed to tolerating the intolerant.[14] Those who attempt to preach or teach intolerance cannot legitimately complain if the state suppresses their efforts; they can only coherently describe such suppression as one side being more powerful than the other, because if they place no value in tolerance they cannot therefore appeal to such a value to condemn the state's reaction. By contrast, the state can appeal to its own concept of tolerance to explain the justifiable limits of tolerance. Tolerance is a principle which is directed towards cultivating the freedom and autonomy of individual citizens. Therefore, whatever directly and immediately threatens to subvert such freedom and autonomy also undermines the rationale for tolerance. One does not successfully cultivate freedom or autonomy by a policy of appeasement toward those who would impose their own totalitarian ideology, by force if necessary, on an ill-defended citizenry. There are obviously subtle political judgments required in determining the importance and the immediacy of attacks on citizens' rights. Tolerance is hardly compatible, for example, with a national paranoia about 'communism' or 'socialism' as was experienced by the U.S. in the 1950s.

Conclusion

Tolerance is a social virtue which, like any other virtue, is acquired by practice rather than by theory. In the case of the individual, this implies the cultivation of a tolerant attitude towards the sincerely held, opposing moral/political views of others; in the case of the wider community, it implies an historical tradition which is less evident in Ireland than in other Western democracies such as Holland. The training of the individual and the traditions of a society determine their respective attitudes towards tolerance in a way which requires a considerable change of perspective in order to modify an already entrenched philosophy of intolerance.

Those who are intolerant often rationalize their limitations by reference to 'principles', with the suggestion that they have to choose between being principled and being tolerant. The argument in this chapter is meant to show the contrary: the issue at stake depends on which principles one ought to endorse, and whether tolerance might be numbered among the principles which a rational agent should adopt.

As Mill argued, intolerance feeds on the illusion of infallibility, explicitly or implicitly assumed. If I believe in my own infallibility, then I will find it correspondingly difficult to accept that anyone else's moral or political views might rival mine as plausible or acceptable. If I know 'the truth', why should I defer to the erroneous beliefs of those who are obviously mistaken? I have argued here that no one can rationally claim to know that he is infallible, although many may hold such a belief for religious reasons. On the assumption that specifically religious beliefs be excluded from determining the policies of a democratic state, one must conlcude that no one has access to the kind of infallible guidance in moral/political affairs which undercuts one of the main defences of tolerance. It is because we *know* that we could not reasonably claim to be infallible, that we allow for the possibility of the moral/political beliefs of others being as valid or plausible as our own.

A second major assumption in any philosophy of tolerance is the practicability of a distinction between 'private' and 'public' actions. At the individual level, this implies minding one's own business about those beliefs and actions of others which minimally, if at all, impinge on my interests or the interests of others who may require my principled support. At the social level, it means a distinction between Church or State, and society. The basic law of the state should explicitly recognize pluralism in deference to a wide range of 'private' actions over which the state has no authority; and the various churches should cease to exploit the power or influence of the state in pursuit of their own religious objectives. Religious pluralism and, more generally, ideological pluralism follows from the political philosophy which recognizes the 'private' range of freedoms which are at least theoretically guaranteed by most Western democracies: freedom of thought, freedom of speech, and religious freedom.

By contrast, intolerance is a characteristic part of the ideological framework of the majority church in Ireland. It is consistent with its beliefs about infallibility; and it feeds on its fear of moral contamination if adult citizens are exposed to alternative belief systems which might challenge the hold of the churches on the minds of the citizens. An insular people, taught by a majority 'infallible' church, and cultivated for many decades by an explicit government policy of fostering a nationalist ideal of religious and cultural homogeneity, is hardly likely to provide a paradigm of political and religious tolerance. We inherit the fruits of an earlier corrupting philosophy in contemporary Irish society's attitude towards tolerance. We can only overcome the more obvious effects of such a philosophy by substituting an alternative concept of man and society in which the autonomy of the individual citizen, rather than the 'truth' of his religious beliefs, is recognized as a basic value.

4

Religious Freedom and the Roman Catholic Church

The interpretation and articulation of a particular religious tradition is an enterprise which characteristically generates disagreement, if not serious dispute. Even the official interpretation by a given church of its own religious tradition can hardly be said to be a simple matter of repeating formulae already endorsed by earlier official teachers. In such a situation as this — where the official teachers reach consensus only by compromise and the unofficial expert interpreters seem doomed to unending discussion — it may seem to be completely misguided to even consider joining the discussion. And yet this is exactly what seems almost unavoidable for anyone who wishes to understand the beliefs of the majority of Irish citizens about religious freedom and tolerance.

The reason for this is straightforward. The majority of Irish citizens are Roman Catholics; therefore, one may assume that their beliefs about religious freedom have been significantly influenced by their church teaching on the subject, even if their number includes many dissenters from orthodoxy. At the same time, the official teaching of the Roman Catholic Church is not so unambiguous on this matter that one can identify it by simply consulting a standard, officially recognized statement of the teaching. Besides, even if a clear statement could be found, it would be differently applied in a country where the separation of church and state is constitutionally guaranteed, such as the U.S.A., than it would be in Ireland where the Constitution explicitly recognizes the role of religious groups in a variety of ways.[1] For this reason we are forced to identify the Church's official teaching, if possible, as a means of clarifying one source of the citizens' beliefs.[2] And even if the attempted clarification is considered by official teachers to be mistaken, the distinctions made here and the questions raised can at least serve as an invitation to the Irish Church to be more explicit about its views on this important question.

This approach to the topic is quite compatible with at least one signpost of the church's stand; the Irish Catholic bishops are not interested in being directly involved in political decisions. At the same time, they clearly continue their role of teaching the members of the Church what they ought to believe in a great variety of different moral or political issues.[3] And religious freedom is one of those. So that we may reasonably assume that the teaching Church will continue to influence the beliefs of the majority of Irish citizens on the topic of religious freedom; it is important to discover what the Church will teach them in this context.

For purposes of discussion I assume that the *Declaration on Religious Freedom* of the Second Vatican Council is the most authoritative recent statement of the Church on the question of religious freedom. Based on that document, I will argue that the Church does not subscribe to religious freedom at all in the usual political sense of that term, and I will try to explain why the Church would find it very difficult to officially teach such a doctrine even if its members, as private citizens, wished to endorse religious freedom. If the Church does not believe in religious freedom, it may also be the case that a majority of citizens in Ireland share the same view.

Religious Freedom

Religious freedom, as a political right, is normally understood as a negative right to non-interference by others in a specific type of individual behaviour or in a range of kinds of behaviour. In other words, to have a right to freedom in this sense is to have a moral claim on others that they refrain from interfering in certain specified types of action by the citizen. Those who press such a claim on others must explain the scope of the claim; they must also explain who has such a right and against whom may it be urged. And finally, they owe us a justification of the claimed right so that those who may not accept it might be persuaded by plausible reasons to change their political philosophy in the direction of increased individual freedom.

It is much easier to concede religious freedom as a political right, than to define it. The most obvious difficulty in trying to explain the scope of religious freedom is the meaning of the word 'religious'. There are no beliefs which could be shown to be clearly non-religious. And therefore the word 'religious', in the phrase 'religious freedom', hardly serves to effectively distinguish one group of beliefs from another.

Part of the difficulty here derives from the word 'religion' itself. It usually connotes something to do with God as a transcendent being, but it need not; there are established religions which do not imply the existence of a transcendent god. Even if the term 'religion' were limited to what pertains to a transcendent god, there are further difficulties in deciding which beliefs are religious and which are not. Is a belief religious because it is (believed to be) revealed by God? How many people need to share such a belief in revelation to make a belief religious; i.e. is it a belief which a group of people, or just one individual, accepts as one which was revealed by God? Even if it is not thought to be explicitly revealed, a belief might be said to be religious because it is included in a coherent set of beliefs which are characteristic of some group which is normally described as religious. In this wider sense, all the factual and moral beliefs which are integrated into a religious group's account of its lifestyle — for example, beliefs about the origin of the universe, or beliefs in the immorality of divorce — would be classified as religious beliefs. And even if the narrower criterion of explicitly revealed beliefs were defended, how might one decide which revelations are authentic and which not? It is scarcely a duty of some institution of state to identify authentic revelations or, more generally, to identify authentic religious beliefs.

This difficulty can be temporarily resolved by shifting the discussion from the scope of the phrase 'religious belief' to trying to answer the question: against whom may one claim immunity from interference in religious matters? If we could agree that whatever else the state ought to do, it ought to mind its own business when it comes to religious beliefs, then there would be no urgency in defining 'religious belief'; no matter what might masquerade as a religious belief, the state should adopt a clear hands-off stance.

But this only provides the appearance of a solution. There is no plausible sense in which one could argue that, however 'religious belief' might be defined, state institutions should be banned from interfering. If I am persuaded by religious reasons that I should not educate my children, or that I should incite citizens to attack members of a different religious group, or that I should persuade minors to commit suicide before reaching an age when they may be 'corrupted' by contemporary culture, then it is not clear how I might justify the claim that the state should never interfere with my religious beliefs or with any of my actions which are motivated by my religious beliefs. The failure to demarcate a range of beliefs which are properly called 'religious' continues, therefore, to block progress even in clarifying the assumed limits of the state's authority.

One way out of this dilemma is to revise the assumption that 'religious freedom' is an independent, specifiable right of citizens which can be adequately defined for the needs of political theory and constitutional law. One might argue instead that there is nothing special about *religiously* motivated beliefs, as contrasted with any other kinds of beliefs, which would justify assigning them a privileged place in political argument. Although abandoning the search for criteria of demarcation may initially appear to downgrade religious beliefs as a privileged class, it may also have many welcome consequences for the traditional defenders of such privilege. For example, if one could establish a more general right to freedom of thought and action within which the scope of the right to religious freedom is contained, it would no longer be necessary to distinguish so carefully between religious freedom and the freedom to entertain and publicly endorse political opinions which may be officially discouraged by particular governments. Some religious beliefs do imply political views which are at odds with the views of governments. At least, some people hold political opinions which are officially discouraged, and which they try to justify by reference to their religious beliefs. For those for whom religious beliefs and political beliefs are thus closely inter-dependent, it seems arbitrary to demand that they should separate the two sets of beliefs and argue, for example: I believe in God and in human dignity as a Christian, and I believe in human rights as a political activist. The interdependence of political and religious beliefs, for many believers, implies that it is useless to even try to separate the two classes of beliefs into distinct categories of 'religious' and 'political'.

This attempt to widen the scope of freedom of thought and expression would precipitate objections from many unsympathetic governments who have worked out a successful *modus vivendi* with defenders of religious freedom. They might urge that whatever else religion is, it is primarily concerned with the after-life or, in general, with various transcendental beliefs which are irrelevant to practical politics. One should be allowed to believe anything one wishes about these matters, they would argue, and congregate quietly in churches or other assemblies to pray, precisely because such beliefs and actions are irrelevant to politics. In other words, restrict religious belief to such a narrow range that it could hardly ever overlap with the more usual business of governments.

Defenders of religious freedom rightly point out that this concedes almost nothing at all; that it is an arbitrary, external limitation of what religion means to religious people; and that it falsely assumes that religious beliefs are somehow independent of appropriate human action in society.

Therefore, rather than pursue the problem of narrowly demarcating religious beliefs or religious action, one might more profitably argue that what is at stake here is an integral part of a more wide-ranging political philosophy which is more or less endorsed, at least in principle, by most Western democracies. One basic assumption of democratic theory is that each individual citizen is entitled to constitutional guarantees of many basic rights and that the state is primarily concerned with the common good. While there may be occasions where the demands of the common good should override the rights of individuals, the rights of individual citizens are independently justified vis-à-vis the common good.[4]

And while there may be room for discussion about the range of rights which the individual legitimately claims, it is usually conceded that the right to freedom of thought and expression is included among basic, human rights.[5] It follows that communist governments illegitimately ban the publication of revisionist political ideas, and that capitalist democracies incoherently ban the dissemination of communist or socialist theories. On this reading, religious freedom is justified on the same grounds as, and is subject to corresponding qualifications as, the more basic right to freedom of thought and expression.

It is important to acknowledge that the beliefs on which modern democracies are founded are, in some sense to be further explained, theories of how the state should be organized and how political communities might live together in relative harmony.[6] As a theory, the belief in freedom of thought and expression is no more sacred than any other political theory; it needs to be justified. But it is the theory to which we normally defer in order to defend individual rights. According to that theory, there are some definite limits to the exercise of individual rights, especially in those cases where the exercise of an assumed individual right encroaches on the freedom of action of others in the community. Religious freedom would therefore be subject to the same limitations or qualifications as freedom of political thought and expression. And those who reject such a political theory would owe us, not only an account of religious freedom, but a more comprehensive political theory within which talk of religious freedom and individual rights might be meaningfully explained.

Thus, in examining the official teaching of the Church on the question of religious freedom, we may anticipate finding one or other of these two strategies adopted. The Church could explain what counts as a specifically religious belief, and then justify the special political and constitutional immunity which such beliefs apparently deserve. In that case, the Church would have to explain not merely what it means by a religious belief, but it would have to provide the civil authorities in a pluralist state with criteria for identifying religious beliefs which are not peculiar to any one church.

Alternatively, the Church might defend religious freedom as a special case of a more wide-ranging right to freedom of thought and action, with acknowledged qualifications or limitations.

Evidently a third possibility is that the Church does not subscribe to the political theory of religious freedom at all.

Roman Catholic Church Teaching

The Church is clearly in favour of religious freedom in some sense of that term. However, it is apparently not in favour of religious freedom in the wide sense of a basic political right to freedom of thought and expression, including religious thought and expression. The evidence of recent official Church teaching suggests that its position is ambivalent between favouring and opposing religious freedom as a fundamental human right. It may also be argued on the basis of Church teaching that the Church could not endorse a theory of freedom of thought as long as it also continues to believe in its own infallibility. This is anticipating the argument; one should begin by consulting the teaching of the Second Vatican Council.

The *Declaration on Religious Freedom*, promulgated by Pope Paul VI on 7 December 1965 on behalf of the Second Vatican Council, is the most authoritative teaching on this subject which is available from the Church in recent years. There are at least two strands of thought in that document which have not been successfully integrated. The two strands of thought are:

    (i)   Each human person has basic rights, the articulation and justi-
          fication of which are independent of Church teaching;
and
    (ii) The Church can only authoritatively teach what is in some sense
          implicit in its own tradition, and this tradition does not include
          the human right *not* to belong to the Roman Catholic Church.
Both of these points need to be developed in some detail.

(i) *Natural Rights*

The right to religious freedom, and the meaning of that right, are
enunciated at the beginning of Chapter 1 of the *Declaration*:

This Vatican Synod declares that the human person has a right to religious
freedom. This freedom means that all men ought to be immune from coercion on
the part of individuals or of social groups or of any human power; so that, in
religious matters, no one is forced to act against his conscience nor is anyone
restrained from acting according to his conscience either privately or publicly,
either alone or in association with others, within due limits (sec. 2, 513).[7]

This right is based, not on any 'subjective disposition of the individual,
but on his very nature' (sec. 2, 514); 'the right to religious freedom is
founded in the very dignity of the human person' (*ibid.*); it is one of the
'inviolable rights of man' (sec. 6, 519); 'it has its foundation in the dignity of the person, the demands of which have become better known to
human reason through centuries of experience' (sec. 9, 522).

If religious freedom is a natural right, the question arises: is the
Council document claiming that this right can be established by reasons
which would be acceptable even to those who do not share the religious
faith of the Council members? The claim that it is a *natural* right need
not imply this. The text might mean that the Church believes, on the
basis of its own religious tradition, that religious freedom is a right which
ought to be conceded even to those who are not Christians; but that it is
necessary to be a Christian to recognize the validity of claims to such a
right. In other words, the word 'natural' may be an indication of the extension of the right to all persons rather than an index of its likely
justification.

The most plausible interpretation of the text is that it is ambiguous between these two meanings. The Church has often invoked 'natural law'
theory as a basis for its moral/political teaching, claiming both that
reason alone is adequate to understand the validity of its claims, and that

the Church has been entrusted by God with the special role of interpreting the demands of natural law.[8] This has the advantage of leaving
room for a ready explanation of those who differ from the Church in its
philosophical reasoning: they lack the appropriate 'faith' to see their way
through the complexities of natural law teaching! I assume, therefore,
that the Vatican Council is at least partly claiming that its theory of
religious faith can be justified by reason alone. This invites a closer look
at the arguments suggested in favour of that theory.

Section 2 of the *Declaration* argues as follows: the human person is
motivated (*impelluntur*) by his own nature and is morally obliged to seek
the truth, including the truth about religion. But he cannot do this in a
manner which is compatible with his nature unless he is both
psychologically free and immune from external coercion. Therefore the
right to religious freedom belongs to every individual human person,
whether or not he satisfies his moral obligations to seek the truth, and it
is based on his nature as a free, rational agent.

Two other arguments are also supplied. The search for truth is a social
enterprise. One can hardly discover the truth without the co-operation of
others and, once discovered, one has a right to express one's beliefs
publicly. So that religious freedom is not limited to the private pursuit of
truth in the security of one's own conscience. Religious freedom,
therefore, must include a right to the public expression of religious
beliefs. The third argument is that the proper role of government is
taking care of the common good ('*bonum commune*', p. 516), and it
would transgress the limits of its function if it attempted to direct or impede whatever pertains to religion, insofar as religious acts directed to
God transcend the temporal or civil order.

In the light of the difficulties already mentioned in defining the term
'religious freedom', it seems as if the third argument here involves an attempt to specify 'religious' acts as those concerned with a transcendental
being, and therefore this argument relies on the first strategy outlined
above. The Church would have to successfully define 'religious beliefs'
by reference to a transcendent god, and it would have to do this without
assuming the truth of its own religious beliefs. This approach would not
convince civil governments who do not share the Church's belief in God.

The first two arguments, however, are very close to the tradition of
political philosophy implicit in the second strategy, which defends the
right of the individual against all unnecessary interference in his pursuit
of, and public expression of, what he understands to be the truth. They

initially appear to be arguments that might have been borrowed from Locke's *Letter Concerning Toleration* or from Chapter II of Mill's *On Liberty*. At least, they are arguments which Mill would recognize as similar to his own.

One comment must be made at this stage about the 'natural law' argument. It is based on the premise that man has an obligation to seek the truth in a characteristically human manner, namely, through free inquiry. It is not based on any assumption that 'truth itself' (in some sense) can make demands on man or that, once the truth is initially believed to have been discovered, an individual has a moral obligation to stay with it rather than to change his opinions. The reason for this is not difficult to find. We never know definitively, at least insofar as we regard ourselves as rational agents, that we have discovered 'the truth'. Evidently when someone believes that he has discovered the truth he then has an obligation (according to this theory) to act according to his current beliefs. The Council *Declaration* reflects this insight as follows: 'Man perceives and recognizes the dictates of divine law by means of his conscience (*mediante conscientia sua*), which he is bound to follow faithfully in all his activity' (sec. 3, 515). Thus, from the point of view of the individual seeker after truth, he can only be guided in a characteristically human fashion by his own beliefs, even if they are erroneous by someone else's standard. Freedom of thought and, more specifically, religious freedom is concerned with the right of the individual not to have his search for truth coerced by any other agent or institution.

While this much is clear in the *Declaration*, there are hints even in the articulation of this argument of another line of thought which compromises the apparent clarity of what has been claimed thus far. In Section 3, the *Declaration* reads:

God made man a participant in his divine law, so that man, gently disposed by divine providence, would be able to increasingly recognize the unchanging truth (sec. 3, 514-5).

This claim completely changes the perspective on the search for truth which operates in the first argument. We are no longer arguing from the perspective of the human inquirer who does not know what the truth is. We are rather being asked to see the issue from God's point of view (insofar as human beings can analogically assume this perspective!), from which alone the truth can be said to be immutable. In another context this might be an innocent blurring of the distinction between our beliefs about what is true, and an ideal of 'objective truth' which is recognized to be unavailable to mere mortals. But later in the same section we find the following:

The exercise of religion, of its very nature, consists primarily of internal, voluntary and free acts by means of which man directs himself to God; acts of this kind can neither be commanded nor prohibited by *a merely human power* (sec. 3, 515-6; italics added).

The implication seems to be that, although the civil powers could not legitimately command such internal, voluntary acts, God could do so, and perhaps even some human representatives of God, such as the Roman Catholic Church. This point is taken up again below.

From the point of view of religious freedom as a political right, the theological question of whether or not God can or should influence human choice by commands or prohibitions is irrelevant. It is irrelevant because we cannot share the perspective of God, as if we could definitively *know* the truth and then only have to worry about appropriately influencing human beings to conduct or pursue their inquiries in the right direction. No matter what approach we adopt to this issue, whether philosophical or theological, we are necessarily restricted to our *own beliefs* about the truth, and these cannot but be fallible. So that the question of religious freedom arises in the context of competing, possibly erroneous, human beliefs about man or God's revelation to man. The right to religious freedom and, more comprehensively, the right to political freedom is based on the individual's right to search for the truth in a characteristically human manner, partly because we have no guarantee of any particular claimant's belief that he or she has definitively discovered the truth about some issue.

The argument of sections 2 and 3 of the *Declaration*, therefore, can be read in two rather different ways, which are distinguished by the choice of perspective — theological or philosophical — which is assumed to be implicit in the two alternatives.

(a) *The theological perspective*: according to this standpoint, every man has a fundamental moral obligation to seek the truth in religious matters (among others) and to believe, and live according to, what he identifies as religious truth. This basic moral obligation cannot be satisfied if the individual is coerced, either in favour of or against some religious beliefs, because the kind of free, voluntary acts which are characteristic of religious faith cannot properly be said to be performed if an agent is coerced. Since each man has a moral obligation (according to Catholic theology) to seek the truth in this way, it would be unacceptable if civil authorities interfered with this most basic moral/religious obligation. Besides, as was made explicit in the third argument above, the very subject matter of these beliefs, since they are concerned with the transcendent, is beyond the competence of civil authorities.

As is evident at this stage, this is a theological argument which would only be found probative by those who share the religious beliefs of the Church on this question. It could hardly constitute an argument in favour of religious freedom which is acceptable to those who dissent from its theological assumptions.

However, there is also another difficulty in this argument which is not alleviated even by adopting its theological assumptions. From the premise that individuals have a moral obligation to follow their consciences, it does not follow that the civil authorities are immoral in constraining those who act according to their possibly erroneous consciences.[9] The moral obligations of individuals and the moral obligations of the state (or its representatives) may have to be reconciled as long as individuals are agreed on the demands of some commonly accepted moral law. If, however, individuals are morally obliged to follow their consciences, even in error,[10] there is no longer any contradiction in claiming that civil authorities are justified in sometimes constraining individuals who act according to their conscience.

Perhaps this is not what paragraph 3 means at all. If not, an alternative interpretation is sketched under (b) below. Whichever interpretation one adopts, it seems to be beyond dispute that theological considerations which are either denied or ignored by many civil authorities are engaged as an essential part of the theory proposed in section 3 of the Council *Declaration*.

(b)   *The philosophical perspective*:   this standpoint assumes that there are plausible or compelling reasons available for a theory of religious freedom and that these reasons are more or less plausible to an impartial reader, independently of his religious faith. If one reads the *Declaration* from this perspective, however, one is disappointed; for we are offered only the suggestion of an argument rather than a rational defence of its views.

However, this seems to be exactly what one would expect from a Church Council, for the following reasons.

No church has any special competence or privileged authority in philosophical discussions. It is almost as if, in response to acknowledging this, that the *Declaration* fails to provide an argument for fear that it may be either insufficiently compelling or incorrect.

Secondly, even though the Church claims to be able to explain what the 'natural law' requires, it does not claim to be able to provide compelling arguments to support its position. Rather, the tradition of the Church has been to claim that certain of its beliefs are within the scope of reason's competence, that they therefore belong to the natural law, but that it is the task of philosophers to discover plausible reasons in defence of its insights into natural law. In other words, the Church claims, for theological reasons, that certain beliefs can be established by reason alone. Hence, there is no obligation on the Church itself to provide such reasons, because its certainty about its own beliefs derives ultimately from theological convictions.

If this interpretation is correct, then the theory which is enunciated in Chapter 1 of the *Declaration* is not proposed at all, despite appearances to the contrary, as a theory which the Church authorities are willing to defend philosophically. Instead, the first chapter claims that it is the belief of the Church that religious freedom is a basic right which should be conceded to all men irrespective of their religious faith. Such a right is a natural right, because everyone who is a person deserves that right, and the justification of such a right may be established, in principle, by reason alone. However, the basis of this last mentioned belief is not the reasons proposed by philosophers or endorsed by the Church, but the religious belief of the Church about the powers of human reason. The Church likewise believes that the existence of God and the immortality of the soul can be established by reason alone, but it evidently does not make these claims on the basis of having provided or endorsed philosophical reasons which are probative. In a similar way, the Church now believes that religious freedom is a human right, that it is part of natural law and can therefore be established by reason alone, but the ultimate basis for both beliefs is theological.

The theological perspective which is not fully explicit in Chapter 1 of the *Declaration* assumes a more central role in the subsequent chapter, in which religious freedom is defended as a corollary of the Church's divinely revealed mission.

(ii)   *The Teaching of Christian Tradition*

The Church authoritatively articulates its own religious tradition in official teaching, such as the *Declaration on Religious Freedom*. It is important to notice that whatever is claimed or taught in this context is
based on religious faith. In plain English, this teaching represents the
religious beliefs of the Church; and no matter how great the conviction
with which they are endorsed, they are still the religious beliefs of one
christian tradition.

Within the context of officially interpreting its beliefs about its own
function, the Church claims freedom to carry out its mission of
preaching, teaching and, in general, organizing the lives of christian
believers in accordance with their shared faith. Here the Church defends
its own freedom of action as primary:

The freedom of the Church is the fundamental principle in relations between the
Church and public powers and the whole civil order (sec. 13, 528).

It is no longer a question of the rights of individuals; the freedom of the
Church is primary, to pursue what it perceives as its legitimate role in
society at any point in history. A subsequent part of the same section (13)
acknowledges the distinctiveness of this claim. After emphasizing the independence from civil interference which is necessary for the Church to
fulfil its mission, the *Declaration* reads:

At the same time the Christian faithful, in common with other men, enjoy the
civil right not to be impeded in living their lives according to their consciences.
There is a harmony therefore between the freedom of the Church and that
religious freedom which is to be recognized by all men and communities and enshrined as a right in juridical structures (sec. 13, 529).

The mission of the Church includes the function of authoritative
teaching:

By the will of Christ, the Catholic Church is the teacher of truth and it is its duty
to preach and authentically teach the truth which is Christ, and at the same time,
to declare by its authority and to confirm those principles of the moral order
which derive from the very nature of man (sec. 14, 530).

This is an expansion of the claim in the introduction to the *Declaration*,
to the effect that the Roman Catholic Church is the one true church:

We believe that this one true religion revealed by God to man subsists in the Catholic and Apostolic Church to which the Lord Jesus entrusted the duty of spreading it to all men . . . (sec. 1, 512).

The *Declaration* specifically 'leaves unchanged the traditional Catholic doctrine on the moral duty of individuals and societies towards the true religion and the one Church of Christ' (sec. 1, 512-13).

Insofar as earlier church teaching is reaffirmed here, it is important to take note of two other Church claims. One is that there is no salvation outside the Roman Catholic Church.[11] This should not be understood negatively as the belief that those who do not formally belong to the Church are denied salvation. It remains for further theological discussion to explain in what sense those who do not officially or formally belong to the Church might still avail of a salvation which is delivered through the medium of the one true church.

The other Church belief which is relevant here is the belief in infallibility, which was defined in the First Vatican Council. It is evident that the claim to infallibility is rather limited in the scope of its possible application, and nothing in this discussion hinges on disputes about the scope of infallibility. The significant point here is that the Church claims infallibilty at all, and that it reaffirms this belief in Vatican II.[12] Some of the consequences of this belief need to be made more explicit.

It is almost redundant to point out that certainty and truth are sufficiently different to leave room for frequent cases where they part company. One may feel very certain of something which is false; and one may feel very uncertain about something else which is true. The kind of certainty which one feels or, more accurately, which one reasonably claims for one's beliefs, is no guarantee of their truth. I assume that the religious beliefs of the Church are held with great conviction or certainty by its official teachers, and that this level of conviction is at least part of what is expressed in the doctrine of infallibility. However, the claim to infallibility is worthless as a guarantee of the truth of any other beliefs which might be taught under its jurisdiction.

The reason for this is that the infallibility of the Church is not something which can properly be said to be *known*, in the sense in which we claim to know many other relatively undisputed facts. The Church does not claim to know that it is infallible; the infallibility of the Church is itself an object of religious faith. Members of the Church are expected to *believe* in the Church's infallibility without being provided with the kind of arguments or evidence which would normally be demanded for a claim to know something. So that if the Church is mistaken in its belief in its own infallibility, its claim to infallibility will not provide independent evidence in its favour. If we knew, on independent grounds, that someone were infallible, we could then claim to have adequate evidence for endorsing whatever they truthfully report. But if we merely believe, on faith, what the Church teaches then it would be fallaciously circular to argue that, since it invites belief in its infallibility, it must indeed be true that it is infallible. In other words, the doctrine of infallibility, just like any other official teaching of the Church, is an object of religious belief. It may be mistaken.

One of the results of the Church's teaching on infallibility has been to camouflage religious faith with an illusory certainty and to mistakenly encourage the belief that the Church, objectively, cannot be mistaken in its more important teaching on faith and morals. Evidently, this was not the intention of the First Vatican Council when it enunciated infallibility as an article of faith. A second consequence of the teaching is that those who officially teach on behalf of the Church find it psychologically difficult to admit, even to themselves, that they could be mistaken in their beliefs. It is difficult to maintain, at the same time, that one is infallible and that one may be mistaken! Hence when the question of religious freedom is at issue, they find it very difficult (although it is logically possible) to say: 'we believe with great conviction that our teaching is true, and we believe that we are infallible in holding this belief; at the same time, we may be mistaken'. The belief in infallibility does not exclude the possibility of being mistaken; it merely makes it difficult to acknowledge this possibility in proportion to the strength of one's religious belief in one's infallibility.

These two traditional beliefs of the Church, on the necessity of the Church for salvation and on the Church's infallibility, are relevant to religious freedom in this way: the Church claims to be the unique, infallible teacher on earth of religious truth, and also to have a privileged authority in interpreting the natural law. Within the Church's understanding of divine law, the duty of the Church to preach and teach is primary, and the obligation of the state not to interfere in religious affairs derives from the pre-eminent authority of the Church to pursue its divinely revealed mission. In this scenario, freedom from civil interference is a corollary of the Church's rights; but only for members of the Roman Catholic Church, because it is the 'true church'. This provides no basis for claiming that members of other religious sects, especially those whom the Church claims are seriously mistaken in their beliefs, have any right to religious freedom. The claim to a right of non-interference by the Church is ultimately based, therefore, on the religious beliefs of that Church about itself and its unique historical mission.

A number of distinct questions seem to be conflated at this stage, and they should be kept separate.

The first is that the Church's teaching, even if 'infallibly' pronounced, cannot claim any more authority in a civil state than the teaching of any other church or religious sect. It would be quite possible for a number of incompatible religious groups to claim to believe that they infallibly teach the truth in religious matters. In that situation the relevant state authorities would have to choose among competing, self-styled infallible religious authorities. From the point of view of civil society and the establishment of human rights, a single majority church which endorses human rights makes many practical political problems of legislation easier. However, it hardly helps to resolve the theoretical constitutional problem of what rights ought to be recognized in civil law. These rights cannot be decided by reference to some self-styled infallible teaching authority, even if there is only one such claimant in any given state. Whatever the Church claims to teach with authority, it teaches exclusively from the perspective of interpreting its own religious tradition, which is ultimately based on religious faith.

The second question to be raised is: what does the Church teach, on the basis of faith, about religious freedom? Here there is some ambiguity. It would appear to be the primary or more fundamental teaching of the Church — and also the interpretation most representative of the tradition of the Church — that the right of the Church to non-interference in its mission is basic. It would be logically possible to maintain this position and at the same time argue that other religious sects should have similar rights. This would certainly be the case if a church accepted a multiplicity of religions as equally acceptable to God. But the Roman Catholic Church believes it is the unique guardian of revealed truth. Since the right to non-interference was derived from this claim, it would at least not necessarily follow from the Church's interpretation of its own role that other religions have equal rights. It is not easy to guess the logic of an appropriate argument for this latter claim. Perhaps the Church might argue that all Christian churches in some sense participate in its own privileged mission. But how then account for non-Christian religious sects, and how explain the rights of religious sects which explicitly oppose the basic teachings of Christian religious groups? This issue underlines once again the difficulties inherent in attempting to say what 'religious' means in the context of religious freedom.

It is at this stage that a third question arises which concerns the Church's attempt to authoritatively teach the natural law theory of morality. The claim to special authority here is an object of faith, and can therefore only be accorded the same status by civil governments as they might accord to the religious claims of any other church. If the claim to special authority is suspended, we have only the arguments or reasons proposed by the Church and we must evaluate them rationally on their own merits.

Evidently the *Declaration on Religious Freedom* is not meant to supply a comprehensive, detailed argument in favour of natural rights. The theory it suggests, outlined in (i) above, is similar to the classic thesis in political theory that man can only reach the truth, if at all, as a result of free inquiry. This at least provides the basis for claiming that the Church extends the rights of religious freedom to all churches. Despite this reasonably clear endorsement of religious freedom as a civil right, there is evidence in the *Declaration* to suggest that radically different lines of thought were somewhat superficially combined, and that the task of providing a coherent interpretation was left to theologians. For example, section 6 — which occurs within the development of the natural law thesis — includes the suggestion that civil governments should help foster religion:

Therefore, the civil powers should . . . provide favourable conditions to foster religious life, so that citizens can truly exercise their religious rights and fulfil their religious duties; and in order that society itself can enjoy the good of justice and peace which derive from the faithfulness of men to God . . . (sec. 6, 519).

The basis of the natural law theory, insofar as it is known by reason, is that a human pursuit of truth cannot be coerced legitimately by any outside agent or group. This would seem to imply that the state should ideally be neutral with respect to religion and that a separation of church and state would most appropriately reflect the assumptions of the natural law theory. If the state should foster religion, which religious tradition should it encourage? If it treats all religious traditions equally, then it clearly is fostering erroneous beliefs on the part of citizens (on the assumption that they cannot all be true). If the state chooses to foster one more than others by giving it a special place in constitutional law, then the Church cannot consistently condone the establishment of what it believes to be erroneous and at the same time claim to be the one true church.[13] Finally, if the state were to give special constitutional recognition to the Roman Catholic Church — as was the case in Ireland before the Fifth Amendment of the Constitution in 1972 — this would seem to be the position favoured by the document. However, this is contrary to the theory that all citizens have equal rights to non-interference in religious matters. The state is expected to be incapable of resolving disputes between the competing claims of different religious traditions; and at the same time it is acceptable that it identify one church rather than another for a privileged constitutional status.[14]

The only options available to the state, therefore, would seem to be: (i) to foster all religious beliefs, no matter what belief is involved. This seems to be so absurd that it hardly merits discussion; (ii) to discriminate among various religions and to foster only those which the state judges to be teachers of religious truth. By the church's own teaching, the state is incapable of making these kinds of judgments or discriminations; (iii) to accept and endorse the religious judgment of one of the competing religious traditions as to which religious group teaches the 'truth'. However, this only repeats the mistake involved in (ii) in a less obvious way. The incompetence of the state in religious matters could therefore only be properly expressed in a clear separation of church and state in which the state neither fosters nor impedes the religious activity of various churches, within the usual boundaries of respect for the rights of citizens.

There is a similar ambiguity in the *Declaration on Religious Freedom* in its references to religious education. On the one hand, any kind of conversion technique which takes advantage of the poor or uneducated is said to be inconsistent with the natural law, because one should only adopt religious beliefs as a result of a free, informed choice (Sec. 4). It is also claimed that parents have the right to determine the kind of religious education which their children are to receive (Sec. 4). It is a violation of parents' rights if their children are forced to attend religious instruction, or if a single system of education which excludes religious instruction is enforced on all (Sec. 5). Two questions arise here: what is the significant difference between taking advantage of an adult's lack of education to convert him to a religious faith, and using a system of education to inculcate a religious faith in children who are equally incapable of a free, informed choice? In the case of education, the text talks about the rights of parents rather than the rights of those who are being converted to christianity, namely, the children.

The second question is one which applies peculiarly in Ireland. There is at least the appearance of collusion between the state and the main churches in not providing any non-denominational third-level educational establishment in which one can train as a primary school teacher. And there is at least a serious impediment of fact, if not of law, in the lack of non-denominational schools at primary and second level. If the text of the Council document is taken at face value, the state should ensure that no students are coerced into attending religious schools by the failure of the Department of Education to provide non-denominational alternatives. Rather than attempt to establish both denominational and non-denominational schools in every district, it seems that in this instance it would only be practically feasible to attend to the rights of all concerned by establishing non-denominational schools with special religious instruction periods which are optional. Otherwise those who are so young as to be equivalent to the 'ignorant and poor' for purposes of religious instruction are exploited by a school system which, in fact, offers no possibility of non-denominational instruction.[15]

A third, and perhaps the most important qualification, of the Church's teaching on religious freedom derives from the apparently intentional coincidence between, on the one hand, the alleged limitations of civil governments in coercing or requiring internal acts of intellect and will and, on the other hand, the denial of similar limitations for the Church. The limits of the civil government's power derive from its inability to command those 'internal, voluntary and free acts' (sec. 3, 515) which are characteristic of religious faith. The Church, however, can demand that Christians 'accept its teaching and hold on to it by a religious assent of the mind. This religious obedience of the will and the intellect must be shown in a special way to the authentic teaching authority of the Roman Pontiff, even when he is not speaking *ex cathedra*.'[16] Thus God is believed to command, through the Church, precisely the kind of voluntary and intellectual subservience which the civil authorities cannot legitimately demand. What God can do is a metaphysical question which could hardly be settled by a simple claim. What is at stake here is what the Church authorities can do or, at least, what they believe they ought to be allowed to do. Some human beings believe that they can command precisely the kind of subservience of will and intellect which a characteristically human, rational pursuit of truth precludes. The apparent liberalism of Chapter 1 of the *Declaration* is swallowed up in the traditional dogmatism of Chapter 2.

The idea that the state should foster religion; that it should facilitate parents by providing religious schools; and that the Church can command the kind of obedience of will and intellect which transcends the competence of the state; these are not incidental slips in a church document which basically teaches the opposite. Rather, these are clear indications of the traditional teaching of the Church which is otherwise camouflaged by the apparently liberal theory of rights in Chapter 1. The Church believes itself to be a unique mediator between God and mankind, the 'one true church' to which all should belong. In the light of this theological interpretation of its own role, it reflects on the duties of state authorities vis-à-vis the 'one true church'. It is neither surprising nor inconsistent, therefore, if the Church teaches that the state should both facilitate the work of the Church and not interfere in religious matters. Both obligations of the state derive from the Church's theological understanding of itself.

The Church and Religious Freedom

I argued at the outset that there seem to be insurmountable difficulties in trying to say what counts as a religious belief as opposed to a non-religious belief, and that the task of demarcating religious beliefs is an unenviable one. Despite that, defenders of religious freedom might assume such a task and then explain the privileged political and constitutional status of religious beliefs. This is one strategy for defending religious liberty. An alternative strategy would be to defend the freedom of thought and discussion of citizens as a basic right, and to include religious beliefs within the scope of protected beliefs. Either strategy might work, on condition that one does not beg the very questions at issue by appealing to the beliefs of one particular church to support one's claims; and the second strategy seems to be more viable than the first.

The *Declaration on Religious Freedom* of Vatican Council II adopts the first strategy, by direct appeal to the religious beliefs of the Church about its own mission. A coherent account of its position would include the following points:

(a)   The Roman Catholic Church is the one true church, which infallibly interprets the more important features of its religious beliefs about itself, including the belief in its own infallibility.

(b)   Among the religious beliefs of the Church is the belief that the Church is necessary for salvation; this implies, minimally, that all churches are not equally competent to lead their members to 'religious truth'.

(c)   Since the mission of the Church includes teaching the truth it infallibly believes, civil authorities should facilitate the work of the Church. They should foster true religion, and they should refrain from interfering in the specifically religious role of the Church in relation to the citizens of any state. One of the implications of this proposal is that all members and potential members of the 'one true church' should not be impeded in any way in their moral obligation to seek and find the truth in the Roman Catholic Church. This is one meaning of religious liberty. Since all human beings are either members or potential members of the Church, the right to freedom from impediments in seeking the truth extends to all men and, in this sense, it is a natural or human right.

(d)   Membership of the Church can only be authentically realized by faith. Therefore any coercion on the part of any other agent or institution in the religious faith of a citizen would compromise precisely what the Church hopes to achieve — namely, the free, voluntary act of will and intellect by means of which a citizen agrees to become a member of the Church and to accept its authority. This is another feature of religious liberty: the absence of coercion even in favour of 'the one true church's' teaching. Again, however, both the understanding of religious conversion and the reason why it must be acknowledged are drawn from the Church's theological understanding of its own mission.

(e)   The claims in (d) about the conditions for freely assenting to 'the truth' are also part of 'the natural law'. However, the Church's claims about the natural law are likewise theological claims about the competence of human reason, rather than a promise of philosophical arguments which are plausible even for those who do not share the Church's beliefs.

(f)   The Church does not urge state authorities to foster 'false religions', whatever that might mean; nor does it acknowledge the rights of individuals to reject the Church's teaching.[17] The reason for this is that the Church finds it difficult to reconcile its belief in its unique, infallible hold on 'the truth' and the possibility that someone could be correct in rejecting the teaching of the Church. If the Church is right, then those who disagree with it must be wrong; perhaps inculpably in error, but still definitely in error. Those who are inculpably in error should be tolerated; but this is not the same thing as recognizing that they may, in fact, be nearer the truth than those who endorse the dogmas of the Church.

Religious liberty cannot be appreciated from the perspective of those who believe that they infallibly know the truth. Freedom of thought and inquiry can only be appreciated from the perspective of those who are not so dogmatically certain of the conclusion of human inquiries about religion. The Church confuses the two standpoints, and expects civil authorities to support its partial judgment.

By contrast, religious freedom implies that the state has no competence to decide which if any of a number of competing religious traditions should be supported, because the state is not burdened with the Church's belief in its own infallibility. Religious freedom, therefore, demands that the state should neither foster nor impede any religious tradition; that the believer and unbeliever have equal rights and privileges in a state; and that the various legal, social, educational and other state-organized facilities should neither hinder nor encourage the religious beliefs of citizens.

The Roman Catholic Church does not subscribe to such a theory. For the Church, the fundamental value for each citizen is the achievement of salvation or, in different language, reaching the truth in religious matters. And religious liberty is endorsed, in a qualified sense, only as a necessary prerequisite for achieving that objective. In the tradition of liberal political theory, freedom of thought and inquiry, together with freedom of expression, are fundamental values in their own right which are not compromised in the interests of some other objective. The Church does not believe in religious liberty as a basic right. It only believes in its own liberty to fulfil what it perceives to be a divinely revealed mission, and in the consequent liberty of individual citizens to freely follow what the Church believes to be their moral obligation, namely, to join the Roman Catholic Church. The liberty of the Church, understood in this way, and the liberty of the individual citizen from state interference, are both compatible with the State's actively fostering the religious beliefs of citizens. The religious liberty of the citizen is reduced to the liberty to practise one's faith without state interference, without the liberty to reject all religion.

5

Private Morals and Public Policy

If morality could be understood in terms of purely personal, private and ultimately religious restrictions on human actions it would be relatively easy, outside the context of a strict theocracy, to argue for the separation of law and morality, and to distinguish the respective competence of each in such a way that any significant overlap is minimized. Likewise, if one supported a positivist approach to jurisprudence, one might reasonably argue that the scope of the law's competence and the justice or injustice of various laws could only be determined by reference to laws actually in force in a state. If laws enforce moral or religious views, then that's the way things are, for better or for worse; there is no room to argue that such laws are unreasonable, unjust or even tyrannical.

The current debate in Ireland on the appropriate extent to which the laws of the state, including the Constitution, should reflect or enforce the moral views of any identifiable group of citizens correctly rejects both of these assumptions. The history of Irish constitutional law makes it abundantly clear that laws which have been properly enacted by the Oireachtas are not guaranteed to be just or constitutional.[1] On the other hand, there are few supporters of the idea that moral considerations are fundamentally irrelevant to law and therefore should be ignored by the law because they are 'merely moral'. In fact, both positions are interrelated; to the extent that morality is not understood as a purely personal or religious phenomenon, then moral questions of justice may be legitimately raised about the reasonableness of laws which are otherwise validly enacted.

The interpretation of morality which was suggested in Chapter 1 above makes it inevitable that law and morality will extensionally overlap. By an 'extensional overlap' is meant that both are concerned with free

112

human actions; with a distinction between those which should be encouraged and those which should be discouraged; with procedures for effecting the relevant encouragement/discouragement; and that many of the same voluntary actions are either encouraged or discouraged by law and morality. Thus, it is both illegal and immoral to murder; it is neither illegal nor immoral to take a walk in a public park. Given the inevitable overlap, the question arises about the rationale for preventing a complete coincidence between the two. Why should we not make all immoral acts illegal, and why not make it always immoral to intentionally act illegally? If we object to such a complete coincidence, what is the rationale for drawing a distinction between those immoral actions which should be made illegal, and those which should not? How could it ever be morally acceptable to break the law?

These are not just abstract questions of jurisprudence and philosophy. Nor are they merely theoretical issues. In one obvious sense they are political issues which will be determined, to a great extent, by political considerations or political factors which are independent of critical analysis. 'Public opinion' will determine, to a large extent, both how and when the legislature decides on questions such as these. However, 'public opinion' is not a homogenised, pre-determined force in the community. It can even surprise those who most rely on its anticipated impact. The public are not so gullible that they fail to see the implications of a policy which, initially adopted for one reason, has ramifications in other equally important political issues. It is therefore worthwhile to make these implications explicit so that, whatever policy is eventually chosen by the electorate, we can only blame ourselves if it is subsequently exploited to our detriment.

The basic pattern of this kind of discussion, about the reasonable limits of legally enforced morality, tends to fall into one of two alternatives. The first claims to have a definitive, coherent and comprehensive policy which can answer all important questions which arise in this connection. The second alternative is very much a matter of trying to balance conflicting objectives in a way which is responsive to the relative maturity of a population and which respects their traditions of democratic, political institutions. The second approach is followed here. The plausibility of whatever suggestions are made hinges crucially on arguments of the form: 'if you agree with that principle . . . look at how it would apply in other cases . . .' If one cannot accept its broader implications, and if one cannot supply an explanation of the difference between the two cases which is not question-begging, then one ought to modify what might otherwise, in the abstract, look like a very plausible principle. The extent to which the first alternative — a definitive, coherent and comprehensive policy — is endorsed by the Roman Catholic Church is briefly examined at the end of this chapter.

As an entry into some of the thorny questions which arise in this context, it may be helpful to consider two of the standard, poor arguments which are used on behalf of the 'law and order' side of this debate.

Two Bad Arguments[2]

It is sometimes claimed that a moral code belongs to the *essence* of a given society and, for that reason, that it ought to be protected by criminal legislation. The idea that moral norms are part of a society's essence might be variously expressed by saying that they are essential to it, that they are defining features of that society, or that they are part of its identity. This is a difficult argument to evaluate because it probably represents a rhetorical overstatement of a rather different thesis, which is described below as the warp-and-woof thesis. If taken at face value, however, the argument about the essence of a society is so implausible that it hardly merits detailed discussion.

The word 'essence' is usually understood in such a way that if something changes its essence, it is no longer the same kind of thing as before. Thus, if the soul (in traditional dualist theories of man) is part of a person's essence, then once the soul departs what remains is no longer a person, but something entirely different. Likewise, if the observance of certain moral norms — usually a quite lengthy list of them — were part of the very essence of a given society, then if the society changed its allegiance to one or more of these moral norms, it would no longer be literally the same society. In other words, no society could ever evolve or gradually change while retaining its identity; any moral change would signal the creation of an essentially new society. What we normally call the change, evolution or even deterioration of a society would have to be re-described as a series of successive, discontinuous societies replacing each other in time. This is so implausible a theory, simply because it makes it impossible to speak about moral changes in society, that it should be rejected a priori.

Besides, this argument also suffers from all the more substantive objections to the second thesis, the warp-and-woof thesis.

The warp-and-woof thesis distinguishes between the alleged harm to individual citizens which is directly caused by moral changes, and the harm which is caused directly to structural or institutional features of a society by similar moral changes. Conservative thinkers often argue that the harm to structures or institutions eventually affects individual citizens. Some institutional or structural features of a society are then described, by analogy with weaving, as the warp-and-woof of a society. The argument for their defence goes as follows: these features of society, such as monogamy or religious schools, are part of the warp-and-woof of a society. To change these is to radically transform society itself and, indirectly, to seriously affect individual citizens. Some moral norms are necessary to maintain the current warp-and-woof; and they are so important that they merit reinforcement by the criminal law. Thus to protect society from radical change and, indirectly, to protect citizens from its ill-effects we must maintain the present warp-and-woof — if necessary, by criminal legislation.

There is a fatal flaw in this argument. It often escapes notice because it is buried in the metaphorical language in which the thesis is usually expressed. The moral/political norms which are structurally analogous to the warp-and-woof of cloth may be so repulsive or unjust that they ought to be replaced by different social norms. One hardly needs to fantasize to think of societies in which racism, various forms of overt, unjust discrimination, religious fanaticism, or institutionalised social injustice, are so integrated into the way in which a society is structured that they constitute its (metaphorical) warp-and-woof. Yet the argument just outlined could be used to defend the status quo in those cases. Therefore, the crucial question for any policy on legislating moral standards is not whether such standards are part of a society's current warp-and-woof; but rather, whether these norms are independently warranted social norms. Being 'part of what we are' is not enough to justify traditional moral norms; the question is — are they part of what we *ought* to be?

A second flaw in the warp-and-woof thesis is the apparent implication that any radical change in a society would be a change for the worse. Again, this is not explicitly stated in many cases, because if it were it would be obvious that such an assumption requires independent justification. The implication is subtly carried in the warp-and-woof metaphor; if certain norms are so structurally important to sustain our society as it is, it looks as if any radical change in these norms would precipitate a society's disintegration. However, disintegration is not the only alternative to maintaining the status quo. For those defending an alternative policy on criminal legislation, the proposed alternative is a different warp-and-woof, not none at all. The real options in such a choice are disguised by those who automatically assume that their version of the correct warp-and-woof for a given society is the only one possible. This is surely begging the question at issue in the whole discussion.

The failure of these two arguments underlines the real source of disagreement on this question. When one asks: 'ought the criminal law reinforce moral standards?' it is not enough to show that certain moral norms are an integral part of the way our society is currently arranged. We can still ask: why ought we maintain the status quo? To answer that question we can hardly avoid the kind of moral/political value judgments which many would prefer to disguise under the apparent wisdom of endorsing what we have become accustomed to.

Moral and Religious Sensibilities

One possible implication of adopting the modified relativist approach proposed in Chapter 1 is to argue as follows about law and morality: there are legitimate disagreements among citizens about what is moral and immoral. There is no reliable method available for resolving such disagreements. At the same time one has to proceed with a fair amount of political expediency to introduce legislation which will at least satisfy the majority of the electorate. This can be done by reference to the 'gut reaction' or the 'moral sensibilities' of the electorate. If a majority of the population regard some form of behaviour as morally repugnant, then it should be proscribed by the criminal law; not necessarily because the majority are right or correct in their moral beliefs, but because we have no other way of proceeding in such issues.[3]

A slightly more subtle version of the same approach is to ignore public discussion of what is just or unjust, and to simply put the issue to a vote. Who could reasonably object to the outcome of a democratic vote?

Consider the following slightly artificial case. There exists a state in which twenty-five to thirty percent of the population are Roman Catholic, and they practise their religious faith in the usual way. Over sixty percent of the population have a religious faith which construes the Roman Catholic liturgy as sacrilegious and grossly offensive to their moral and religious sensibilities. Both groups are sincere in their respective beliefs. The question arises: ought the liturgy of the minority be legally suppressed, with criminal sanctions, because it grossly offends the moral and religious sensibilities of the majority? The answer is surely 'No'. The degree of revulsion experienced by the majority is not, in itself, an adequate reason for 'democratically' enacted legislation to suppress the cause of their revulsion.[4] Some other kind of argument is required, preferably one supported by a principle which continues to apply even if the relative size of different sections of the electorate is changed, and if their moral revulsion is triggered by different kinds of 'objectionable' behaviour.

The reason for this is that the moral and religious beliefs of citizens are influenced by non-rational factors. If we simply consult their current beliefs and draw inferences about how we ought to legislate from the factual data we gather, then we are committing a form of the naturalistic fallacy. We cannot derive moral guidance from counting the numbers who support various beliefs. The mere fact that a majority of an electorate shares a belief tells us nothing about its validity or reasonableness. Since the degree of revulsion they experience vis-à-vis certain kinds of behaviour is directly proportional to their moral/religious convictions, it follows that this experience of 'moral revulsion' is no more a guide to reasonable legislation than the beliefs which give rise to it.

Even the classic utilitarian is embarrassed by any other outcome to this question. The utilitarian might argue that the morality of an action should only be decided by examining the amount of pain or pleasure which it causes. If a majority of the electorate feel revulsion towards certain actions, then the fact that they know these actions are performed causes them a lot of pain. If this pain is severe enough, it follows that more people experience pain as a result of knowing something is allowed, than others experience pleasure by being allowed to act in that way. Therefore the act is immoral, on utilitarian grounds, and may even be legally prohibited on similar utilitarian considerations.

The utilitarian need not be constrained by the logic of this argument. He may agree with John Stuart Mill that if utilitarianism results in this conclusion, then it needs to be modified to avoid such an implausible conclusion. In Mill's language, what is wrong with the conclusion is that the immorality of some type of behaviour is being determined exclusively by the fact that a lot of people believe it is immoral, and consequently experience mental anguish at the very thought of its occurrence. If the mere beliefs of a majority of the electorate could determine the morality of an action, the result would be: something is immoral because people believe it is immoral! Even the utilitarian, and certainly Mill, would prefer to avoid the arbitrariness which is implicit in this conclusion.[5]

By a judicious choice of examples from Irish historical experience or from more recent political events in the Middle East, it is relatively easy to reject any principle which tries to determine the criminal law by just consulting the moral sensibilities of the electorate. There is always a prior question about the validity or reasonableness of the moral beliefs to which the electorate appeals as the source of their moral revulsion.

Immoral implies Illegal

The sophisticated proponent of the thesis that the law should be used to support moral values is rightly unimpressed with the moral revulsion argument. To support the same conclusion, however, without the weakness of the previous argument, he might argue that the moral revulsion is warranted because the moral norms which are violated are valid or reasonable. The moral revulsion is merely a symptom of valid moral objections to certain kinds of behaviour. The latter is the real reason why some kinds of human behaviour ought to be proscribed by law.

Few people would suggest that all moral obligations should be reinforced by criminal legislation. There is a number of reasons for this. The most obvious one is that many moral beliefs derive their force from religious beliefs. Any attempt to legally enforce these moral beliefs is, by implication, a legal enforcement of religious views. It is patently unacceptable in a modern democracy to legally enforce religious beliefs, for reasons discussed in Chapter 4 above.

If one could separate moral values based on religious beliefs from other moral values, then the question arises about the reasonableness of any policy which would legally enforce even the latter group of moral norms. We have two questions to ask here, of any given type of human behaviour: (1) is it immoral? (i.e. have we any reasons for proscribing such behaviour?) and (2) if it is immoral, should we use criminal legislation to enforce our moral values? (i.e. have we any moral justification, not only for proscribing the behaviour in question, but for subjecting those who fail to observe our moral standards to criminal punishment?).

I argued in Chapter 1 above that the obligatory force of many moral norms depends on the appropriateness of such norms for guiding individuals towards goals which they themselves would wish to achieve. In other words, it is only because one wishes to realize a certain objective that one ought to do this or not do that. If one fails to follow the moral guide, one risks failing to realize some important human objective. This is roughly analogous to giving someone instructions to guide their safe arrival at a chosen destination. If he fails to follow the directions, he risks getting lost, and he is the only one to directly suffer the ill-effects of his failure. A person's failure to follow such individually oriented moral guidelines may be explained in a variety of ways: he does not accept the reasonableness of the moral guidelines; he does not place a high value on the goals such guidelines lead to, or he values a competing objective more highly; or simply, he suffers from a lack of moral virtue or moral strength. If some moral norms are understood in this way, it is difficult to see any reason for enforcing them with legal sanctions. We could no longer say: this must be done and that must be avoided, and we are justified in using whatever means are necessary to make sure such obligations are honoured. Such an approach fails to take account of the source of such moral obligation.

If an individual is willing to risk the personal ill-effects which are said to befall those who ignore moral obligations, what benefit could be realized for that person by forcing his compliance? This is especially true if the moral value of actions is thought to depend on the voluntary and intentional co-operation of the individual agent. Forced moral virtue is no virtue at all. The only response which seems plausible here is a paternalistic one. One hopes to realize certain goods for another, if necessary against his will, because these goods are more important than the evil of coercion which is involved in the course of their realization. The reasonableness of paternalism is discussed in more detail below.

There are other moral standards — such as the obligation to keep a promise or the obligation to be honest — which represent community-based conventions for facilitating the realization of basic human values for all those who share these conventions. Failure to observe these standards to some extent undermines the conventions on which the success of such moral norms depends. Yet, it can be argued that in many cases the harm done to other individuals by non-observance is not significant enough to warrant criminal punishment. Those who fail to observe such moral standards can be 'taken care of' by the community by being considered dishonest or unreliable; their exclusion from the benefits of the moral convention is an adequate response to their rejection of the community's standards.

In a great variety of other cases, however, the failure by one individual to observe a moral norm causes serious harm to others in the community. In those cases, and only in those, the community may reasonably argue that it needs the threat of criminal sanctions to protect itself against the harm caused by the non-observance of moral standards. Of course the same kind of argument may be used to protect citizens against harmful behaviour which may not be otherwise immoral. For example, there is nothing immoral about driving on one side of the street rather than the other; however if doing so is likely to cause serious injury to others, it is reasonable for citizens to protect themselves by traffic legislation against the possibility of injury.

The difficulties in applying this principle mostly derive from problems in explaining what is meant by 'harm'. In general, an individual may be harmed in either of two ways: *directly*, as for example when another physically injures me; and *indirectly*, when another's action causes me injury only through the mediation of some institution or third party. Thus, if one were to act in such a way that respect for the law were significantly diminished in a community, then one's action indirectly harms all those who are eventually affected, to their detriment, by the diminished respect for law. This indirect harm may be less obvious than the first one, but it is hardly less real on that account. In fact, it is precisely this kind of relatively invisible, institutional or indirect harm which is the focus of many conservative positions in favour of the legal enforcement of morals.

Once 'harm' is understood to include both direct and indirect harm, it still remains to explain what is meant by 'harm'.

Any attempt to explain 'harm' will involve a value-judgment about what kinds of events, actions or experiences are detrimental to the good of an individual. The problems which arise here cannot be avoided by changing terms to talk about, for example, the interests of individuals. Interests are similarly value-laden. Therefore any account of 'harm' and, consequently, any justification for invoking criminal sanctions to enforce moral standards cannot avoid the kind of value-judgments which were already alluded to in Chapter 1. A society must decide, either implicitly or explicitly, what counts as 'man's good' and, by implication, what may be classified as harm. This question is taken up again in Chapter 6.

One approach to this question which should be rejected is any attempt to include *moral harm* in the scope of 'harm', and then to define 'moral harm' by reference to some religious faith. This was Aquinas' strategy when he recommended capital punishment for apostates from the Roman Catholic faith in order to protect other faithful members of the

Church from moral contamination.[6] This kind of argument is a confused form of religious imperialism.

If moral values are not defined in terms of the religious faith of a particular church, however, then the question arises: would it be morally justifiable to enforce moral values because, if many people ignored them, they would fall into disrepute, and this in turn would cause 'moral harm' to others? There is something odd about a positive answer to this question, which makes it close to being a vicious circle. The situation envisaged is something like this. I hold certain moral views which I think should be shared by others in the community. You don't share them, or at least your behaviour falls far short of my moral values. I may live my life according to my own moral standards without interference, but I perceive your behaviour as a temptation to me to fall short of my own ideals. So I appeal to my moral standards to force you to behave in the way I would like you to behave. In that way, your forced co-operation will at least not tempt me to behave against my own standards. If you ask for a moral justification for the legal enforcement, I refer to my own moral values. But those are precisely what is in dispute between us! In other words, I force you to behave in certain ways to reflect my moral standards, and when you object, I rely on the disputed moral standards to support my own coercing behaviour. It is difficult to see how you could ever find that kind of argument plausible.

It follows that, unless I can appeal to some other kind of 'harm' apart from the mere harm of being challenged in my moral beliefs, I have no justification for coercing the behaviour of others so that it conforms to my moral standards. As soon as other people's failure to observe moral norms causes me some independently specifiable harm, however, then I have some justification for invoking criminal sanctions.

There are two qualifications on this conclusion which should be added, both of which concern the relative 'privacy' of what is believed to be immoral behaviour.

There may be good reasons for proscribing public behaviour which the majority of citizens believe is offensive. The reason for this restriction on *public* behaviour is perhaps more aesthetic than moral; for example, behaviour which is perfectly moral and commendable — such as sexual intercourse between married partners — may still be proscribed if done in public. The level of tolerance accepted by different communities in this matter is obviously subject to variation; it was not until relatively recently in the twentieth century, that bathing in shorts was permitted for men on public beaches in the U.S.! What is acceptable or unacceptable as a gross offence to decency can only be determined by local standards of decency. Evidently, considerations of what is 'offensive' only limit public actions, where 'public' is understood as 'performed in a place where the public cannot reasonably avoid noticing the behaviour'.[7]

There is another case in which a plausible argument could be made for restricting public actions, in the same sense of the term 'public'. Parents may reasonably claim that they have a right to educate their children according to moral standards which may not be shared by others in a society. There are surely limits to even parents' discretion in this matter, but these may be left for later discussion in connection with education. If parents have such a limited right, then they may also reasonably claim that their educational efforts should not be unduly compromised by *public* actions which they claim to be seriously immoral. This kind of argument could degenerate into a cloak for arbitrary legislation. If the moral beliefs of a majority of parents are strange enough, they might use this kind of argument to ban the public performance of the most trivial and morally neutral actions. However, within limits which would be subject to rational criticism, parents might reasonably claim that the law may allow immorality (in their view), but that it should not tolerate public immorality in deference to their rights to educate their children. This involves a political trade-off between the rights of individuals to act 'immorally', and the rights of parents to decide the moral education of their minor children. Again, this kind of argument, like the previous one, would only support the legal restriction of public behaviour which many people believe is immoral. It does not support the view that immoral actions should be legally proscribed because they are immoral (in the view of many citizens). Nor does it support their proscription in order to lessen temptation to morally sensitive adults.

As in any other case of criminal legislation, there are other questions which must be addressed before rushing into law. The most obvious one is: would the proposed legislation be enforceable, and would it generally be obeyed? Unenforceable legislation, or legislation which fails to win the respect of citizens, is bad law. Likewise there is a delicate political balance between the likely gains from a given piece of legislation compared with its negative consequences. This was Mill's point about comparing the good and evil consequences of legislating even for those actions which are agreed by all to cause harm to others. We cannot successfully prevent all harm to others, and criminal laws are not always an effective means for trying to do so.

The argument up to this point could be summarized as follows. We ought not to legally enforce any moral beliefs because they are essential to a given way of life; nor should we enforce moral values because they are institutionally established as the warp-and-woof of a society. To legally enforce moral values, we must at least explain why those values are worth defending, whatever their role in the history of a given society.

Nor should we adjust legislation to reflect the moral sensibilities of a majority of the electorate. A majority of citizens may have very irrational moral sensibilities.

The basic principle which should guide legislation is the one proposed by Mill: that we are only justified in legally controlling human behaviour when it is necessary to prevent harm to other members of a society. 'Harm' includes both direct harm to individuals, and also the harm which indirectly affects individuals as a result, for example, of undermining various institutions of the state. However, we cannot include moral harm in applying this principle, if 'moral harm' means tempting people to disobey traditionally accepted moral principles. To do this is equivalent to legally enforcing something simply because people believe it is immoral.

Finally, it is justifiable to control behaviour which takes place in public more stringently than what people do in private. The reason for this is to protect citizens from having to witness what they consider to be offensive, and to protect the rights of parents to control the education of their minor children. Both of these reasons for restricting public behaviour need to be discussed in detail; however, they are not the main point at issue here.

Since Mill's principle is based on the prevention of harm, the question arises: is the state justified in legislating for human behaviour so as to prevent individuals from causing harm to themselves? This raises the issue of paternalism.

Paternalism

'Paternalism' means coercing someone to do something (or to refrain from doing something) for his own good.[8] It is probably true that, in most cases where we coerce another to act in a certain way, our motivation is considerably more complex than this simple definition suggests. We might force someone to do (or avoid) some action partly because any other course of action would adversely affect us; partly because it adversely affects others; partly because . . .; and partly because we think it is in the interests of the agent to act as we direct. Thus paternalism may often be only one strand of our motivation for coercion; it still needs to be examined to see what measure of justification it brings to our coercing behaviour.

The paradigm of a paternalistic action presupposes the following conditions: (i) an agent, *A*, decides to perform an action *voluntarily*. That means that his performance is not unduly influenced by factors which would compromise his freedom, such as passion, the influence of drugs, etc. (ii) *A* acts *intentionally*. That means that *A* realizes what he is doing, or he correctly describes the significant implications of his proposed act. By contrast, one might voluntarily but *un*intentionally hold up a bank and mistakenly think that one is taking part in shooting a movie. (iii) *A* understands the more likely consequences of his action. Thus, if he voluntarily and intentionally crosses a bridge, he also realizes the danger from the imminent collapse of the bridge. If *A* satisfies all three conditions, at least to the extent to which the average human agent does, and if someone else, *P* (the paternalist), tries to force *A* to act otherwise because it would be better for *A*, in *P*'s judgment, to do so, then *P*'s intervention is said to be paternalistic. It is essential to the definition that *P*'s motivation derives from his own perception of what is good for *A*; otherwise *P* might be moved to intervene for any number of alternative possible reasons, and none of these would make his intervention paternalistic.

It is customary in this context to excuse or condone a weak form of paternalism, if the agent *A* does not satisfy all three of the conditions listed. Thus we often justifiably coerce children for their own good, because they are defective with respect to all three conditions. Likewise with those whose judgment is seriously impeded by drugs, or those who suffer from serious mental or emotional retardation. However, even in these cases it is not clear that one can simply assume that such agents are completely incapable of having any significant input in decisions affecting themselves. The justification for weak paternalism allows us to override the express wishes of others about their own welfare only in proportion to the seriousness of the decision in question, and in proportion to the independently judged diminished capacity of the other person.[9]

The kind of paternalism which is at issue in political philosophy is often called 'strong' paternalism. Here the first agent makes a voluntary, intentional and adequately informed judgment about some matter which directly affects only himself; or at least, the extent to which it affects others is not at issue at this point. Another agent or institution, *P*, overrides *A*'s decision because *P* decides that an alterntive course of action would be better for *A*. And then *P* tries to coerce *A* into acting according to *P*'s decision. The analogy with the discussion of causing harm to others is clear. If it is justifiable to coerce someone to behave in a certain way in order to prevent harm to others (apart from the agent), why is it not justifiable to coerce *A* to act in a different way in order to prevent harm to *A*? In each case the prevention of harm is the justification, and 'harm' can be defined in the same way in both cases.

Of course the 'prevention of harm' is ambiguous. One might suffer harm positively by being deprived of some good which one already possesses. Or one might suffer harm negatively by failing to realize goods which, by a different course of action, could be realized with an equal amount of effort. If *P* acts 'for the good of *A*', it may mean that he is trying to prevent the occurrence of positive harm to *A* as a result of *A*'s free actions. For example, *P* might prevent *A* from smoking in order to prevent the usual risks to health associated with smoking. *P* might also be motivated by *A*'s interests if he anticipates that *A*'s intended course of action will fail to realize goods which he could easily enjoy by a different course of action. Thus, an unemployed *A* might decide to take a walk in the park and miss the opportunity to meet a potential employer. *P* might then coerce *A* to stay at home in order not to miss the chance of employment. In the first case, *P* is trying to prevent the positive occurrence of some harm to *A*; in the second case, *P* is trying to prevent *A*'s failure to realize some good which he could easily achieve and which (in *P*'s judgment) would be desirable for *A*. In either case, *P* is attempting to prevent either positive or negative harm to *A*.

What reason might *P* give *A* for a paternalistically motivated coercion of his behaviour, which would seem plausible to *A*? It won't do to argue, as above, that *P* is ultimately trying to protect himself; if he is, then this is not a case of paternalism at all. Nor could *P* claim that he is protecting the 'moral environment' from *A*'s evil influence, because this kind of argument also depends, when analysed, on the motive of protecting individuals apart from *A* who might be harmed by *A*'s immoral influence. Again, this is not a paternalistic action at all, but something quite different which only looks like paternalism. To properly focus attention on a strongly paternalistic action, one must isolate the relevant motivation and ask: if *P* had no other reason for interfering in *A*'s action except to prevent harm to A, what reason might he give to A which would be plausible from A's point of view? If we cannot provide such a reason, then why should we not think of P's interference as a blatant exercise of power, perhaps with the co-operation of the law, to determine the behaviour of another free agent?

Any answer to this question will involve a value-judgment about the relative worth of A's autonomy compared with other goods which might be realized by compromising his autonomy. The Inquisition-type answer is this: A's eternal salvation is more important than his autonomy (although it is difficult to imagine any coherent explanation of how A could be saved without his free consent!). Therefore, while it is true that A's autonomy as a person is compromised in forcing his behaviour in a certain direction, and while this would normally be immoral in other circumstances, in those serious cases in which A's salvation is at stake, it is preferable that he lose his autonomy rather than 'lose his soul'.

Two questions come to mind. For whom is it preferable to make this decision? And according to what theory, or whose theory, is it preferable? In response to the first question, the answer must be: preferable for P. A knows what he is doing and prefers his intended course of action to that proposed by P. How could P be justified in forcing his own value-judgment on A? There is no need at this point to assume that all value-judgments are completely relative to individual choices, and therefore A's judgment is just as valid as that of P. Even if A's decision is a patently poor decision or a defective value-judgment, as long as he is the only one who suffers the ill-effects of his decision, what justification can there be for constraining his judgment in the direction of community-endorsed standards? The only thing P might say is: you think your choice is good for you, but we know otherwise. A might respond: I know it is bad for me to act in this way, but I still choose to act as I wish. P's only reply can be that he (P) chooses one good over another, for A; the good he thinks A will realise by following P's coercion rather than the good of autonomous choice.

The second question was: whose set of values does P rely on to make such a choice (for A)? According to whose theory is it so clearly better for A to be constrained to act 'correctly' rather than freely? Evidently, the answer must again be: P's theory. Why is P so confident about the validity of his own theory that he is willing to override someone else's autonomy on the basis of his theory? The typical 'Inquisitor' would appeal to the infallibility, explicitly or implicitly claimed, of his sources, which are often religious. There is no rational gainsaying such an internally consistent, power-supported ideology.

There is one other subterfuge available to P to justify his use of force against A. He might try to re-describe the coercion as weak paternalism, because the kind of decision being made by A is 'obviously' not one which would be made by an ideal rational agent. A, in other words, would not have made the decision he did if he were either better informed or more adequately in control of himself. What looks like freedom or autonomy is, in fact, the end result of a distortion of A's freedom by various factors which have undermined his true freedom. True freedom is only manifest in those who at least intend to do what they ought to do; those who *apparently* choose to do what they clearly ought not to do are not truly free or autonomous.[10]

The dangers of this type of reasoning are so clear that they hardly need elaboration. According to this criterion of true freedom, a society, a state, or a religious institution might list what it considers to be political virtues. Those who fail to acknowledge those virtues would be judged 'insane' or in some way mentally defective and therefore in need of corrective therapy. It would clinch any argument in favour of the coherent totalitarian if he could not only justify his actions in terms of some higher good but, besides, if he could show that those who disagree with him are not fully competent to make the decisions on which their disagreement is based. Actual cases are usually not as clear-cut as the religious persecution of the Inquisitor, or the psychiatric treatment of political dissidents. Those who argue in favour of paternalism would claim that the values by which the competence of A is judged are neither arbitary nor speciously camouflaged political or religious judgments. However, that is exactly the nub of the issue. In order to describe one's paternalism as weak (and justifiable) one needs to supply *independent* evidence of A's incompetence to make the decision he apparently makes freely and intentionally. 'Independent' here means: independent of the particular decision which is being judged incorrect and therefore worthy of being paternalistically overridden.

Another way of seeing this point is to ask: is it possible to be competent (in the relevant sense) and still make a decision which most normal people would regard as so detrimental to oneself that the very decision one makes causes doubts about one's competence to make it? For example, is it possible to competently decide to commit suicide, or to competently decide to inflict severe pain on oneself? We often decide com-

petence, not by reference to the choices made by another, but by examining the internal logic of the choice. Irrational connections between
beliefs are easier to diagnose than irrational beliefs. If someone's system
of beliefs is internally coherent, and if their factual beliefs about the
universe are consistent with available evidence, could we still decide their
competence by reference to the 'strangeness' or 'abnormality' of their
value-judgments? Here the concept of 'independent' criteria can do some
work.

If someone were reasonably consistent over a period of time in their interests, choices and decisions, and then made a decision which was
radically out of character with their usual pattern of value-judgments,
one might plausibly argue that, on that basis alone, the single aberrant
decision is defective in competence. One might therefore override such a
decision, for the good of the other person, in the anticipation that when
he returns at a later stage to his usual pattern of choices he would
retrospectively confirm the decision made by others on his behalf. The
anticipation of such retrospective confirmation would justify overriding
A's decision; P would characterize his intervention as weak paternalism.
However if A's value-judgments were reasonably consistent over time
and simply diverged from those which P endorses, it would be the merest
subterfuge on P's part to attempt a similar reclassification of his strong
paternalism in that case. For in this second case, there is no independent
reason to believe that A would share P's values; the mere fact that A's
decision disagrees with P's (rather than with A's usual pattern of
choices) is being used to characterize A as incompetent.

Thus strong paternalism is unjustified. The law should not be used to
prevent competent agents from causing moral or other harm to
themselves. And strong paternalism should not be redescribed as weak,
when the alleged incompetence of an agent is decided exclusively by
reference to the disparity in value-judgments between a dissident agent
and a paternalistic community. Independent evidence of incompetence is
required.

Individualism

The argument to this point defends a position which is similar to J.S.
Mill's:

. . . the sole end for which mankind are warranted, individually or collectively, in
interfering with the liberty of action of any of their number, is self-protection.

. . . the only purpose for which power can be rightfully exercised over any member of a civilized community, against his will, is to prevent harm to others. His own good, either physical or moral, is not a sufficient warrant.[11]

In coercing the behaviour of others by law, we should make the following distinctions:

(a) if *P*'s moral beliefs are primarily inspired by religious faith, he cannot justifiably coerce *A* to endorse this faith;

(b) if *A* ignores moral obligations which are primarily oriented towards *A*'s own welfare, then again *P* is not justified in coercing him;

(c) many moral obligations are directly related to facilitating a harmonious realization of human objectives which are thought to be common to all citizens. If *A* ignores these moral obligations, in many cases his lack of co-operation can be dealt with by depriving him of the benefits which are believed to follow, for the moral community, from observing moral norms. One can lose many community-based benefits by simply being classified as dishonest, unreliable, and so on;

(d) finally, if *A*'s immoral behaviour significantly affects others apart from himself adversely, and if the harm he thereby causes is greater than the costs of criminal sanctions, it is justifiable for the community to protect its members against the ill-effects of *A*'s behaviour.

One of the standard objections to this is that it is so abstract that it is irrelevant to the complexity of actual political decisions. Just as the line between weak and strong paternalism proved, on closer analysis, to rely on a disputed concept of competence, so likewise (it might be objected) the apparent distinction between adversely affecting oneself and adversely affecting others is a purely theoretical distinction which is too difficult to draw in practice. Hence, Mill's proposals are inapplicable, and the safer course is to act conservatively. In case of danger to the body politic, bring in appropriate restrictive legislation!

The premises of this type of objection should be conceded, in a modified form; but the conclusion does not follow without begging the question which is highlighted by the discussion of strong paternalism.

There are clear cases where immoral behaviour (immoral as judged by plausible, rational standards) is primarily self-regarding; i.e. the only specifiable ill-effects of the immoral behaviour are suffered by the agent. There are also clear cases where others, apart from the agent, suffer a specifiable and significant amount of harm, and in those cases there is no dispute about the appropriateness of criminal sanctions. Most disputed cases seem to fall somewhere in the middle, when the likely, foreseeable effects of actions affect the interests both of the agent and of many others in the community. In other words, most human actions are not private in a sense which is relevant to libertarian principles. They are public insofar as they directly or indirectly affect, for both good and ill, many citizens. Therefore the relative merits of their effects on others must be taken into consideration by appropriate legislation.

There is a real danger here of distorting the complexity of this question in favour of simplistic solutions. This is a temptation on the part of both conservatives and classic liberals. Whatever solution is eventually endorsed must represent an attempted balance between conflicting values in a society, rather than the mechanical application of any one general principle. If we consider the activity of begetting children within a legal marriage, and then contrast this with contraceptively 'protected' fornication, there is an obvious sense in which many would regard the latter as immoral (perhaps for two reasons). Yet the moral behaviour of the married couple is much more *public* or other-regarding than the allegedly immoral behaviour of the unmarried couple. Begetting children, especially if the example is complicated by financial dependencies on others in the community, eventually affects the lives of many other citizens in a way which fornication may not. If others are adversely affected by a couple's begetting a child, then one might argue that such a conception may be subject to legal interference.[12] The very suggestion of such a possibility would make some people quake; 'if we could not make room in our legislation for a mother-and-child medical scheme, we could hardly condone the totalitarian attitude of a government which would attempt to influence the birth-rate of legitimate children in the state.' This only shows, however, that we have separated the alleged 'right to procreate' from the many other rights of individuals with which it may conflict. Because it is insulated as a 'natural right' or as an 'inalienable right', we put blinkers on the extent to which it is a public or social act, with significant and obvious consequences, both economic and social, for many other members of a community. By contrast, we might be willing to uncritically criminalize all sexual behaviour outside of marriage simply because we think it is immoral, and without being able to explain how such behaviour adversely affects others.

If we change focus for a moment, away from conventional norms of morality and immorality, to examine the relative 'publicity' or social implications of actions, then we may need to change our list of difficult cases which require legislative decisions. Smoking causes ill-health and, in many cases, it puts a financial burden on one's family and on other tax-payers. Likewise for careless or even just incompetent driving of motorized vehicles on public roads. There is a wide range of actions which, by ordinary standards, are voluntary and intentional, and which typically cause an imminent threat of harm to others in society. For example: the unmerited certification of any professional or specialized worker who offers his or her services to the public; the election of incompetent or uncritical legislators; the organization of social services, by those responsible, which are demonstrably below the level of efficiency which is warranted by the finances made available for them; incompetent managerial decisions which are at least partly remediable, and which eventually cause unemployment and its attendant hardships to an almost incalculable extent: the provision of deficient schools or other social services to those in need; and so on almost indefinitely. The conservative's premise is therefore well placed. There are many actions, which we might uncritically imagine are almost exclusively private or self-regarding and therefore only the concern of individual agents, which have repercusions for many others in the community. Indeed, we might begin to have trouble in thinking of clear cases which are, in the relevant sense, 'private'. Many of the actions with obvious social implications were ignored by traditional moral casuists; by the canons of traditional morality, they are morally neutral. But that does not imply that the state should be uninterested in their regulation, in the interests of the common good.

Any regulation of human actions with definite social consequences, in the interests of the common good, will involve not only the kinds of value-judgments already mentioned, but also rather delicate questions involving a comparative evaluation of conflicting values. The liberal tradition inspired by Mill is based on the recognition of individual autonomy as *one* of the basic values which must be respected in resolving conflicts of interest. It is therefore consistent for Mill to claim that society has no legitimate interests in controlling the behaviour of individual citizens unless and to the extent to which their exercise of autonomy causes harm to others. Thus Mill's thesis does not depend on any counter-factual assumptions about the relative isolation of individuals' actions, and their consequences, from other members of society. All human actions, whether moral or immoral by the standards of traditional morality, are subject to social control to the extent that they cause harm to other members of a society. In making the decision to control them, however, one needs to question whether criminal sanctions are necessary or justified, and whether the same objectives (of minimizing harm) might be adequately accomplished without the use of legislation.

Thus Mill's thesis does not presuppose some kind of theoretical individualism, according to which most of the actions we perform affect only ourselves. He can be a robust realist in describing the extent to which most of our actions rather significantly affect others, both directly and indirectly. Once this is recognized or agreed, it still remains to decide when society is justified in interfering in individuals' choices. Mill has a coherent answer to this: society is justified in interfering to the extent that an individual's action causes harm to others.

This changes the focus of our social concerns away from the traditional morality of actions to concentrate on their causality of social harm. It also means that we can no longer easily isolate some actions as 'natural rights' just because we have traditionally thought of them in that category, and therefore not scrutinize their effects on society. In a paradoxical way, the result of Mill's thesis is to enlarge the scope of justified social control over human actions by changing the criterion for interference from 'immorality' to 'harm to others'. The question of balancing the conflicting demands of individual rights and of social control, in the interests of the common good, is taken up again in Chapter 6.

Church Teaching

The Roman Catholic Church apparently endorses Mill's thesis. For example, the statement of the Irish Episcopal Conference, in 1973, concerning proposed changes in the law regarding the sale of contraceptives, includes the following:

There are many things which the Catholic Church holds to be morally wrong and no one has ever suggested, least of all the Church herself, that they should be prohibited by the State.

Those who insist on seeing the issue purely in terms of the State enforcing, or not enforcing, Catholic moral teaching are therefore missing the point. The real question facing the legislators is: What effect would the increased availability of contraceptives have on the quality of life in the Republic of Ireland? That is a question of public, not private, morality. What the legislators have to decide is whether a change in the law would, on balance, *do more harm than good*, by damaging the character of the society for which they are responsible. (Italics added)[13]

What this means depends on how the bishops understand 'harm'. There is a strong tradition in the Church of interpreting 'harm' by reference to the moral/religious teaching of the Church. Thus whatever directly or indirectly weakens the religious beliefs of members of the Church would be construed as harm. That is certainly the exact opposite to Mill's doctrine.

For example, Pope Pius XI, in his encyclical *Casti Connubii*, wrote:

Governments can assist the Church greatly in the execution of its important office, if, in laying down their ordinances, they take account of what is prescribed by divine and ecclesiastical law, and if penalties are fixed for offenders. For as it is, there are those who think that whatever is permitted by the laws of the State, or at least is not punished by them, is allowed also in the moral order . . .[14]

Pope Paul VI makes a similar appeal to civil governments, in his encyclical *Humanae Vitae*, to support Church laws by civil legislation:

To rulers, who are those principally responsible for the common good, and who can do so much to safeguard moral customs, we say: Do not allow the morality of your peoples to be degraded; do not permit that by legal means practices contrary to the natural and divine law [as interpreted by the Church] be introduced into that fundamental cell, the family.[15]

The Irish Catholic Bishops, in their statements in the past decade, have been careful not to explicitly demand civil penalties for those who reject the Church's view of natural or divine law. However, many of their comments fit into the category which includes 'moral harm' among the harms caused by defective legislation, and 'moral harm' in turn is understood by reference to Roman Catholic theology. Thus:

Young people in Ireland have high moral standards but it may be felt that legislators ought to think very carefully before making the *environment for moral living* more difficult for them. (Italics added)[16]

The same sentiment is expressed in the 1978 Episcopal statement on family planning:

Laws can affect people's attitudes about relations between the sexes, both within marriage and outside it. Laws affect the *moral environment* in which we live. Laws can make decent living for the young more difficult or less difficult. The law-maker has to consider the effects which new legislation in this area is likely to have. He must weigh the good against the bad. The good which a law may do must be set against the harm which it can do. (Italics added)[17]

Again the assumption here is that, since the beliefs of the Roman Catholic Church on the morality of contraception are obviously true, any changes in people's beliefs or moral attitudes about contraception would represent a deterioration in the 'moral environment'. The metaphor about a moral environment is a picturesque way of describing a change in moral beliefs which is partly influenced by the changed beliefs of others. Such a change of attitudes could only be described as 'harm' by first assuming the correctness of the Church's teaching!

The bishops have also defended the warp-and-woof thesis with respect to our current marriage customs. Thus:

> Every broken marriage inevitably brings suffering to the couple themselves, . . . (and) serves to *undermine* the very society in which they live. (Italics added) [18]

In the same statement, the bishops claim that their teaching about the indissolubility of marriage is not simply based on the religious teaching of one church; however, that claim can only be plausibly understood as a slip of the pen:

> . . . a validly contracted marriage is not dissoluble by any merely human authority. It is essential to recognise that this conclusion is not dependent merely upon the teaching of a particular Church, but is based also upon any unprejudiced consideration of the grave social evils which inevitably follow from what the Council calls 'the plague of divorce'. [19]

The available evidence on the Irish Catholic Church's position indicates a change in rhetoric from explicit moral imperialism to an apparently compromising, liberal attitude. The change is only a change in rhetoric; the underlying doctrine is the same as that enunciated by Pope Pius XI or Pope Paul VI. This doctrine involves a number of inter-related assumptions, which include the following:

(i)   The Church is the final, authoritative decision maker on moral issues; its verdict is guaranteed to be correct. Those who disagree with its moral judgments are either mistaken or else motivated by immoral desires or objectives. In either case their recommendations should be ignored.

(ii) Governments have an obligation to safeguard not only the material interests of citizens, but also their moral or spiritual interests.

(iii) Any legislation which condones immorality (as defined by the Roman Catholic Church) causes a deterioration in the moral environment in which citizens live. That means that the civil law encourages immoral behaviour, and this in turn encourages immorality in others.

(iv)   Therefore, civil governments should legislate in such a way that immorality (as defined by the Church) is not encouraged. They should make many moral acts (which?) illegal — not simply because they are immoral, but because publicly tolerating them causes the grave social harm of a deterioration in the moral environment. In less metaphorical language, the legal tolerance of immorality encourages immoral behaviour.

It is difficult to avoid the conclusion that the Church is doing precisely what it says it is not doing: it is looking for support, from criminal legislation, to sustain the moral traditions which it endorses. The only difference between this and a straightforward theocracy is a matter of degree. The Church does not make this request for all immoral actions; partly because the civil law would be ineffective in many cases, and partly because such a blatant attempt to influence civil legislation would be recognized for what it is. Nor does it request the criminalization of immoral acts simply because they are immoral. However, the Church does ask that they be criminalized because they tempt citizens to act in a way which is believed, by the Church, to be immoral. Since the authority of the Church ultimately rests on its own religious beliefs about itself,[20] the demand that civil legislation reinforce the Church's views on morality is a form of moral and religious imperialism.

6

Human Rights and the Common Good

Respect for human rights is the touchstone of democracy in contemporary politics. Even those governments which flagrantly violate human rights try to explain their actions by arguments of expediency in the interests of the common good, national security or the like. The agreement in principle to uphold human rights and the signing of international agreements to that effect do not guarantee unanimity in our understanding of human rights, nor uniformity of interpretation of the international agreements. Despite this, however, there is a non-trivial sense in which human rights occupy a central place in the political consciousness of contemporary mankind.[1] In deference to this raised consciousness and to our own national traditions of demanding freedom from any form of oppression, it is appropriate to ask: to what extent are human rights legally guaranteed in Ireland?

The language of human rights is a controversial part of our more wide-ranging language of evaluation. When someone has a right to something, there is nothing which is had in any ordinary sense of the word 'have', as when one has a house or a pain. To have a right is to be justified in making a claim. The kind of justification one appeals to and the extent to which it is recognized by the relevant community decide whether one has a right or not, and what kind of right it is.

If someone claims to have a right, he may justify the claim by reference to the law or some quasi-legal institution, or by reference to moral values. In the former case, one claims to have a *legal* right, and in the latter a *moral* right. The force of this distinction clearly depends on one's understanding of morality and of the law, and assumes the possibility of making a workable distinction between them. Human rights claims are characteristically *moral* in the sense that they are

136

justified, in the first instance at least, by reference to our moral conventions. Any given legal system may or may not incorporate human rights into its framework; so that it is not incoherent to speak of human rights which are not legally recognized in a given jurisdiction.

In discussing the legal protection of human rights in Ireland, one must consider both the impact of international law on citizens' rights, and also the kind of protection which is afforded by domestic law, both statute and constitutional. Neither the *United Nations Universal Declaration of Human Rights* nor the *European Convention on Human Rights and Fundamental Freedoms* are part of the domestic law in Ireland.[2] An argument might be made that both of these legal instruments are part of international law, and that Ireland is bound by its own constitution to respect and enforce international law. Even if this argument is rejected by the Courts, it is still true that Ireland is bound by its legal commitment to international conventions to provide the protections which they guarantee to Irish citizens. In those cases where Irish courts refuse to legally protect rights which are guaranteed, for example, by the *European Convention on Human Rights*, an Irish citizen may have recourse to the European Commission.

Apart from the significant implications of international law on the legal protection of rights in Ireland, the Constitution also guarantees 'Fundamental Rights' to citizens in Articles 40 to 44. It is not surprising, given the important developments in the recognition of human rights since 1937, that the Constitution does not explicitly mention many of the rights which are listed in the United Nations *Declaration*.[3] However, the failure to mention specific rights does not imply that they are not constitutionally guaranteed in Ireland. Article 40 implies the existence of a residue of implicit rights which are constitutionally protected. Section 3 of Article 40 reads:

(1)   The State guarantees in its laws to respect, and, as far as practicable, by its laws to defend and vindicate the personal rights of the citizen.
(2)   The State shall, in particular, by its laws protect as best it may from unjust attack and, in the case of injustice done, vindicate the life, person, good name, and property rights of every citizen.[4]

This text has been understood since *Ryan* v. *Attorney General* to mean that the personal rights which are guaranteed by the Constitution are not limited to those which are explicitly mentioned in the text, but that they include 'all those rights which result from the Christian and democratic nature of the State'.[5]

One of the implications of this interpretation of Article 40 is that there is no clearly defined list available of individual rights which are legally recognized as human rights in Ireland. In reaching decisions on specific claims, Irish courts have been guided by decisions of the U.S. Supreme Court, by international law, by philosophical claims about the 'natural law', and by a variety of other arguments.[6] Therefore, in order to construct a profile of the legal protection of human rights in Irish domestic law, and to compare it with corresponding legislative guarantees in international law, one must try to describe the philosophy of rights which is implicit in the Irish Constitution. Evidently, the courts are restricted in their interpretation of constitutionally guaranteed rights by other provisions of the Constitution, apart from Articles 40 to 44, and these are relevant to any profile of rights which might be proposed. But apart from such explicit restrictions, the courts are principally guided by the philosophy of rights which is implicit in the Constitution and which was described in the phrase 'the Christian and democratic nature of the State'.[7]

This chapter suggests one interpretation of the philosophy of rights which is implicit in the Constitution. Is is not directly concerned with the impact of international law on the protection of rights in Ireland, except to compare the provisions of domestic law with those afforded in other jurisdictions.

In comparing the Irish Constitution with international human rights conventions I adopt the following strategy. The concept of a human right, as that concept operates in modern democracies, is clarified by reference to the equality of members of political communities as moral agents. With this concept in mind the Constitution is then examined and is found to contain two categories of individual rights: (a) those which are inalienable or antecedent to all positive law, and (b) those which are subject to qualifications by reference, for example, to the common good or to public order and morality. I then argue that the choice of rights which are included in the first list indicates a significant confessional influence on the drafting of the Constitution and that the confessional imbalance could only be rectified by a compensatory weighting of other individual rights by the courts, or by constitutional amendments. In relation to the qualification of rights by reference to the common good, there is reason to believe that constitutional provisions for so-called 'emergency legislation' are subversive of basic rights to a degree which no Irish government, to date, has fully exploited. The commitment of any constitution to human rights can be gauged by its willingness to compromise rights in the interests of the common good and by the theory of the common good to which it appeals, implicitly or explicitly, in such compromises. By this criterion, the Irish Constitution is schizophrenic.

Human Rights and Equality

A human right is a moral right which every individual has in virtue of being a human being. One does not claim to have a human right because of one's citizenship, nor because of one's function in a society, nor because of any features of race, colour, religious belief, intellectual or other abilities, nor because of the significance of one's contribution to the community. One claims to have human rights because one is a human person. This does not justify one's claim, nor explain why one has the specific rights one has — it merely identifies those who have human rights, and even here there are still some residual problems.[8] Nor are human rights conferred by some institution on the person who has them; hence they cannot be taken away by a similar institution.[9] Rather, human rights are such that each person has them independently of any particular legal recognition of them, and independently of any of the features which distinguish people and which may be used to discriminate against specific groups. If human rights are so basic and so independent of the law, it is important to see why one may justifiably claim such rights against all attempts to subvert them by the state, the churches or any other institution.

The concept of a human right is closely dependent on the equality of persons as moral agents. There is an unavoidable danger of obfuscating the issue rather than of clarifying it by relating human rights to equality; it looks like trying to explain something which is poorly understood by reference to another concept which is even less clear and less tractable. In the present case this is a risk which cannot be avoided.

The idea of equality is useful because it leads the discussion in the direction of specifying what it is about persons which underlies human rights, and what it means to attribute equal rights to all. There is no easy way out of this mutual clarification of concepts. For example, it would not help, as Melden has pointed out, to say that persons have rights because they were created by God.[10] Those who believe in God as creator also tend to believe that God created trees, and fish, and everything else, and we are presumably not tempted to ascribe rights to all these creatures also *because* they were created by God. For whether created by God or not, human beings are sufficiently different from other creatures to have rights, and it remains to be seen what it is about them which justifies that kind of claim.

The basis of human rights is the common interests and capacity for moral judgment of human beings. To support a philosophy of human rights one must assume that various differences among individuals — such as national, cultural, religious, or racial distinctions — are not sufficient to completely displace what individuals, world-wide, have in common. One needs to assume that there are various basic goods which human beings characteristically desire; in some cases these will be negative goods (such as the desire to avoid serious pain) and in other cases positive goods (such as a desire for adequate nutrition or autonomy). This is not to argue fallaciously that because something is desired, that it is therefore desirable. To say what is desirable is to make a value-judgment, and such judgments can only be made relative to some moral convention. What is at issue here is more basic than moral conventions; it is an attempt to explain the reasonableness of the moral conventions to which we freely give our allegiance.

If I imagine a group of individuals getting together to draft moral conventions which they will then freely endorse, it is reasonable to assume that the success of their efforts would presuppose some preliminary agreements, such as:

(1)   the recognition of all members as equal with respect to their input into the deliberations and their subsequent recognition as moral agents in a moral community;

(2)   agreement with respect to a significant number of characteristic human goods which are the subject of guaranteed protection by the conventions adopted. If there were no agreement on this point it is difficult to see why participants in the moral community would be motivated to honour their commitment to its conventions.

The first pre-condition for any moral agreement specifies the extension of human rights to all and only those who are capable of moral actions. The exceptions and difficult cases would have to be defended independently. Apart from such cases, human rights are assumed to extend to all persons insofar as they are capable of moral judgment and activity. Thus, we do not first establish a particular moral theory and then argue for certain moral rights on the basis of the theory, no more than we can successfully argue that people have rights because of any natural qualities which they might have. On the contrary, we could not establish a moral community at all unless we first granted that all moral agents are recognized as equal precisely insofar as they are moral agents. This explains why we traditionally correlate human rights with being a person rather than with being intelligent, or strong, or white, or anything else. Insofar as an individual is a moral agent or a person, he is of equal status with others, and the mutual recognition of this equality as persons is the *sine qua non* for establishing a moral community and evolving conventions for human conduct which could function as moral norms.

The second pre-condition specifies the range of goods which are basic enough to deserve serious moral control, and the minimal standards which would have to be satisfied in order to both win and keep the allegiance of members of a moral community to the conventions which it endorses. It is impossible to avoid the conclusion that any attempt to fill in a list of 'human rights' in this sense is historically conditioned. It is an illusion of metaphysical imagination to think that there is some objective standard available (where?) by reference to which we could relatively easily decide which human goods are basic, and what 'amount' of such goods is minimal for human living. There is no sharp line of demarcation between basic human rights and those which, being less fundamental, are subject to political or legal compromise. Where one draws the line here depends on the distinction between fundamental and reasonably vague moral demands for treatment as a human person, and the moral demand for equality of access to whatever conditions are required for exercising these basic rights.[11] Even guaranteed equality of opportunity will not deliver any of those goods which are necessary for a human life: in a situation of famine, for example, people might be said to have an equal right to a daily ration of food without the slightest chance of getting anything to eat.[12] Equal rights to a share in some good are compatible with no share at all when there is nothing to divide.

Absolute Rights

The language in which rights are expressed tends to be unconditional. For example, one might say: 'I have a right to strike' or 'I have a right to say what I think'. The grammar of such claims does not imply that the rights themselves are absolute or unconditional, because the legitimate rights of different individuals may conflict. Thus the right to freedom of speech does not imply freedom to libel someone because the someone in question also has rights, including the right to his or her good name. It would be naive to think that one might specify in advance all the possible ways in which rights may conflict, so that the enunciation of each right would include a qualifying list of all the situations in which it must cede to other rights. In the case of moral principles, to say that something ought (or ought not) to be done does not usually mean that there are no conceivable circumstances in which the contrary would not be morally tolerated. Likewise, to have a right is to have a moral or legal justification for a claim; and moral or legal counter-claims of comparable significance must be considered before my right unequivocally justifies my actions.

This raises the question of the relative significance or weight of different rights. If, despite their unqualified expression, rights are not unconditional justifications for actions; if the exercise of legitimate rights may conflict with those of other individuals, then we need some criterion for deciding which rights are absolute, if any, and which are more or less basic.

The utilitarian tradition in political philosophy is able to make distinctions between more or less basic rights, and to define these rights in terms of the minimal conditions necessary for satisfying human interests. However, utilitarians cannot use the concept of an absolute right. No matter how unjust, cruel or inhuman an action may be, it might be required (on a utilitarian calculation) for the greater good of the greatest number. If the objective to be realized is important enough, the putative rights of individuals may always be compromised.

Non-utilitarian political theories are not forced to this conclusion. They claim to be able to identify some human goods which are so basic that nothing could ever conceivably justify their denial to an individual. It is clear that the *European Convention on Human Rights* is non-utilitarian in this sense. For example, Article 3 reads:

No one shall be subjected to torture or to inhuman or degrading treatment or punishment.

Article 15 reinforces the unconditional character of Article 3 by precluding the possibility of derogating from its observance even 'in time of war or other public emergency . . .'

(1) In time of war or other public emergency threatening the life of the nation any High Contracting Party may take measures derogating from its obligations under this Convention to the extent strictly required by the exigencies of the situation, provided that such measures are not inconsistent with its other obligations under international law.

(2)   No derogation from . . . Articles 3, 4 (paragraph 1) and 7 shall be made under this provision.

This means that one may not derogate from Article 3 (nor from the other articles mentioned) for any reason, whether it is the public good, or national security, or anything else. It follows that one cannot consistently be a utilitarian and subscribe to the European Convention. A government could, of course, subscribe to the Conveniton for political reasons with mental reservations, i.e. with an implicit understanding that it would cease to be a party to the Convention whenever it could be shown to be derogating from its unconditional prohibitions. Such political manoeuvering does not affect the philosophy of rights which is explicit in the Convention: that some rights are so basic that no political or national emergency justifies their suspension. Some human rights are absolute.

Any attempt to provide an adequate philosophical explanation of which rights are absolute and which are relative would divert our attention at this stage from the main question at issue, namely: the philosophy of rights which is implicit in the Irish Constitution. Two standard distinctions, however, may help focus the discussion of that topic. One is the distinction between negative and positive rights; the other is the distinction between political and economic rights.

The United Nations covenants on human rights are distinguished into two sets: one on Civil and Political rights, and the other on Economic, Social and Cultural rights. The distinction partly reflects the ideological disagreement between East and West as to which kind of right is most fundamental. The Eastern bloc countries tended to argue that civil rights are useless if one is so economically deprived that one is not in a position to effectively exercise any of the rights which are legally guaranteed in theory. Western countries generally argued that civil or political rights did not cost anything to grant, and therefore there was no good reason (apart from ideological ones) for not recognizing them immediately. By contrast, economic rights depend on various economic factors over which governments may have little direct control. The choice between the two categories of right is complicated because of the real possibility of a trade-off between the two; one might surrender some personal freedoms in exchange for increased economic or social welfare. It is hardly feasible to discover some abstract criterion which would convincingly settle the variety of possible disagreements which are generated by this distinction.

The other distinction which is helpful here is the distinction between positive and negative rights.[13] If someone has a positive right to do something, then he has a moral or legal basis for claiming that he is free to act in a certain way. In this sense of 'right', one has a right to do anything which is not either illegal or immoral, and this includes a rather comprehensive and diverse class of rights. The concept of a negative right, on the other hand, is used to mark off limits to the extent to which others may justifiably infringe on the freedom or autonomy of an individual. Thus, if someone has a negative right to do something, then no other person or institution is justified in preventing him from doing what he has a right to do. In this sense of the term 'right', rights mark the minimal conditions for the kind of autonomy and respect which are presupposed in any moral community. Positive rights tend to be more subject to compromise than negative rights; absolute rights, where they exist, tend to be negative rights.

Given the almost innumerable ways in which a country's constitution might express the rights of its citizens and provide legal mechanisms for resolving conflicting rights claims, one might approach the problem of examining a given constitution by asking two questions: does it recognize any absolute negative rights? If it does, which ones are they? In the case of those rights which are legally recognized as subject to compromise, the question arises about the relative ease with which such compromises are constitutionally permitted, and the kind of justification which is required to allow them.

Inalienable and Imprescriptible Rights

On first inspection, the Irish Constitution reflects the non-utilitarian philosophy of rights which is characteristic of the *European Convention on Human Rights*. It identifies some individual rights as so important that any contrary legislation may be ruled to be invalid by the High Court or the Supreme Court. It provides definite constitutional limits on the powers of the Oireachtas vis-à-vis the individual citizen, and it provides clear procedures for testing the validity of acts of the legislature, either before they are signed by the president into law, or even after being duly enacted as law by the Oireachtas.[14] The strength of these constitutional limits on government is even more evident in recent developments in Irish jurisprudence, where many rights which are not explicitly mentioned in the Constitution have been recognized as fundamental rights of individuals which provide the legal basis for overturning contrary legislation.[15]

Among the fundamental rights which are constitutionally protected, some are more fundamental than others and therefore less subject to compromise. These include those rights which are said to be inalienable, imprescriptible, or 'antecedent to positive law'.

Basic human rights are often said to be inalienable in the sense that, even if one tried, it would be impossible to give up or lose such rights because they are part of what it means to be a human person.[16] The inalienability of rights, in other words, is an index of how central they are to being a moral agent. On the other hand, the relative ease with which a right may be relinguished is an indication that it derives from a more or less changeable social or political contract between people.[17] Besides being inalienable, some constitutional rights are qualified as imprescriptible, and the two words do not mean the same thing. One could conceive of a right which was alienable but imprescriptible; such a right may be given up by whoever has it, but it could not be taken away by anyone else.[18] The inalienability or imprescriptibility of rights are both indicators of the relatively fundamental status which such rights are accorded. Human rights would seem to be both inalienable and, in general, imprescriptible, so that either index would provide some insight into the constitutional status of human rights in Ireland.

The Constitution recognizes two rights as inalienable: in Article 41, the family is said to have 'inalienable and imprescriptible rights, antecedent and superior to all positive law'. However, the Constitution does not give any indication of what these rights are. In Article 42 parents are said to have 'the inalienable right' to provide for the education of their children. Article 42 also establishes that children have 'natural and imprescriptible rights' vis-à-vis the educational arrangements of the State. The only other rights mentioned in the Constitution on a par with these in terms of their independence of positive law is 'the natural right, antecedent to positive law, to the private ownership of external goods'.[19]

It has already been noted by Declan Costello that these rights are different, in their relative immunity from interference by the State, from the personal rights listed in Article 40,[20] and that this suggests a difference in their philosophical ancestry. This is a fair comment but not a reason for unmitigated enthusiasm. Those rights in the Constitution which come close to being recognized as absolute, negative rights are limited to those which were important to the tradition of Roman Catholic moral theology which was current in the 1930s.

In the case of education, the rights of parents are not qualified by the rights of children, although the State's concern for educating children is qualified by the 'natural and imprescriptible rights of the child'. And with the exception of the unspecified rights of the family, the right to own private property is the only right in the Constitution which is endorsed as a 'natural right, antecedent to positive law'. The effect of this hierarchy of rights in Articles 40 to 44 is to give an unwarranted emphasis to Catholic Church fears about socialism and secular education. This is even more apparent in Article 44. The right to own property had already been guaranteed in Article 43. Despite that, Article 44 takes two more subsections to guarantee that religious communities may own property and that they may not be deprived of it except by law and on payment of compensation. It appears that those rights which were important in Catholicism in the early part of the 20th century were emphasized and reinforced in the Constitution as natural, inalienable or imprescriptible; while those rights which are less important in the same tradition, such as the right to free speech, freedom of association and assembly, freedom of conscience, freedom of access to the courts, and the satisfaction of those material needs which are presupposed for any exercise of rights, were not equally established as natural or imprescriptible.

The natural law tradition on which these inalienable and imprescriptible rights are based is a moral theory of man's ultimate end and of the duties which that end imposes, in the form of moral obligations, on man's actions. This natural law theory did not originally include the concept of a right at all. This is not merely a historical comment. The Thomistic Natural Law theory was fundamentally a theory of man's duties to God and to his fellow man. When the language of rights was introduced into this theoretical framework, rights were defined in terms of duties. Therefore the concept of a moral duty is primary. The conceptual liaison between rights and duties is reflected in the Constitution when the 'rights of the family' are linked with the mother's 'duties in the home', and 'the inalienable right' of parents to educate their children is expressed as 'the inalienable right *and duty* of parents . . .'[21] The significance of this conceptual shift from rights to duties is that the natural law theory which partly supports the constitution's defence of rights is not a theory of rights at all, but a theory of moral duties and, by implication only, of rights to the necessary freedom to fulfil one's duties. This implies that we must first discover what one's duties are before we can know what rights one has. The decision on this point is very much open to the direct influence of religious belief.

Modern theories of rights are inspired by a different philosophy. They are based on the assumption that moral agents require a guaranteed measure of autonomy in their pursuit of what they believe to be worthwhile in life. The exact scope of this autonomy or freedom is subject to dispute, but the reason underlying it is still reasonably clear. Individual freedom is not provided merely as a necessary condition for doing one's duty. The exercise of freedom is itself a fundamental value which is presupposed by any attempt to justify moral conventions and the moral duties which they define. This is the exact opposite of the tradition which first defines moral duties for human agents, and only then provides them with enough freedom to perform their duties. It is therefore ironic that those rights which are classified as antecedent to positive law, as inalienable or imprescriptible rights, in the Constitution were derived from a political and moral theory which gave priority to moral duties over moral rights.

Constitutional Limits of Individual Rights

Even the most ardent proponent of human rights must concede that the exercise of rights by different individuals in a society gives rise to conflicts of rights. Any plausible theory of rights needs to take account of such conflicts and to acknowledge the reciprocal limitation of individuals' rights which results from social interaction. Likewise, with some notable exceptions, any constitution which includes legal guarantees of rights must stop short of making rights absolute and therefore not subject to compromise.

Those fundamental rights which are constitutionally protected in Ireland — a rather open-ended list because of the courts' interpretation of Article 40 — are subject to a great variety of limitations. Some of these have been worked out in detailed cases in which both a right, and some of its relevant limitations, have been defined by the courts. There are other limitations on rights which are explicitly recognized by the Constitution; the subsequent discussion is confined to these in an effort to disclose the philosophy of rights which is implicit in the Constitution.

Before looking at specific limits on rights, it is important to identify one general qualification which could conceivably apply to any right. This is the distinction between a right and the exercise of a right. This distinction is found in two places. In Article 40, section 6, subsection 1 (iii), 'the rights of the citizens to form associations and unions' is qualified by: 'laws, however, may be enacted for the regulation and control in the public interest of the exercise of the foregoing right'. Likewise in Article 43, section 2, subsections 1 and 2, the Constitution provides for State regulation or limitation of the exercise of the right 'to the private ownership of external goods'. This distinction, between a right and its exercise, may be taken as an indirect way of introducing problems of conflicting rights. As such it would have no special significance. The distinction also has more disturbing connotations, however, to the extent that it implies the possibility of non-trivially having a right without the relevant freedom to exercise it. And this second interpretation must be resisted to maintain any semblance of significance for the language of rights.

Evidently, there is a distinction from the point of view of an agent between having a right and exercising it. However, there is no correspondingly simple distinction between limiting someone's right and merely limiting the exercise of that right. To have a right is not to have something which is logically independent of that freedom to act in terms of which the right in question is defined. The language of limiting the exercise of rights seems to imply that there is something which is had, and which is not affected by the limitations imposed on its exercise. If having a right is being morally or legally justified in doing something, then to limit or prevent someone doing what they have a right to do is, to that extent, to limit the right itself. It would be a cynical witticism to tell someone: 'I know you have a right to freedom and I'm not denying you your rights in any way. I am merely controlling the exercise of your right by confining you in prison for a few years.' While I may have a right and not exercise it, no one else can intentionally restrict my exercise of this right without thereby limiting or, in more drastic circumstances, denying it altogether.

This interpretation of the Constitution is corroborated by the decision in *National Union of Railwaymen* v. *Sullivan and Others:*

Both logically and practically, to deprive a person of the choice of the persons with whom he will associate is not a control of the exercise of the right of association, but a denial of the right altogether.[22]

This decision accurately focusses on the implications of limiting the so-called exercise of rights. 'Logically' here means that there is a conceptual relation between having a right and being justified in exercising the right. Therefore, it is incoherent to concede rights to people, to limit the freedom to act in terms of which these rights are defined and then to suggest that one is merely limiting the exercise of the rights. 'Practically' means: that whatever the niceties of philosophical or legal argument, from the point of view of the agent who is trying to exercise his rights, there is no difference in his freedom of action between limiting a right and merely limiting the exercise of a right.

An alternative, coherent understanding of the distinction between rights and their exercise is to see this distinction as another way of talking about the limitation of rights. The Constitution mentions seven ways in which individual rights, or their exercise, may be constitutionally limited:

1. By the need to respect the rights of others: Article 42, 5; Article 44, 2, 4°.
2. By considerations of the common good: Article 42, 3, 2°; Article 42, 5; Article 43, 2, 2°.
3. By the requirements of the 'public interest': Article 40, 6, 1°, (iii).
4. By law: Article 28, 3, 3°.[23]
5. By the proviso not 'to undermine the authority of the State': Article 40, 6, 1°, (iii).
6. By the requirements of social justice: Article 43, 2, 1°.
7. By the demands of 'public order and morality': Article 40, 6, 1°; Article 40, 6, 1°, (i); Article 44, 2, 1°.

The first kind of qualification of the citizen's basic rights, which we might expect to play a more significant role in this context, occurs where the exercise of one's rights interferes with the rights of others. Yet this is only mentioned in two places in the Constitution, and on both occasions it concerns the rights of children. In Article 42 'the natural and imprescriptible rights of the child' qualify the State's educational policies, and in Article 44 'the right of any child to attend a school receiving public money' qualifies the claims of various denominational schools to equal support from the State. Apart from these two cases the possible clash of individual rights is not mentioned as such in Articles 40 to 44 of the Constitution.

Rather than examine each in turn of the other six types of constitutional limitations of rights, I will concentrate on three of them, 'the common good', 'law', and 'public order and morality'. The kinds of issues which arise here will be applicable, with appropriate modifications, to the others.

Rights and the Common Good

According to the Constitution, the State is 'guardian of the common good'.[24] However the common good is understood, the Constitution

allows for the possibility of a conflict between the fundamental rights of
the citizens and the interests of the common good and, at least in some
cases, concedes that basic rights may have to be qualified in terms of the
common good. At the same time the common good is not defined in the
Constitution. 'Common good' is susceptible to a wide spectrum of more
or less different interpretations; to help focus the discussion three rather
different conceptions are introduced and each is discussed in turn. From
the point of view of the appellant to the courts, the only relevant interpretation is the one which is likely to be officially adopted by the courts.
But from the point of view of making explicit the underlying moral and
political philosophy which is inherent in the Constitution, any interpretation which the text will reasonably support is significant.

The 'common good' may be understood as:
  (i) a collective noun which denotes the result of summarizing the in-
      dividual goods of all the members of a given class or group;
 (ii) a general term which, despite grammatical appearances to the con-
      trary, refers to a specific political or social objective which is
      logically independent of the individual goods of the members of a
      society or group;
(iii) a term which refers to the cluster of social and political institutions
      which are thought to be necessary prerequisites for the exercise of
      basic human rights. In this sense, the common good is not logically
      independent of (i.e. it cannot be defined or explained without
      reference to) basic human rights.

There is scope for interpreting the Irish constitutional sense of 'the common good' in all three ways; and it is the second one listed above which
potentially causes most problems for anyone who does not share the
political and cultural values of those who drafted the Constitution in
1937. In the following discussion each of the three interpretations of
'common good' is taken up in turn in conjunction with relevant sections
of the Constitution.

One further preliminary note before the main part of the argument:
what is at issue here is the relative priority of basic human rights over
other considerations. Evidently one can disagree as to which human
rights are basic, and there are presumably alternative, and equally
reasonable, compromises possible in any constitutional effort to
safeguard such rights. However, it is also possible that a facade of apparently reasonable qualifications can systematically undermine what
seems to be constitutionally guaranteed for individuals. In that case, it is

the pattern of systematic qualifications and the proposed justification for them which is important. The common good is a suspicious and likely candidate for undermining basic rights in this way. What one needs to know is: if individual rights are systematically subject to the demands of the common good, and if the latter is a rather flexible concept in the political and judicial traditions of a country, in what sense are any fundamental rights constitutionally guaranteed at all?

(i) *A Utilitarian Common Good*

The first interpretation of the common good is utilitarian, both in its method of identifying the common good and in its implied justification for the priority of the common good over the rights of individuals. This understanding of the common good is collective in the sense that one summarizes what is assumed, on independent grounds, to be good for each individual. Any arrangement for allocating goods to members of a society raises problems about discovering what, in fact, is good for individuals (as distinct from what the members of the group might believe is good for them), and what are the likely effects for some members of the group of allocating 'goods' in different ways to other members. Both of these problems can be avoided by recourse to a ballot of members, in which one hopes to determine only the beliefs of the group in question. A sufficiently sophisticated ballot comes as close as is practicable to determining what the members of the group believe is good for themselves as individuals and, secondly, what particular disposition of these 'goods' they believe is in their own interests. Assuming at least some disagreement among members of the group on both questions, the ballot is designed to satisfy most of the people on most of the goods at issue. The term 'common good' then applies to whatever disposition of goods results from this type of arrangement. It is the disposition of what most of the members consider to be goods, in a way which the majority believes will satisfy them as individuals. The 'majority vote' approach reveals the latent justification for this concept of the common good. It is based on a utilitarian political philosophy in which the concept of a basic right has no place, and in which decisions of principle are reached only by reference to the putative interests of the voting majority.

The utilitarian concept of the common good operates in the Irish Constitution in two ways: in some cases where the common good or its equivalent is explicitly mentioned as a limitation on fundamental rights, and in other cases (especially under the rubric of 'law') where a collective common good argument seems to be at work in justifying the limits imposed on the exercise of individual rights. Since the limitations on rights derived from law are discussed separately below, the remarks made at this point are concerned with explicit constitutional appeals to the common good.

Article 43, section 1 acknowledges the 'natural right, antecedent to positive law, to the private ownership of external goods'. Section 2 of the same article reads:

1°   The State recognises, however, that the exercise of the rights mentioned in the foregoing provisions of this Article ought, in civil society, to be regulated by the principles of social justice.

2°   The State, accordingly, may as occasion requires delimit by law the exercise of the said rights with a view to reconciling their exercise with the exigencies of the common good.

These qualifications should be read in conjunction with the 'Directive Principles of Social Justice' in Article 45, in which the State is charged with promoting 'the welfare of the whole people' (in Irish: *'leas on phobail uile'*, which is equivalent to the common good). Specific recommendations to the State include Article 45, section 2 of which states:

The State shall, in particular, direct its policy towards securing . . .

ii.   That the ownership and control of the material resources of the community may be so distributed amongst private individuals and the various classes as best to subserve the common good. . . .

iv.   That in what pertains to the control of credit the constant and predominant aim shall be the welfare of the people as a whole (*'leas on phobail uile'* = the common good).

Article 45 implies that the principles of social justice and the exigencies of the common good in Article 43, section 2, are equivalent. The possibility of an economically powerful minority exercising economic and political control over a whole community on the basis of the right to ownership could compromise many guarantees of basic rights to individuals. Hence the common good restriction on the exercise of the natural right to ownership should be interpreted as a qualification in the interests of social justice.

Who decides what is demanded by social justice? The introductory paragraph of Article 45 explicitly precludes any role for the courts in implementing the principles of social policy:

The application of these principles in the making of laws shall be the care of the Oireachtas exclusively, and shall not be cognisable by any Court under any of the provisions of this Constitution.

On the other hand, the text of Article 43 seems to imply that nothing is inconsistent with the guarantee of this fundamental right except the unqualified abolition of the right itself or of its normal legal consequences.[25] This leaves open the possibility that 'social justice' is determined exclusively by the Oireachtas, and this in turn represents the majority view in the electorate. In other words, we have a clear case of the common good being understood in the first of the three senses listed above; the majority of the electorate decides what restrictions may be imposed on the exercise of an acknowledged fundamental right, and whatever restrictions are imposed can be justified by reference to the common good.

This interpretation of the Constitution was adopted by the Supreme Court in *In re Article 26 of the Constitution and the Offences Against the State (Amendment) Bill 1940*:

The main object aimed at is the promotion of the common good, which, it is contemplated, will assure the dignity and freedom of the individual, the attainment of social order, the restoration of the unity of our country, and the establishment of concord with other nations. . . . There is nothing in this clause of the Preamble which could be invoked to necessitate the sacrifice of the common good in the interests of the freedom of the individual. . . . The duty of determining the extent to which the rights of any particular citizen, or class of citizens, can properly be harmonised with the rights of the citizens as a whole seems to us to be a matter which is peculiarly within the province of the Oireachtas, and any attempt by this Court to control the Oireachtas in the exercise of this function, would, in our opinion, be a usurpation of its authority.[26]

It is tempting to assume that this is precisely the way in which those who drafted the Constitution intended it to be understood. If that is correct, their text was self-contradictory. The Constitution clearly assigns the task of interpreting the Constitution, with the exception explicitly mentioned in Article 45, to the courts; and one of the sections which is more obviously open to interpretation because of its relatively high 'philosophical' content is the section on fundamental rights. If the courts are the acknowledged official interpreters of the constitutional guarantees of basic rights, it follows that the courts can legitimately rule on the extent to which any legislation, even legislation concerned with social justice, infringes on constitutional guarantees of fundamental rights. So that while the courts may not be constitutionally competent to decide the relative merits of different social policies, they are constitutionally empowered to recognize when legislation of whatever kind infringes on the rights guaranteed in Articles 40 to 44.

This alternative interpretation of the role of the courts in balancing the opposing claims of the common good (in the first sense) and individual rights was adopted by the Supreme Court in 1950, in *Buckley and Others* v. *Attorney-General and Another*:

> It is claimed that the question of the exigencies of the common good is peculiarly a matter for the Legislature and that the decision of the Legislature on such a question is absolute and not subject to, or capable of, being reviewed by the Courts. We are unable to give our assent to this far-reaching proposition.[27]

This position was re-affirmed by the courts in *McDonald* v. *Bord na gCon, McGee* v. *Attorney-General,* and more recently in *The State (Healy)* v. *Donoghue:* 'The promotion of the common good so that the dignity and freedom of the individual may be assured, being the objective stated in the Preamble to the Constitution, is as much a function of the judicial organ of the State as of the legislative or the executive.'[28]

It may seem unreasonably contentious to demand explicit and clear guidelines on the question of who decides what is required by the common good. One might argue that there are two distinct questions involved here: (a) what is demanded by the common good? and (b) in cases of conflict of opinion, who resolves disagreements about (a)?, and that the courts are only validly concerned with (b). This is a specious distinction because it implies that we have some commonly acknowledged way of discovering the answer to an apparently factual, empirical question (that is, 'what is demanded by the common good?'), and that we may only need recourse to the courts in very unusual or difficult situations of conflicting interests. The situation is rather the converse. The demands of the common good cannot be determined as if it were an empirical question, and we have no generally accepted means of determining what the common good requires. We could simply accept the decision of a majority of the electorate. However, since the voters do not have to justify their voting behaviour, this procedure would be equivalent to allowing the voting majority to decide, for whatever reasons of personal advantage, short-term interest, religious or ideological prejudice, or whatever, what the common good requires in a given set of circumstances. And if the common good, decided in this way, conflicts with fundamental rights, that procedure is equivalent to rejecting the concept of constitutional rights for individuals. Whatever the authors of the 1937 Constitution might have meant, they cannot have consistently provided constitutional guarantees of basic rights and also precluded the courts from defending individuals against alleged intrusions by the Oireachtas on those same rights. Individual rights which are subject to the electorate's unchallengeable determination of the requirements of the common good are worthless.

(ii) *The Common Good as a Political/Social Ideal*

The second concept of 'the common good' is one which establishes a certain moral, social or political ideal as a community objective to be realized, in such a way that the individual rights of citizens are not relevant to its definition. This is very different to the first concept of the common good discussed above in that, at least in the first concept, what the majority of the citizens believed to be in their own best interests was collectively summarized under the title 'common good'. The second concept of the common good is much less empirical than the first one. It is also correspondingly more ideological insofar as it implies some specific political or social goal as the primary objective for the community while the individual's good or rights are granted only a subsidiary role, if any. As in the first concept, it is crucially important to determine *who* decides what this common good is, because a reasonably critical and free society will not normally surrender the right to decide what it thinks is good for its members. By contrast, the ideologist of the common good tends to urge that what is good for the individual can be defined as a function of a political ideal, just as individual freedom can be defined as the liberty to do what one ought to do. If what one ought to do is also decided by whoever defines freedom in this moralizing way, there is a real danger of sophistically redefining actual slavery to an imposed ideal as freedom to do what one ought to do.

This second view of the common good is the most dangerous to human rights because it seems to grant rights to individuals, and is very often presented in the guise of a liberating social philosophy. Besides, the concept of a right has a definite, although secondary role here, but it is not apparent in advance that the rights which are conceded are subject to review in the interests of the social or political ideals which are the primary objective of the ideology which supports this understanding of the common good. In this approach one first specifies what is good for man and society, and one then defines human rights in terms of the freedom necessary to cultivate the goods already decided. Clearly, this rules out in advance any difficult problems of reconciling individual rights with the common good because one only has rights to do what ought to be done; and we no longer have moral problems of tolerating actions which we consider to be against the interests of the common good.

Among those outside the Republic who are reluctant to put their trust in the 1937 Constitution, there is commonly a feeling that the text of the Constitution is an expression of a relatively homogeneous culture which provides insufficient safeguards to minorities against the dangers of being forced into accepting the legislative implications of that culture. In religious matters the Constitution is officially pluralist.[29] This religious pluralism, however, is narrowly interpreted in terms of freedom of religious beliefs and practices. The legitimate source of concern for the outsider is not so much that he might be prevented from practising his religion. It is rather that the religious and cultural values of the majority in the Republic will be reflected in a wide variety of laws which are not specifically concerned with the practice of religion at all. And when these kinds of issue arise, there is no room in the Constitution to offset the obvious influence of confessional beliefs on the type of legislation which is likely to be passed by the Oireachtas.

This well-founded unease may be answered by an appeal to democratic principles of majority rule, and this suggests a collapse between the first two concepts of the common good. However, further analysis indicates that this kind of argument short-circuits an important point which needs to be made explicit. In the case of most pieces of proposed legislation, one anticipates that there is significant fluctuation among individuals in their endorsement of such proposals, and that different members of the community have a variety of distinct reasons for either supporting or opposing different bills. For want of a better, or more practicable, system for deciding legislative questions the 'rational man' is normally willing to operate by majority rule. If one finds by experience that there is no variation in voting patterns and if one discovers, instead, that there is systematic bloc-voting on many issues, one reasonably asks why. If there is a constant conjunction between the voting patterns of a majority of the electorate and their religious or cultural/political values, it is impossible to avoid the conclusion that the explanation of the voting pattern is the cultural/religious ideals shared by those in specifiable sub-groups of the population. Those concerned about basic freedoms or fundamental rights can then ask: 'To what extent might one anticipate that such religious/cultural homogeneity in the population would override the legitimate interests of minorities?'

The most explicit invocation of the 'common good' to justify constitutional restraint on fundamental rights for ideological reasons occurs in Article 40, section 6, subsection 1°, which reads:

1°   The state guarantees liberty for the exercise of the following rights, subject to public order and morality:—

i.   The right of the citizens to express freely their convictions and opinions.

The education of public opinion being, however, a matter of such grave import to the common good, the State shall endeavour to ensure that organs of public opinion, such as the radio, the press, the cinema, while preserving their rightful liberty of expression, including criticism of Government policy, shall not be used to undermine public order or morality or the authority of the State.

The publication or utterance of blasphemous, seditious, or indecent matter is an offence which shall be punishable in accordance with law.

All three freedoms listed in sub-section 1° — freedom of speech, of assembly, and of forming associations and unions — are guaranteed 'subject to public order and morality'. This qualification may be an unimpeachable reference to the need for order in our social lives and the need to respect the rights of others in public behaviour which may offend the common morality of our society. Thus only acts which are predominantly public are subject to restriction in terms of 'public order and morality'. One might even compare the text in the Irish Constitution with a similar qualification in the *U.N. Universal Declaration of Human Rights*, Article 29, (2) of which states:

In the exercise of his rights and freedoms, everyone shall be subject only to such limitations as are determined by law solely for the purpose of securing due recognition and respect for the rights and freedoms of others and of meeting the just requirements of morality, public order and the general welfare in a democratic society.

However, there is a crucial difference between the U.N. Declaration and the Irish Constitution. It is partly a matter of emphasis on the relative priority of rights over the common good, and partly a matter of the tradition, both political and legal, in which the otherwise innocuous reference to public morality occurs.

The U.N. Declaration lists various fundamental rights and freedoms, including freedom of speech, without any reference to the common good. Likewise, the United States Bill of Rights is unambiguous about freedom of speech. Article 1 reads: 'Congress shall make no law . . . abridging the freedom of speech, or of the press.' By contrast, the 1977 USSR Constitution also grants freedom of speech, but only subject to the common good:

Article 50: In accordance with the interests of the people and *in order to* strengthen and develop the socialist system, citizens of the USSR are guaranteed freedom of speech, of the press, and of assembly, meetings, street processions and demonstrations.
Exercise of these political freedoms is ensured by putting public buildings, . . . at the disposal of the working people, . . . (italics added).

With appropriate changes in ideology, the Irish 'common good' might equally determine the scope of freedom which is allowed under the law. This kind of fear is suggested by the response of the President of the Dáil in discussions during the drafting of this article: 'I say that you should not give to the propagation of what is wrong and unnatural the same liberty as would be accorded to the propagation of what is right.'[30] This suggests that we first decide what is moral or natural and only allow citizens freedom to propagate views which are compatible with our prior moralizing. This in turn implies that one of our moral principles is that others do not have the right to express opinions which, according to our moral views, are immoral or obscene. And this view is tantamount to giving the voting majority in a democracy the legislative power to control the freedom of speech of a dissident minority. It is suspiciously like the principle which underlies any totalitarian system's control of what may or may not be expressed, when the government or the legislature decides what is good or bad for people to hear. The pattern of argument in each is the same: freedom of speech is granted *only* as a means of realizing some other end. Since the other end or objective is primary, freedom of speech is revocable to the extent that it does not help in achieving some social objective, whether this is a socialist state or a Christian and culturally pure Ireland.

Two other factors which makes the Irish constitutional limitations on free speech worthy of concern are the tradition of emergency legislation (which is discussed below), and the influence of the churches in determining what might be counted as being in the public interest. Thus, for example, one could in good faith define the political life of the citizens in terms of a specific religious ideal, and then argue that 'since the order of nature is subordinate to the order of grace, the common good of civil society is subordinate to the common good of the Church.'[31] If this view is accepted on faith, then we should also believe that 'the province of the State is to foster natural virtues in its subjects.'[32] And this implies that it is inconsistent for the State to tolerate whatever hinders the cultivation of these natural virtues. Therefore the legislator

should try to prevent or remove all major incentives to immorality and crime. With regard to literature, art and public entertainment, the common good requires that nothing should be tolerated in public that is a grave incentive to sin.[33]

It is apparent in this kind of ideology that what constitutes a sin is also determined by the religious faith of the protagonist, so that the function of the State and the limitations this implies are all based on the religious belief of the proponent of such views. What is good for the individual and how the State should cultivate this good are equally defined by religious faith, and in such a closed circle the rights of individuals can only get a secondary place.

Given the Irish experience of censorship and the churches' attempts to define the common good by reference to their respective religious beliefs, there is a real danger of subverting freedom of speech, and similar freedoms, by reference to the constitutional provisions for safeguarding 'public order and morality'. This would not be a mere limitation of the exercise of one's rights. It would effectively constitute a denial of such rights in the interests of the common good as defined by religious faith. This is not to suggest that those who defend this position do so because they wish to impose their faith on others; rather, they genuinely believe that their concept of the common good is valid. Most committed ideologists, on the left or the right, do likewise.

(iii)   *The Common Good as a Safeguard of Rights*

There is a third sense of 'the common good' which is compatible with a less compromising attitude towards human rights. In this sense 'the common good' refers to the complex of arrangements in any society which must be established if all the citizens are to enjoy the necessary freedom to exercise their basic rights and to pursue their interests without unnecessary infringement from others. An obvious example of the common good in this sense is national defence, for the defence of a country is not logically analysable into the individual efforts of each citizen to defend his own plot of land. Just as evidently, basic rights and freedoms would be difficult to exercise in a community without a set of laws to regulate life in the community, and this presupposes a legislature to enact laws, a judicial system to interpret and implement the laws, a police force to enforce the laws, and so on. One could more generally and vaguely refer to all those institutional features of our community life which are a necessary prerequisite for the exercise of the basic human rights of individual citizens as the common good.

What is characteristic of this third concept of the common good is that it is defined in terms of the assumed priority of basic human rights. Even if there is considerable disagreement in specifying which individual rights are fundamental, there may still be agreement on the relative priority of individual rights. And however agreement is reached on which of them are subject to more or less compromise, one defines the common good, which varies correspondingly in its specific content with the specification of which rights are basic, as one of the social/political means for safeguarding and facilitating the exercise of those rights which are regarded by the community as fundamental.

This does not imply that fundamental rights are absolute, or that they are never subject to compromise. It is a familiar conclusion of moral and political philosophy that attempts to implement principles invariably give rise to conflicts in which there may be no decisive meta-principle available to resolve a conflict. Human rights claims can hardly be understood any more stringently than that. They represent fundamental moral principles which express what human beings are least willing to compromise about. Some principles may be such that the members of the community are never willing to compromise them, no matter what the outcome. Thus the *European Convention on Human Rights* includes some principles of this kind from which signatory nations are not permitted to derogate in any circumstances. Apart from exceptional rights such as, for example, the right not to be tortured, most basic human rights are understood as liable to compromise at least to the extent to which their exercise conflicts, in some situations, with equally important rights of others.

If the common good, in this third sense, is understood as a set of institutional procedures which are necessary for preserving basic human rights, then it is inevitable that occasions will arise when there is a conflict in practice between specific rights and the requirements of the common good; that is, a conflict between the exercise of rights by an individual and the social prerequisites for the exercise of equally fundamental rights by others. Such a conflict may be resolved in a number of ways. What is characteristic about the third concept of the common good is that such conflicts are resolved by analogy with situations of conflicting basic rights, rather than by automatically conceding priority to the common good as understood in either of the first two senses. Thus, in a situation of extreme national emergency, one could envisage a conflict in practice between the long-term defence of human rights and the short-term overriding of some of these rights in the interests of the common good. In such a context one might anticipate agreement from the members of a political community to suspend some fundamental rights temporarily in order to defend these same rights in the long term. But this is done reluctantly, not because the common good as something logically distinct from basic rights is more important than individual rights, but because the long-term defence of rights unavoidably demands a suspension of some rights in the short term.

The 1937 Constitution is reasonably explicit in proposing this concept of the common good in those cases where the concerns of the common good are acknowledged to be secondary to the requirements of individual rights. This is most evident in the Article on education which contains three references to the State's concern with the common good, each of which concedes the priority of the individual rights of parents or children. Sections 3, 4 and 5 of Article 42 read:

3. 1° The State shall not oblige parents in violation of their conscience and lawful preference to send their children to schools established by the State, or to any particular type of school designated by the State.
    2° The State shall, however, as guardian of the common good, require in view of actual conditions that the children receive a certain minimum education, moral, intellectual and social.
4. The State shall provide for free primary education and shall endeavour to supplement and give reasonable aid to private and corporate educational initiative, and, when the public good (*leas on phobail*) requires it, provide other educational facilities or institutions with due regard, however, for the rights of parents, especially in the matter of religious and moral formation.
5. In exceptional cases, where the parents for physical or moral reasons fail in their duty towards their children, the State as guardian of the common good, by appropriate means shall endeavour to supply the place of the parents,

but always with due regard for the natural and imprescriptible rights of the child.

Apart from these clear cases of acknowledged priority for individual rights, there are two other references to the common good in the Constitution which may also be interpreted in the third sense of the term. The first of these occurs in the Preamble to the Constitution, which includes the following passage

We, the people of Éire . . . seeking to promote the common good (*an mhaitheas phoiblí*), with due observance of Prudence, Justice and Charity, *so that the dignity and freedom of the individual may be assured,* true social order attained . . . Do hereby adopt, enact, and give to ourselves this Constitution (emphasis added).

This suggests that the common good is a means to a series of ends, one of which is 'the dignity and freedom of the individual', or at least that the common good is a subsidiary end relative to the other objectives for which the Constitution was adopted.

Another reference to the common good is found in Article 6, section 1:

All powers of government, legislative, executive and judicial, derive, under God, from the people, whose right it is to designate the rulers of the State and, in final appeal, to decide all questions of national policy, according to the requirements of the common good.

This is much less clear than the Preamble on the relative status of the common good vis-à-vis individual rights. It does clarify the common good as the objective towards which 'all powers of government' are directed. While it is not inconsistent with the third concept of the common good, it is not clear how it should be interpreted.

Rights and the Law

Apart from Article 40, section 5, which allows for the forcible entry of private homes 'in accordance with law', the Constitution provides for two very significant qualifications on fundamental rights which were originally justified by reference to emergency situations obtaining in time of war. These two legal qualifications on fundamental rights occur in Article 28, 3, 3° and in Article 40, 4. Their combined effect on the Constitution is effectively to abrogate all guarantees, in Irish Constitutional law, of basic human rights.

As amended in 1939 and 1941, Article 28 precludes the possibility of a successful court challenge to any law 'which is expressed to be for the purpose of securing the public safety and the preservation of the State in time of war . . .' 'Time of war' is defined in the same sub-section to include 'a time when there is taking place an armed conflict in which the State is not a participant but in respect of which each of the houses of the Oireachtas shall have resolved that, arising out of such armed conflict, a national emergency exists . . .' The *Emergency Powers Bill (1976)* is a recent example of emergency legislation which took advantage of this constitutional provision for a declaration of a state of emergency. When referred by the President to the Supreme Court, it was judged to be constitutional because of the immunity granted by Article 28 to emergency legislation.[34]

The implications of Article 28 are of paramount significance for the protection of human rights. Whatever the political realities of such a manoeuvre, it is at least constitutionally possible for an Irish government to subvert *all* guarantees of fundamental rights in Articles 40 to 44 by introducing emergency legislation which effectively overrides them. This can be done in two stages: (1) by getting the two houses of the Oireachtas, by a simple majority vote, to declare that a national emergency exists; and then (2) by introducing legislation which 'is expressed to be for the purpose of securing the public safety and the preservation of the State'. The declaration of a state of emergency is not part of the emergency legislation; it is merely a necessary preliminary to avail of the constitutional immunity from court challenge. Hence one could speculate about what factual situation would warrant such a declaration. For example, could a government with a reasonably safe majority of votes in the Oireachtas declare a state of emergency when there is nothing remotely like an armed conflict occurring in the state? Or could a government use the occurrence of an armed conflict in another country, for example in the Middle East, to declare a state of emergency in Ireland and then introduce arbitrary legislation under the umbrella of constitutional immunity? In the case of the *Emergency Powers Bill (1976)* the Supreme Court held that there was a presumption of fact in favour of the declaration of the Oireachtas, but the Court also expressly reserved the right to consider similar declarations in future with a view to deciding its own jurisdiction in the matter.[35]

Assuming the existence of an authentic state of emergency and the appropriate declaration by the Oireachtas, any legislation which is passed by the Oireachtas for the purpose of coping with the state of emergency is immune from the normal constitutional provisions for judicial review. The major flaw in this arrangement is that the Constitution does not specify the content or the limits of emergency legislation, and this implies that it is at least legally possible (even if politically improbable) that emergency legislation could make it legal for the police to torture suspects, for the army to arbitrarily arrest and imprison people in military institutions, and for the government to effectively deny all those rights which are internationally recognized as minimal conditions for treating someone as a human person. The failure of the Constitution to put any limits or qualifications on the scope of emergency legislation, its extreme vagueness in specifying the conditions which would warrant its introduction, and the fact that it provides immunity from judicial review for emergency legislation effectively undermine all constitutional guarantees of human rights in Ireland. One's only legal recourse, in these circumstances, is to the European Commission.

One could argue, in the opposite direction, that the Constitution recognizes natural moral rights as antecedent and superior to any legislation which is introduced by the Oireachtas. This was the interpretation which emerged from *Buckley and Others* v. *Attorney General and Another*,[36] and was made even more explicit in *McGee* v. *Attorney General*:

Articles 41, 42 and 43 emphatically reject the theory that there are no rights anterior to the law. They indicate that justice is placed above the law and acknowledge that natural rights, or human rights, are not created by law but that the Constitution confirms their existence and gives them protection. The individual has natural and human rights over which the State has no authority; and the family, as the natural primary and fundamental unit group of society, has rights as such which the State cannot control.
The very structure and content of the Articles dealing with fundamental rights clearly indicate that justice is not subordinate to the law.[37]

The text of the Constitution and its interpretation by the courts suggest that natural rights, or human rights, are more basic than any legislation which may be passed by the Oireachtas, or any other body for that matter.

It appears that the Constitution is not consistent on this point.[38] To the extent that the Constitution recognizes the priority of fundamental human rights and endorses natural rights as constitutional rights of Irish citizens, it establishes human rights as constitutionally superior to any legislation which is passed by the Oireachtas. On the other hand, the Supreme Court has also endorsed the obvious implications of Article 28 in virtue of which the Court has no constitutional jurisdiction to examine the validity of emergency legislation which satisfies the conditions set out in Article 28. The Constitution cannot coherently establish the legal priority of basic human rights and, at the same time, grant the government power to undermine these rights without the possibility of a court challenge.

To safeguard human rights and to make the Constitution coherent, Article 28 would have to be amended. This does not imply that the Constitution should preclude all possibilities for emergency legislation. Our political experience in Ireland includes a residual tradition of small armed groups trying to achieve political objectives by force, and there is no guarantee that those who subvert the Constitution in an effort to improve, in their estimation, the political and social life of the country would change their philosophical allegiance at a later stage in favour of personal freedoms and human rights. The defence of personal freedoms against violent political activists may sometimes warrant otherwise intolerable legal compromises between the demands of the common good and the fundamental rights which are assumed in a modern democracy. There is no justification, however, for a constitutional *carte blanche* for emergency legislation. Even if the Constitution were not to put specific limits in advance on what could be legislated under the provisions of Article 28, it could at least provide for a constitutional test of emergency legislation to safeguard human rights. And to the extent that it specifically precludes such a court challenge, the Constitution is inconsistent on the so-called antecedent and superior status of basic moral rights.[39]

Article 40, section 4 of the Constitution establishes the constitutional right of access to the courts in cases of alleged illegal custody, i.e. the right of *habeas corpus*. Under the provisions of sub-section 1, 'No citizen shall be deprived of his personal liberty save in accordance with law.' This guarantee of appeal to the High Court is fundamental to controlling the government or its representatives if they use the police or army to illegally imprison citizens. Despite the seriousness of the issue, the Constitution provides two very important exceptions to this constitutional right: under Article 28 emergency legislation could be introduced which specifically precluded appeals to the courts; and in sub-section 6 of Article 40, section 4, the actions of the Defence Forces 'during the existence of a state of war or armed rebellion' are immune from *habeas corpus* appeals.

Derogation from the right of *habeas corpus* can come about by being explicitly written into emergency legislation. If it is not explicitly included in emergency legislation then, despite Article 28, anyone who is deprived of his personal liberty may appeal to the High Court directly and have the legality of his detention investigated. In that case, the court would have no jurisdiction to question the validity of the emergency legislation itself, but it would have jurisdiction to examine whether the legislation was correctly applied in the case of any given appellant.[40] Emergency legislation could conceivably go even further, however, and abolish the courts to which an appellant would normally apply for *habeas corpus*. Although this sounds far-fetched, it seems to be implied by Article 28 where it says: '*Nothing* in this Constitution shall be invoked to invalidate *any* law . . .' Presumably the 'nothing' and the 'any' leave room for laws which would directly suspend the right of *habeas corpus*, or would make it ineffective by suspending the courts to which one might appeal.

Apart from the possible consequences of emergency legislation, Section 4 of Article 40 includes the following exception:

Nothing in this section [on *habeas corpus*], however, shall be invoked to prohibit, control, or interfere with any act of the Defence Forces during the existence of a state of war or armed rebellion.

The comparable section of Article 28 reads: '. . . in time of war or armed rebellion'.[41] This phrase is defined in Article 28 to include states of emergency when there is no armed conflict in existence in the State. However, the widening of the extension of the terms is expressly introduced 'In this sub-section'. Therefore, sub-section 6 quoted above from Article 40, section 4, would not be applicable merely in a state of emergency declared by the Oireachtas. There would presumably have to exist 'a state of war or armed rebellion' in some ordinary sense of these words, and any suspicious widening of their scope could be appealed to the courts.

Granting even that much — and it would hardly take a full-scale war to merit the title 'armed rebellion' — the Constitution then gives the Defence Forces an unwarranted immunity from court investigation into the way in which they might deprive citizens of their personal liberty. This immunity could be further insulated in a situation of an actual armed conflict, even on a minor scale, by the introduction of emergency legislation. Thus, it would be constitutionally possible for the Oireachtas during the existence of an armed conflict to: (a) declare an emergency, (b) introduce legislation granting powers of arrest and indefinite detention to the army and (c) avoid *habeas corpus* appeals by reference to Article 40, section 4, sub-section 6, and avoid challenges to this latter manoeuvre by appealing to Article 28, section 3, sub-section 3. If such unusual powers could be justified in terms of the common good, appropriately understood in the third sense mentioned, then even the champion of human rights might reluctantly agree to them. But when the Constitution allows such extreme measures and at the same time grants them immunity from court challenge, we have reason to worry at the risk of abuse which such constitutional arrangements imply. As in the previous example of possibly abusing Article 28, what is wrong with Article 40, section 4, sub-section 6 is not the latitude it provides the Defence Forces in time of war or armed rebellion. It is the fact that it precludes any judicial review of whatever actions they might take whether or not these are justifiable by the seriousness of an armed rebellion and the demands of the common good.

Conclusion

The status of human rights in any political community depends on at least two factors: (a) its constitution or fundamental law, and (b) its legal and political traditions of respecting human rights and individual freedoms. By either one of these standards, the status of human rights in Ireland presents conflicting evidence which remains to be resolved in favour of one or other of two quite disparate traditions.

The text of the Constitution provides a lead in the kind of ambiguity to which we have become almost accustomed. On the one hand it recognizes the existence of some rights which are so basic that they are described as inalienable, imprescriptible or antecedent to positive law. These texts have provided the courts with a constitutional basis for expanding the list of constitutional rights of citizens by reference to the natural law tradition of jurisprudence which those texts clearly reflect. This is a welcome development for any proponent of strong human rights legislation. On the other hand, these same texts derive from one strand of a complex natural law history which was primarily committed to moral duties, rather than to moral rights. This is not just a historical or semantic point. What was basic in that tradition were man's duties, interpreted by a religious tradition; rights were merely the freedoms required to observe one's duties. It follows that one does not have a right to do those things which one has a moral obligation to avoid. The idea that one should first decide what is moral or immoral before granting various freedoms, including freedom of thought, of speech, and of assembly, is perhaps reflected in the Constitution's concern to limit these freedoms in the interests of the common good, and in keeping with the community's standards of public order and morality.

A more serious and more definite challenge to individual rights is found in the Constitution's provisions for emergency legislation. Since the Supreme Court has only recently interpreted those provisions of the Constitution, it is clear that the fears expressed here are not purely academic. A majority of the Oireachtas can effectively subvert all the Constitution's safeguards for human rights by a judicious use of emergency legislation.

While this may seem far-fetched, the point is only reinforced when one considers the political history of the State during the past half-century. Ireland has been in a permanent state of emergency since 1939. Therefore, all the necessary conditions are permanently satisfied for introducing emergency legislation at any time. When one looks to the political and legal traditions of the State in respect of basic freedoms, the overall picture one gets is not that of a modern, pluralist democracy in which the rights and freedoms of individuals are respected and cultivated. Instead one gets a general impression which matches the reservations already expressed about the Constitution. It is a picture of a State which is confessional rather than pluralist; timid and reluctant about individual freedoms; favouring censorship rather than freedom of thought and speech; and overly concerned about its perceived role as a civil handmaid to the theological demands of an infallible church. In short, it is exactly the kind of state which would endorse the confessionally prejudiced Constitution of 1937.

The only encouraging sign in the history of human rights in Ireland is the leadership of the judiciary in many cases where the legislature should have taken the lead. Irish courts have creatively interpreted the Constitution in a way which guarantees more rights to citizens than those who wrote it might ever have imagined. And where Irish courts have failed to find a constitutional basis in domestic law for claimed rights, the European Court of Human Rights has obliged Irish citizens with a legal defence of their claims. The frequency with which the courts have intervened to correct the Oireachtas' perception of the common good and to modify it in defence of individual rights is a convincing argument in favour of the need for constitutional limits to the legislative power of governments. In Ireland, the recognition and defence of human rights is almost exclusively due to the courts. Hence the justified fear for human rights when the Constitution explicitly precludes any recourse to an Irish court to defend one's rights against emergency legislation.

7

Equality of Opportunity

The word 'equality' has the ring of a philosophical term. It is ideal for slogans and perfect for campaigns. Yet it is subject to a thousand qualifications and can mean almost anything to those who are adept at semantic manipulation. Part of the ambiguity or indeterminancy of the word derives from its generality. This is compounded by the variety of cases in which what is apparently unequal can be construed as equal as soon as a relatively indeterminate number of compensating factors are taken into account. This kind of open-ended, necessary qualification on what might be construed as 'equal' is reflected in the Irish Constitution. Article 40, section 1 states:

All citizens shall, as human persons, be held equal before the law.
This shall not be held to mean that the State shall not in its enactments have due regard to differences of capacity, physical and moral, and of social function.

Before we can say what counts as equal treatment, or equal rights, or equal opportunity, we need to make explicit what kinds of consideration may be legitimately taken into account in our 'measuring'.[1] It quickly becomes clear that this is the main source of our difficulties.

There is a whole range of issues, legal, political and moral, raised by the concept of equality. This discussion is limited to explaining what kind of equality of opportunity is implied in the convention theory of morality which was proposed in Chapter 1.

Equality of Opportunity

It is patently clear that with respect to almost all natural qualities, such as athletic ability, musical talent, theoretical intelligence, good looks or other physical attributes, most people are unequal. This needs to be made very explicit even if it seems obvious. Otherwise we fail to look in the right direction to identify what it is about people which makes them

170

equal in any significant sense. On failing to identify a plausible basis for equality claims, we might be tempted to assume that equality, in the relevant sense, can only be real if we are all equal in intelligence, or income, or whatever. Some egalitarian programmes seem to make this mistake, of confusing the equality which is a basis for rights-claims with a kind of equality which is simply not true of human beings.

However, to exaggerate the opposite thesis is just as counterproductive for human rights. Some kind of unquantifiable, metaphysical equality might be predicated of all individuals in such a way that it has no empirical implications at all for how we ought to treat others in a society. We might be willing to define 'equality' in terms of a metaphysical nature and then imagine that the theoretical concession of such a metaphysical thesis is all that might plausibly be required for equal rights.

Both of these options fail to do justice to the moral/political status of any egalitarian policy. Whatever else equality-claims mean, they are not merely factual claims about the present condition of human beings, whether empirically or metaphysically described. They are claims about how we ought to treat one another in society. The first thesis claims too much; by confusing empirical claims with political ideals, it assumes that we will never be equal in the relevant sense unless we are (almost) equal in every possible respect. The second thesis demands too little; by conceding that we are already equal in some metaphysical sense, it implies that there is nothing more to be done. Equality as a social policy or as an implication of justice falls somewhere in between the two. It is because we are equal in some significant sense (to be specified) that we ought to be treated as equals (in ways to be specified). Such equality of treatment is compatible with continued inequalities among individuals.

A convention-based theory of morality depends on the assumption that human beings are equal as moral agents. This is a more contentious claim than its generality might suggest. It is clear that very young children are not moral agents in the sense at issue here; if they are to mature into moral agents they need to benefit from a rather lengthy moral education. It is also reasonably clear that the efforts at moral education which many children expereince are unsuccessful to a greater or lesser extent. This raises the question about the cause of the failure in such cases. Does one fail to mature into a moral agent because of innate (genetically controlled) factors, or does one fail to become a moral agent exclusively because of social conditioning? This is not an irrelevant theoretical quandary. If the former is true, then even the slim metaphysical basis for egalitarianism is upset in favour of a contrary thesis; not all human beings are capable of developing into agents who are, as moral agents, equal. If the second alternative is true, then we might at least hold on to a counterfactual thesis about equality, which could be expressed as follows: if moral education were equally available to all (which it is not), all mature human beings would be *equal* insofar as they are moral agents. What does 'equal' mean here, and what kind of evidence or reasons could help decide between the two theses?

'Equal' must be understood in this context in a fairly flexible way. 'Equal' does not mean that different individuals have the same 'quantity' of moral virtue, if such a metaphorical measuring makes any sense at all. That is surely false in comparing those of outstanding moral strength with those who only recognize moral obligations by breaking them. And it seems to be equally implausible to explain such discrepancies in performance exclusively in terms of extrinsic influences. If egalitarian policies are not to rest on very implausible counterfactuals, then the concept of 'equality' must be appropriately amended in the direction of a flexible interpretation.

'Equality' might be defined in terms of satisfying minimal conditions for being a moral agent. All those who are capable of voluntary, intentional actions might be said to be moral agents, and they are all equally moral agents to the extent that they equally satisfy minimal conditions for acting morally. Thus, some might be much more moral than others, but if we lower the threshold of 'moral agency' far enough to a set of minimal conditions, then all would equally pass that test. However, even this only gives the impression of a solution, as long as one avoids the problem of specifying where this minimal threshold is set.

Traditionally the threshold problem has been avoided by contrasting two classes which indisputably fall on either side of the threshold, despite variations in how it is defined. One class includes normal adults who perform actions which are voluntary and intentional by standard criteria. The other class includes those individuals who are apparently incapable of ever acting in this way. This would include non-rational animals, and perhaps some uncontentious examples of human beings who are so obviously incompetent that there is no real dispute about their responsibility for their actions. The law has followed this tradition by allowing that some people are incapable of intentionally breaking the law. Between the paradigm cases in each class, there is a critical problem of assessing the extent to which any individual satisfies some minimal standards of competence which would make his behaviour voluntary, intentional and therefore responsible. This is not a problem for which there is any agreed solution. Since exactly the same type of issue re-occurs in trying to explain equality of opportunity, the difficulties experienced at this point might be deferred for further discussion below.

A convention-based moral/political theory assumes that there is a non-arbitrary solution to the threshold problem, and that once the threshold is established, there is a sense in which one can say: all moral agents (i.e. all those above the threshold) are equal insofar as they all pass the same test of moral autonomy. They are all capable of acting morally by reference to the same minimal criteria of moral agency. Those who do not, in fact, exhibit the properties which are claimed for them by this thesis are still 'capable' of moral agency. That means that we have independent evidence for saying; if they had been educated morally and if . . ., then they would have exhibited exactly the same symptoms of moral agency as those we normally take to be paradigm cases of moral agents.

Equality as moral agents implies equality of opportunity. A convention-based theory of rights and justice includes, as a crucial element, this assumption: that the members of a moral community would not be willing to endorse typical moral conventions unless all the members were recognized by others in the community as having an equal claim on those goods which the conventions are designed to realize. One does not willingly agree to a set of arrangements which operates to one's own detriment. Therefore, in order to win the support of potential members of a moral community to any conventions which are typically classified as requirements of justice, one must first acknowledge that all those who subscribe to the conventions enjoy an equal opportunity of realizing those goods which are protected by the moral/political conventions. Which goods are those? And how do we know that opportunities are equal among those who do not (apparently) enjoy equal shares of these goods?

Equality of Opportunity in Education

There are three quite distinct concepts of equal opportunity available, which depend on the extent to which an individual is compensated for those personal and social factors which inhibit his access to various goods. Rather than explain these in the abstract, it may clarify the discussion to apply the three different concepts to equality of opportunity in education.

One background assumption of 'equal opportunity' discussions is that, whatever good is at issue, there is not enough of it available to satisfy all those who want it. Thus, there are more people who wish to be educated than our educational resources can accommodate. The intuitive idea in equality of opportunity is that all those who wish to be educated should have an equal chance of achieving their goal, and that we can give a non-arbitrary explanation of what 'equal' means here. However, even before opportunities are equalized in the first sense, there are some restrictions on who may apply for inclusion in the equalized stakes. These initial restrictions have to be explained without begging too many obvious questions.

In the case of health-care, considered as a limited social good, we do not normally assign every citizen an equal number of units of health-care, independently of his or her state of health (although that would be one kind of equality). We usually think that the provision of health care should depend on individual need. Some people need more than others, and we might define 'equal health-care' as equally satisfying the objective medical needs of all. This might mean expending £10,000 worth of health care on one citizen and none on another, in any given year. In a similar but less obvious way, we tend to define the educational 'needs' of citizens partly in terms of their innate ability, partly in terms of their career objectives, and partly in terms of the needs of the community. Thus, with limited resources available, we might exclude various classes of people before the equal opportunity lottery begins. Those who are advanced in age or who already enjoy a career might be excluded first, because they do not 'need' further education. Likewise if the community is paying most of the financial costs, through taxes, for education in the State, the community might reasonably decide on limits to the number of applicants each year who may be trained in any specific skill, because the community does not 'need' any more, and is therefore not willing to pay for their training. These preliminary exclusions are reasonable because they are appropriately related both to the needs of the community which funds education, and to the needs of the applicants who wish to benefit from the public purse. By contrast, excluding people on the basis of colour, religion or other irrelevant features is clearly discriminatory in an unreasonable way. If, having excluded some on reasonable grounds, there are still more applicants than positions available, we then define equality of opportunity in terms of the criteria applied in selecting the eventual beneficiaries of publicly financed education.

It has already been mentioned, in the discussion of human rights, that an equal share of some good is compatible with none at all in cases of total deprivation, such as extreme famine. Therefore, there is another background assumption in operation here: viz. that the State has the financial resources to provide the educational opportunities to which equality of access is demanded. It can be plausibly argued that some kind of basic education is a minimal prerequisite for living in a modern democracy, and therefore that the State ought to supply such education for all, irrespective of the native talent of individuals and irrespective of more specific requirements of the community, such as teachers, plumbers, carpenters, dentists, etc. Wherever the limits of this basic education are set, once it is provided for all citizens, there is no question about equality of opportunity. This question only arises for the first time, in education, at the point at which there are more applicants than places available in a given educational field or level. The attempt to resolve the discrepancy between competent applicants and places available produces the first definition of equality of opportunity.

Equality of Opportunity I

Definition: The opportunity to avail of educational resources is equal among competing applicants, when the selection of applicants is made only on relevant academic or educational criteria.

This concept of equal opportunity is similar to the standard definition of equal opportunity in employment. It assumes that the only *just* criteria for employing one person rather than another are those which are determined by the requirements of the job to be done.[2] The skills required to perform a given job may be specifiable in terms of a definite threshold. In that case, those above the threshold may be more or less qualified, but all are sufficiently qualified to perform the job in question satisfactorily. Therefore, employees might be justly hired either on a first-come first-hired basis; or all applicants (before a given date, for example) might be randomly processed and only the lucky ones get a job. All those who are competent have an *equal* chance of being hired. There is a rather different situation where the skill requirements of a given job are open-ended. Then the more skilled can do a better job than those less skilled, and there is no non-arbitrary point at which all might be said to be equally skilled. One might assume that original research in any field falls into this job-classification. In that case, it would be just to hire the most skilled applicants first, and then hire others in descending order, on a scale of less skilled, until all positions are filled.

By analogy with the employment example, one might select applicants for educational opportunities in either of two ways. If the education in question only presupposes a specifiable level of skill, then all who satisfy the basic requirements might be included in a lottery from which the limited number of places would be randomly filled. On the other hand, if open-ended academic criteria applied, the places available should be filled by those best qualified first, and then by others in descending order of competence until all places are filled. In either case, those who are excluded may still be said to have enjoyed an equal opportunity of sharing in the good of education, because they were not excluded on arbitrary or discriminatory criteria. There was a fair competition for the places available and equal opportunity is defined in terms of fair competition.

Of course, those who are excluded on this kind of selection procedure need not so readily agree that the competition was indeed *fair*. Attempts to explain how it is still unfair and how to make it less unfair give rise to a second concept of equal opportunity.

Equality of Opportunity II

If one administers a standard competency test at any given age for a whole population of applicants for a limited number of places — such as an admission test for secondary schools, the points system of evaluation for university admission, or any comparable test for access to other educational resources — the relative success of different students is partly determined by various factors which are morally neutral with respect to the fairness of the testing procedures adopted. These extrinsic factors may be sub-divided into two groups: those which are believed to be innate in an individual, and those which are thought to be acquired or socially determined by one's overall environment. This distinction is the basis for two other concepts of equal opportunity.

It is well established that the performance of different individuals on a standard educational test is partly determined by such factors as the following: the educational background of one's classmates or peers; the quality of teaching to which one is exposed; the educational facilities to which one has enjoyed easy access, and so on. Perhaps more fundamentally, the home environment of children significantly affects their school performance by either providing a secure, encouraging atmosphere for studies or, at the other extreme, the kind of home in which studies are discouraged and perhaps even impossible. Some of the factors which are influential on this list are in turn determined by the relative wealth or poverty of one's parents or guardians. Even if it does not determine the kind of encouragement or challenge provided for young students, a relatively wealthy home environment at least provides access to expensive educational resources; these may include books, private extra tuition, educational travel, and so on.[3] When all these factors are taken into account, it is not unreasonable for unsuccessful applicants for educational opportunities to argue: those who are socially privileged in any of these ways are competing in a standard test, on *unequal* terms, with those who are socially deprived. Since the latter group are handicapped in comparison with privileged children, the outcome of any standard test is determined, in part, by educationally irrelevant factors, such as the relative wealth or disposition of parents, for which the students themselves are not responsible. From a moral point of view, this outcome seems to be just as arbitrary as selecting students for scarce educational opportunities on the basis of hair colour or religion. Therefore, we need a new definition of equality of opportunity to compensate for these morally irrelevant factors which load the dice against the socially deprived. Equality of opportunity II is defined as follows:

Definition: Applicants for scarce educational resources enjoy equal opportunity of access to them if, and only if: (a) the first definition is satisfied; and (b) if the actual performance of the applicants in a standard test is adjusted to compensate for their socially induced deprivations, or if the applicants themselves have been effectively compensated by counteracting social influences which neutralize the debilitating effects of those factors which detrimentally affect their performance on a test.

Thus if two students are competing for a single educational opening, and if one of them is educationally deprived in the sense just indicated, one might equalize opportunities between the two by either of two strategies. One could consider the performance of the deprived applicant as equal to that of the other if he/she achieved (for example) a 25% lower mark on a standard test. Or one could intervene early enough in the student's studies and provide the kinds of opportunities and encouragement to study which the other student enjoys. For example, one might provide extra tuition, free transport to a better school, and so on. Then when the two students take the same examination, their scores are taken at face value. The student who scores highest deserves the one available place, because the competition between them is fair.

The problem for the egalitarian with these suggestions is that they are not radical enough. The attempt to get to fundamentals involves introducing a third concept of equal opportunity.

Equality of Opportunity III

The compensatory efforts introduced in the second concept of equal opportunity only took account of *socially* induced impediments. There is a further class of personal impediments which are usually believed to be innate or genetically controlled. There is no important issue, for this argument, of trying to decide which factors are innate and which are social; the distinction between II and III only relies on a decision to compensate for some, or all, of the factors which apparently impede individuals in their access to certain goods. Nor does the distinction hinge in any important way on the truth or plausibility of the community's beliefs about which factors belong in either of the two classes of impediments. Whether their beliefs turn out, in the long run, to be true or false, they can currently make a distinction (on the basis of possibly erroneous beliefs) between some impeding factors for which they are willing to compensate and others which they are willing to ignore. The rationale for a third concept of equality of opportunity derives from denying that there is any morally relevant distinction between the two classes of impeding factor, and that an adequate theory of equal opportunity would attempt to compensate for all impediments, whatever their alleged source.

The move from I to II depended on an argument such as the following. The relative wealth of one's parents, or the propinquity of one's parents' domicile to a good school, are completely fortuitous events from the point of view of justice, and therefore they should have no influence in determining the access of an applicant to scarce educational resources. The individual student is no more responsible for them than he/she is for hair colour, and therefore such factors should be excluded from determining one's educational opportunities in competition for scarce resources. The move from II to III only needs the same argument, widened in scope to include so-called innate impediments.

If one's health is poor enough to impede one's academic progress in school; if one is born with any congenital impediment to learning; or even if one's native intelligence is either below average or at least below that of one's competitors for access to some educational field; then the radical egalitarian's argument can be put to work again. All of these factors are morally irrelevant to considerations of justice. They are completely fortuitous occurrences for which one is not in any way responsible. Being born somewhat less intelligent than others is no more fortuitous than being born less wealthy or less socially privileged, and the victim of either type of misfortune is no more responsible for one condition than the other. Therefore, if equal opportunity requires us to compensate individuals for those impeding factors for which they are not responsible, then this should apply across the board to all such impediments, whether they are socially or genetically caused. This suggests a third concept of equal opportunity, which is defined as follows:

Definition: Those who compete for limited educational resources enjoy equal opportunity of access to such resources if, and only if: (a) the requirements of I are satisfied; and (b) if *all* those factors which handicap the efforts of one applicant relative to another are appropriately compensated for in either of the two ways mentioned under II above.

If we were led by the logic of this argument to endorse equality of opportunity III, two other questions would immediately arise: (i) How would we know when we have equalized opportunities in the relevant sense; (ii) Who would pay for the costs of equalizing the opportunities of those who are deprived?

Effective Equality of Opportunity

In answer to the question about knowing when we've done enough, in terms of strict justice, to equalize opportunities among unequal competitors for limited resources, two contrasting philosophical assumptions about human choices determine two very different responses.[4] One assumption is to think of human choices as completely autonomous, as the act of pure wills in Kant's sense. The model which is implicit here is of some kind of activity which completely transcends the causal influence of physical or psychological factors. The will, in its activity of choosing, is completely 'outside' the influence of any determining factors. It is therefore quite possible that two wills might be presented with exactly the same range of goods and that their opportunities for choosing would be exactly equal, and yet one would choose one course of action, and the other may choose something quite different. The two wills might still be said to have enjoyed equal opportunity in the sense that, on condition that they *first* choose to do something, their respective chances of realizing their objectives would be exactly equal. Choice comes first, as something which wills autonomously perform; equality of opportunity then comes into operation, as a description of their relative chances of successfully implementing a previously made choice.

On this model, many of the more obvious differences between individuals — for example, in careers, in their relative wealth or success — would be explained by saying simply: 'they chose not to do this or that.' There is no room for the counterfactual argument: 'if he had enjoyed an equal opportunity of pursuing such a career he surely would have. Since he did not follow that career, he must not have had an (equal) opportunity of doing so'. On this model of human choice, we can only know that we have equalized opportunities by examining the relevant conditions in which a given choice is implemented. If two students, for example, have approximately the same mix of health, intelligence, access to good schools, library facilities, etc., then we know we have equalized opportunities between them and the final result of their choice is irrelevant. Whatever differences survive between them is explicable by reference to the indeterminancy of human choice.

There is another model of human choice which is both more plausible and more compatible with our usual intuitions about degrees of responsibility. In the application of criminal law or in the social study of human behaviour, we assume that the choices people make are often influenced or determined by various factors over which they have little or no control. Without at least a weak version of this assumption any attempt at constructing a social explanation of human behaviour, or even of attempting to discern patterns in human behaviour, would be entirely misguided. On this second model of human choice, the actual choices made are (at least partly) determined by a series of factors which are not under the control of the agent who chooses. Therefore, it is no longer sufficient to monitor the input into, for example, educational choices and then explain the resulting differences in choice by 'free will'.

A strong version of this model would argue: if two agents do not choose alike, it is most likely because their choices were differently determined by various factors which may even be unknown. In the example at issue here, if two potential applicants for limited educational resources choose differently and therefore avoid any competition between them, we might argue: 'because they chose differently, they must have been subject to different motivating influences.' Since this is always a viable argument in every case of unequal final conditions of individuals (we can never simply say: 'they chose differently'), we could only assume that opportunities had been *effectively equalized* between different individuals if they all choose alike and if their respective personal efforts are rewarded with exactly equal end-results. The counterfactual argument, on this model, is: 'if two individuals had enjoyed effective equality of opportunity, they would have achieved equal end-results. Since the latter is not true, we must conclude that the opportunities were not equal, even if they appeared to be so from an inspection of the "input" to the individuals' careers.'

This may seem like an absurd conclusion when applied to individual cases, for two reasons. It leaves no room for random differences between individuals which result in their choosing different life-styles which are more or less equally satisfactory. Secondly, it seems to be motivated not just by the injustice of unequal opportunities, but by some kind of totalitarian ideal which would result in our all wearing exactly the same clothes, reaching the same level of education in schools, and so on. Such a perfectly homogeneous world is so repulsive to most people that they might reasonably prefer the alleged injustice of the status quo rather than follow the logic of the argument to its unacceptable conclusion.

However, the same argument is not so implausible if applied to groups or classes, as it normally is by social scientists. If there is a discernible class stratification among those who avail of higher education, for example, it is a poor explanation to say: members of one class just choose differently from those of another! Individuals might just choose differently, but why would members of a given socio-economic class coincidently all choose the same way? Such a coincidence is more plausibly explained by unrecognized factors which systematically influence or determine their choices and which are therefore relevant to equalizing opportunities between members of different classes. Alternatively, the coincidence between membership of a class and the use of educational resources might be explained by class-relative innate factors. This is a hypothesis which is worth considering; the predominance of black athletes in short distance races on the U.S. Olympic team is hardly an indication of racism. Thus, without endorsing the second model in its strongest form, one could learn this lesson from the concept of effective equality of opportunity: the monitoring of the known input to career choices, for example, is no guarantee of equality of opportunity. If there remains any systematic pattern of failure to choose a limited good in a given class of individuals, then one might seriously question the assumption that we have in fact equalized opportunities. The pattern of choice may be an indication of an unrecognized bias in favour of one group rather than another.

The concept of equal opportunity has been articulated so far in terms of a single example, access to education. This is a central example, in many ways, because one's educational level (understood in a broad sense) significantly affects one's career opportunities and consequently one's access to a wide range of other goods, such as wealth, prestige, or even political office. The consistent egalitarian, however, must expand his list of human goods and correspondingly widen the scope of equal opportunity. He must defend the justice of equal opportunity in citizens' access to all those goods which are plausibly construed as significant for human flourishing. As already indicated, this is not equivalent to a demand that the state provide services or goods which it cannot afford, nor that the state completely satisfy all the citizens' reasonable requests for goods. The background assumption in equal opportunity discussions is that most of these goods are so limited that only some of those who wish to share them will in fact realize their objectives. Equality of opportunity operates to monitor the *distribution* of limited goods according to principles of justice. What is so unjust about those distributive procedures which were challenged under I, II or III as morally objectionable? In other words, what theory of justice is the defender of equal opportunity working with, and how is it justified?

There are two related intuitions implicit in the equal opportunity thesis, and both can be accommodated in a contract or convention theory of justice. One is an objection to huge discrepancies in the personal wealth of individuals; the other is motivated by a desire to decrease conflict between social classes.

The more basic intuition is that there is no rationale for the scale of the discrepancies among individuals, in their shares of human goods, which results from a laissez-faire market theory of distribution. Locke's theory of a limitless supply of natural goods (including land), which could be justly appropriated by the work of individuals and then bequeathed to their legal succcessors, is as inapplicable in the twentieth century as it was in the seventeenth. Therefore if we expect members of any community to endorse a convention which will allow very significant discrepancies between individuals in their supply of human goods (comprehensively understood), we need to provide convincing reasons for such a convention.

It should be remembered that this question arises more acutely in some ethical/political theories than in others. If someone believes, as Locke apparently did, that various rights come from God, then there is little more to be said about distributive justice except that God distributes things rather unequally. In a similar way, if we believe that justice is determined by an objective moral law or by any other extra-terrestrial rules, there is nothing more to be said or done, except: justice demands that I do this, or accept that, and it is irrelevant if it seems rather unfair to me, or if I starve to death while my neighbour suffers the ill-effects of gluttony. Likewise, if one relies on Nozick's premise, that what we lawfully own we can lawfully bequeath and that this right is one of the absolute side-constraints on any political theory, then there is no need to look into the history of how I came to have what I lawfully own.[5] Nor is there any need to worry about the long-term distributive effects of such an arrangement in a given country. Perhaps those who are already rich will get much richer, and those with political power and ingenuity will consolidate their position in the society; and those with a firm hold on almost any social good will continue to prosper at the expense of those who are unlucky (or those who were born of unlucky ancestors). From the point of view of a contract theory, however, we need to distinguish between the following: (i) what the law of any country currently accepts; (ii) what the common morality or religious morality of a community endorses; and (iii) what a society of more or less rational agents would be willing to accept as a fair distributive principle for human goods. The contract theory of justice relies exclusively on (iii). Even if the law allows something and if it is acceptable to the common morality, do I have any reason for endorsing the procedures which result in a significantly unequal distribution of social goods? And if I do, what kind of reasons are they, and what kind of disparities should I be willing to rationally accept?

The standard argument in favour of a differential distribution of social goods is utilitarian. Society at large and the individuals who compose it need the dedication and hard work of its more talented members in every profession or specialty. In order to encourage such dedication, one needs to reward it in proportion to the effort involved in each individual's contribution to the common good. This will inevitably lead to some individuals enjoying a greater share of human goods than others. The only other alternative, it is argued, is to equalize the rewards of all and thereby abolish the incentives to hard work on which the well-being of the whole community depends.

This conclusion might also be expressed in terms of the concept of desert. Those who work hard and contribute significantly to the common good 'deserve' their rewards. There is an issue of justice involved here too, in the sense that it would be unjust to deprive anyone of the deserved fruits of his labour. There are further difficulties with the concept of 'desert', however; what one deserves is to a great extent determined by the conventions in force in a society at the time one initiates one's efforts. It may be the case that these conventions are in turn established for utilitarian reasons along the lines just suggested. So that the concept of desert, while it appears to be an independent justification for rewarding individual effort, may in fact collapse into a utilitarian rationale for rewarding contributions to the common good. The following discussion is simplified, therefore, by ignoring it.

Even if the utilitarian theory of rewarding effort is accepted, there is still a major problem in accepting discrepancies among individuals which are hardly required by any theory of encouraging individual effort. There is no significant difference, in effort, between the average contributions of sanitation workers and university professors to the common good. Nor is there a significant discrepancy in effort between the work of an industrial worker and the professional or managerial workers who earn perhaps ten times his salary. Such discrepancies would have to be otherwise explained, perhaps in terms of professional closed-shops and self-regulation. The scale of these discrepancies within any given society is made even more obvious if one compares under-privileged workers in a poor society with those who are most privileged in a rich society. No plausible theory of justice, and no plausible utilitarian considerations, will justify the kinds of differences in acquired wealth which are found in that case.

Thus, if one grants the need for a differential distribution of goods to encourage effort and to reward individual contributions to the common good (on a scale which more reasonably reflects our intuitions about justice rather than the insatiable acquisitive instincts of individuals), we cannot hope to produce a society in which everyone has more or less the same amount of social goods. This remains true even if the lack of effort of many individuals is explained by reference to various factors for which they are not responsible. The relative 'poverty' (in terms of goods in general) of some individuals is a utilitarian trade-off for the benefits which accrue to society from the incentives provided for the well-motivated (even if their motivation is also causally explained).

There is a second, perhaps more basic, reason for rejecting any attempts on the part of the state to exactly equalize the end result of social interaction in terms of one's relative share of goods. It is a basic tenet of liberal, democratic theory that individual citizens ought to enjoy the greatest amount of personal freedom which is compatible with a corresponding level of freedom for others.[6] The autonomy of the individual is logically compatible with stringent controls on economic activity and personal wealth; however, such logical possibilities are irrelevant to political realities. In fact, the autonomy of an individual is unreasonably limited when he is prevented from exploiting his talents and interests in a variety of different ways, and thereby increasing his share of human goods and lessening his share of others. Individual autonomy implies significant discrepancies, in fact, between different individuals in their relative share of society's goods.

These two reasons are sufficient to reject any social policy which is based on a concept of effective equality of opportunity, as applied to individuals. This policy implies that we have effectively equalized opportunities only when the end result of implementing the policy achieves equality in fact among individuals. If we cannot justify effective equality of opportunity for individuals, it remains an open question as to whether we might justify a similar policy for various groups or classes.

The rejection of obscene discrepancies between individuals in their respective shares of social goods as an arrangement which is fundamentally unjust, is one of the intuitions which motivates equal opportunity demands. The other main source of discontent with unequal opportunities is its tendency to reinforce a stratification of different classes in a society and thereby to promote the kinds of class conflict which undermine many of the constitutive features of the common good.

This second argument assumes the context of a modern democracy in which citizens contribute, through their taxes, to finance various state-funded services which are provided on a limited basis to only some of those who may wish to avail of them. If one examines the net effect of state intervention in what might otherwise, at least in theory, be a free market, the available evidence sometimes points in a direction which is the exact opposite to the intended purpose of the state's policy. The funding of educational facilities provides a good example of this, although the same point might be made more generally for the effect of a state's economic policies on the distribution of goods in a more comprehensive sense.[7] State financing of education in Ireland has not

significantly affected the class distribution of those who avail of it.[8] This
means that the real advantages which accrue to already privileged
students who avail of subsidized education are being financed by those
who are less privileged in society. The net effect of such a policy is to
systematically transfer wealth from the poor to the (relatively) rich.

This raises the obvious question for a convention-based theory of
justice: why should those who are already disadvantaged — through
whatever complex combination of factors which determines their
chances of success in social competition — why should they agree to sub-
sidize the efforts of others who, relative to them, are socially privileged?
If they could be persuaded of the following thesis, they might accept it:
'subsidizing the educational ambitions of privileged students will eventually redound to the improvement of the lot of all members of society,
and is therefore a policy which one should endorse for reasons of self-
interest.' This argument might seem plausible in the case of those who
are especially talented and obviously necessary for the improvement of
the common good, if they did not subsequently exploit their opportunities to their own personal advantage. Apart from such exceptional
cases, therefore, it is doubtful if many underprivileged citizens would accept this kind of argument. And for that reason alone, such a policy is
unjust in a contract theory of justice. It is unjust because it is not a convention which most people would willingly endorse if they had the opportunity of choosing, and if they realized the likely implications of their
choice. Since any social arrangements which have a similar effect, of
transferring wealth (broadly understood) from the underprivileged to
those who are relatively privileged, will be equally unacceptable and unjust, the minimal demand that any theory of justice makes on the state is
to refrain from implementing policies which have this result. A more ag-
gressive form of the same thesis is some version of an equal opportunity
policy, defined in terms of one of the three concepts outlined above.
Which concept of equal opportunity can be defended on this argument
depends on other considerations which are more contentious than the objection to policies which cultivate class differentiation.

Two broad sources of discontent, or two objections based on a
convention-theory of justice, have been briefly outlined up to this point:
the objection to unreasonable discrepancies in wealth between individuals, and the objection to social policies which reinforce class
distinctions. Neither one of these, however, is enough to identify and
justify any specific theory of equal opportunity. A third consideration

comes into play at this stage, which has figured in the articulation of the three concepts of equal opportunity; that is the idea that the distribution of goods in society should not be a function of 'morally irrelevant' factors.

Morally Neutral Causes

One of the standard moves made in defending equal opportunity is to object to someone's being deprived of some good because of determining factors for which he cannot be held personally responsible. Such factors are classified as morally irrelevant from the point of view of justice. For example, it is often said that it is unfair that young people are deprived of an opportunity to continue their education simply because their parents cannot afford the financial costs involved. This seems plausible enough on first reading. On further analysis, however, it loses the lustre of self-evidence and unfolds into a complex thesis about who should pay for a student's education. Likewise, for corresponding claims about equal opportunity of access to any human good, the economic cost involved is an intrinsic part of any argument based on 'justice'.

The first difficulty with the 'morally relevant' objection is that it implies an infinite regress in any attempt to justify a differential treatment of competing applicants for a limited good.[9] The educational example runs: one student should not have a better opportunity of availing of advanced education or training simply because his/her parents cannot afford the financial costs involved. Why? Because the wealth of one's parents is an irrelevant factor on which to base a selection of applicants for higher education or training. Why is it irrelevant? Partly because the unsuccessful applicant is not responsible for it; and partly because the obviously relevant criterion is 'ability to make use of educational resources'. What determines the 'ability to use educational resources'? Presumably, many other factors, some of which are genetically determined, and others socially determined. The potential student is not responsible for these either. There is no clear starting-point in this regress of explanatory factors at which one could stop and say: 'the potential student was clearly responsible for that, and therefore whatever arrangements we make by reference to this factor will be such that the student deserves the outcome. It is therefore a fair arrangement.' There is surely something random — and therefore outside the scope of considerations of justice — about the differential aptitudes, interests, degrees of motivation, etc. of young citizens. The objection of the equal opportunity thesis seems to rely on the following premise: if someone is not responsible for some condition which enhances his opportunities, then he should not be allowed to exploit it to his advantage in a competition for limited resources. This premise, consistently applied, leads to an infinite regress. The argument which relies on it is doomed to failure. In fact, it was a consistent application of this premise which inexorably drove the analysis of equal opportunity in the direction of Equality of Opportunity III.

A second problem with this type of objection is that it substitutes one random distribution of goods by another, equally random distribution. The only difference between the two random distributions is that we can guess the outcome of one of them before the results are in, whereas the other seems to be more open or fair because we do not know the results in advance. It should be kept in mind that there is no question of equal opportunity if everyone can in fact have access to whatever goods they aspire to. Equal opportunity is meant to give competing aspirants an equal or fair chance of achieving their common objective. The argument against any system which selects on the basis of criteria for which individuals are not morally responsible implies that we ought eventually to. select people, for any limited good, by some kind of random procedure. For example, all the names of those who wish to proceed to higher education are put in a randomizing machine and the first number of names it produces which correspond to the number of places available are chosen. Why is this any more 'morally relevant' than the random factors which determine the genetic and social conditioning of each applicant? It only seems more fair because in the one case, genetic or social conditioning, we can anticipate the result of any selection procedure since we already know the end result of random determining forces; whereas in the case of putting names in a machine, we only know after the machine does its job. However, random selection is morally neutral, whether the randomness involved comes from a machine or a gene pool.

And yet, despite these arguments, there still seems to be something worthwhile about this objection: 'the parents' income should not determine the educational opportunities of their children.' There is a genuine basis for this objection which can be accommodated without a thoroughgoing theory of equal opportunity. Part of the reason why we find the objection plausible depends on a background utilitarian assumption; another part of its plausibility derives from the implicit demand for reverse discrimination to compensate innocent victims of social injustice.

The background utilitarian assumption is that a society should select applicants for any scarce resource on the basis of criteria which are relevant to the good in question. Thus, access to medical resources is normally based on the medical needs of people. In the educational example, one should select among applicants for limited places in a school or college on the basis of their likely performance in the studies in question. The reason for this is that, as rational agents, we are only willing to finance the studies of those who are likely to benefit from such studies or those who are likely to make a subsequent, useful contribution to the common good. There is no point in wasting scarce resources in the musical training of someone who completely lacks the relevant talent; nor is there any reason why we should finance the engineering studies of those who have neither the talent nor motivation to pursue their studies to a successful conclusion. Relative to these kinds of selection criteria, the wealth of someone's parents is irrelevant. Thus while the lack of appropriate talents in one applicant is a random, natural occurrence, the lack of financial backing from parents is both random *and irrelevant* in the case of the talented, poor student. Part of the rationale for the objection at issue, therefore, is that a talented student should be encouraged to exploit his/her talents for both personal and social reasons, and the relative poverty of parents should not be allowed to jeopardize his chances of success.[10]

The same objection also relies, in part, on an assumption that remediable, social causes help determine the underprivileged student's lack of opportunity. To the extent that social arrangements, for which the members of society are in some sense responsible, have determined the parents' poverty (for example), then society has thereby effectively diminished the poor student's chances of availing of education. This is unfair in a way which the genetically-caused lack of talent of another is not unfair. It is unfair because it results, at least in part, from the intentional actions of many different members of society. To the extent that 'society' has negatively influenced the students' opportunities, society ought to compensate him and arrange that he enjoys the same opportunities as he would have enjoyed had society not diminished them.

This kind of argument, if successful, would support some version of Equality of Opportunity II. However, even before reaching this conclusion there remain some standard difficulties with any form of reverse discrimination or compensatory programme of social reform. Two such problems are worth mentioning: (i) the likely beneficiaries of a compensatory policy; and (ii) the responsibility of 'society' for an individual's lack of opportunity.

As A. Goldman has convincingly argued in his discussion of reverse discrimination, if a society decides to compensate individuals for the negative effects of intentional social factors on their opportunities, the most likely beneficiaries of such a programme are those who are least affected by society's harmful influence. The assumption on which any such programme is based is that the opportunities of young people are negatively affected more or less seriously in proportion to the detrimental effect of social factors (among others). Those who are most seriously affected, therefore, are less likely to be in any position to compete with 'privileged' members of society, than those who are only slightly affected by adverse circumstances. If we are selecting applicants for admission to college or university, it would make no sense (on this argument) to compensate those who performed slightly less well than others because they were reared in disadvantaged conditions. Those who were most seriously affected by disadvantageous circumstances are not even in the running for admission; and they surely have a more serious claim, in justice, to be compensated for society's adverse influence.

It follows that any kind of compensatory evaluation of applicants for admission to schools or colleges — with corresponding implications for any competition for limited goods, such as hiring or training employees — is likely to favour those who were least disadvantaged by the influence of social factors. This is clearly evident in the current debate about financing third-level education in Ireland. The most vocal proponents of equal opportunity are those who have been privileged by a whole cluster of factors which bring them within reach of a third-level education, at which point they claim to be unable to finance their education any further. However, any consistent compensatory social programme, which is concerned with justice rather than political pressure, would look instead to those who have been so disadvantaged by society (among other factors) that they have not come close enough to even qualify for admission to higher education. This conclusion will be taken up again below in discussing the financial cost of equal opportunity.

The second qualification on society's obligation, in justice, to those whom it has intentionally inhibited is concerned with the question of social responsibility. If the parents of a child fail to provide the kind of home environment in which the child's natural talents will develop, and if their failure can be correctly described as voluntary and intentional, then it follows that they are responsible for whatever ill-effects the child suffers from their neglect. A similar kind of statement could be defended in respect of anyone else who may detrimentally affect the child. It would apply to incompetent teachers, ineffective school administrators, and so on — everyone who adversely affects the educational opportunities of an individual child. Apart from those who are directly responsible, in what sense do other members of society share responsibility for the intentional behaviour of those individuals who adversely affect the child?

This question can hardly be resolved favourably for victims of adverse social influence within an ethic of purely individual responsibility. There is a clear and obvious sense in which I am not responsible, in justice, for my neighbour's intentional neglect, no more than I am morally responsible for the contingencies of genetic determination. If I cannot be held responsible for the latter, why should I be held responsible for the former? Besides, any social arrangement which glosses over these distinctions would seem to provide an easy way out for those who are irresponsible: 'my neighbours will take care of it!' This kind of question can probably only be resolved by reference to the kinds of conventions which members of a society may be willing to adopt, in order to protect innocent children from at least the more deleterious effects of human agency. The intentional neglect of some people and the random ill-effects of purely natural contingencies, will both be taken into account from the perspective of the innocent victim. If that is the case, there is no way in which one can avoid the issue of the relative cost, to society, of whatever policy it might be willing to implement.

In fact, apart from the utilitarian argument in favour of exploiting the talent of individuals in the interests of the common good, and the argument in strict justice that those who intentionally harm others should compensate them for the effects of their intentional actions, all the issues which are raised by proponents of equal opportunity seem to converge on questions of cost. This is an issue which can no longer be avoided in choosing between alternative concepts of equal opportunity.

The Cost of Equal Opportunity

As already mentioned, the argument in favour of Equality of Opportunity III relied on the premise that people should not be adversely affected by those morally irrelevant factors which seem to determine their chances of access to limited social goods. I argued above that this is an implausible claim if it is taken as a general premise which applies to every case of competition for limited goods. At the same time, it seemed as if some criteria of selection were not only random but also irrelevant to any rationale one might give for a particular selection procedure. Evidently, hair-colour is irrelevant in this sense for admission to college, whereas the ability to benefit from a college education is not irrelevant. Both factors may be equally the effect of random, natural causes, and therefore equally outside the scope of an individual's responsibility. Given the relevance of 'ability to benefit from higher education' as a criterion of selection, there remains the question of who should pay the financial costs involved in applying such a criterion.

This is not an issue of strict justice in the sense in which, for example, returning a stolen item to its owner is normally believed to be demanded by strict justice. What will count as just, or unjust, can only be determined by the kinds of conventions which members of a society might be willing to reasonably adopt. We cannot discover these conventions in some natural law which is already in existence, nor in any other objective set of norms. Those who assume that their own principles are self-evident or patently true are only avoiding the difficulties which are obviously involved in providing a coherent account of our intuitions about justice.

Among the objectives which a society might endorse, I have so far included the following: (i) minimally, to avoid any social policy which has a net effect of transferring real wealth from the relatively poor to the relatively rich; (ii) to discourage social arrangements which allow some individuals to become obscenely rich while others lack the barest necessities for a human existence; (iii) to avoid policies which facilitate significant class distinctions and the resulting frictions which they are likely to cause; (iv) for utilitarian reasons, to provide incentives which encourage the efforts of individuals to improve both their own lot and to contribute to the common good; and (v) to compensate those individuals who are adversely affected, to a significant extent, by intentional human actions. If a society were to adopt these principles of social policy, it would still be far short of anything like Equality of Opportunity III. The extent to which it may, or may not, be willing to endorse a stronger programme of equalizing opportunities is very much a question of deciding priorities in the use of public funds.

This is a rather different conclusion about equal opportunity from one which seems to be suggested by the rhetoric of rights. If someone is owed something strictly as a matter of right, we usually argue that it must be provided for him no matter what the cost involved. It is in this sense, for example, that the intentional adverse effects of human agency on the opportunities of another citizen must be strictly compensated by those who were responsible for the damage. Apart from this case, however, all the other contingencies which differentially affect the opportunities of competing individuals are randomly determined by natural causes and therefore morally neutral from the point of view of justice. To compensate individuals for the effects of any of these contingencies — such as being born a citizen of one country rather than another; being born intelligent or otherwise; being born rich or poor; and so on — requires both a decision on the part of society, and a choice of priorities in using the limited funds available.

The kinds of consideration which come into operation at this point are detailed empirical and normative beliefs which may reasonably vary from one society to another without necessarily implying a greater or lesser commitment to some ideal of justice on the part of contrasting societies. This follows from the argument in Chapter 1. In making decisions about competing priorities, the following kinds of normative consideration should be included: (a) to identify some conditions of the individual which are so necessary that one could be said to be in serious need if they were lacking. For example, an adequate supply of food and shelter and also some less material needs, such as freedom and autonomy, would be included here. These basic needs should be satisfied first, before looking to such luxuries as the cultivation of someone's musical talent or the development of another's expertise in nuclear physics at great expense to the tax-payer. (b) To identify skills and abilities which are especially beneficial to the common good, and to facilitate the appropriate training of those who are most likely to contribute to the common good. The justification of this priority ranking is not some abstract right to equal opportunity of talented individuals, but rather the needs of society at large. (c) In attempting to equalize opportunities among individual citizens, to identify those social factors which are likely to do most damage to individuals at an age when they are least capable of protecting themselves. This implies, for example, concentrating limited educational resources at first level — by supplying young students with whatever is needed to make their chances of success comparable to those of their more privileged peers. In a competition for limited funds, this might imply that most of the remaining finances for education would be channelled into second level schools, to the detriment of those at third-level. Again, the rationale for this choice is that the vocational and academic training of the majority of second-level students is more important, for the common good, than subsidizing the educational pursuits of adults.

Whatever concept of equal opportunity is adopted by a society, it is clear that the costs involved in implementing it will increase exponentially in proportion to the degree of success aimed at. Thus, what was called 'effective equality of opportunity' above is a limiting case which is unrealizable in practice. Any practicable policy will be confined to some version of Equality of Opportunity II. Even here the extent to which society can compensate individuals for socially induced unequal opportunities will be limited by the priority decisions which allocate resources to other urgent social problems. In a compensatory programme for equalizing opportunities which reflects principles of justice, it is also likely that those who are most aware of the need to equalize opportunities will be least likely to benefit; for those most likely to complain about unequal opportunities are those who just marginally fail to succeed in their attempts to gain access to some limited good. If the thesis of social causality, on which Equality of Opportunity II is based, is plausible, then those most adversely affected by social causes will be least likely to figure in the final selection of applicants for any limited good. Equality of opportunity, therefore, should be understood less in terms of equalizing the chances of success of those who are already close to achieving their objectives. It should be understood, rather, as a more radical theory of social justice from which many would benefit who might not otherwise have even known what opportunities they were missing.

Education is a special case in considerations of equal opportunity because of the significant link between a person's standard of education and his long-term prospects of career success. As a good in its own right, citizens ought to have an equal opportunity of access to all educational resources which are publicly funded; but this is a mere slogan without a detailed calculation of the costs involved and a clear explanation of which kind of equal opportunity is demanded. I have argued that, apart from a basic education, and apart from those skills which the community requires to foster in its own interests, any attempt to equalize opportunities in education will have to compete with many more urgent demands on the public purse and will probably loose out in the competition. Nevertheless, as a means to other goods — especially as a determinant of one's income in later years — education raises questions of basic justice. The analysis of the links between education and career success by

Jencks suggests that equalizing educational opportunities would have a rather small effect on the eventual disparities between people in their earned income.[11] Since this was one of the fundamental motivations for equal opportunity demands, it seems preferable to tackle this question directly and to take steps to equalize earned income rather than to distract the public's attention with talk of equal opportunity. And as long as that issue is not confronted, it is both ineffective and unjust to fund higher education completely from the public purse.

On the particular issue of public financing of third-level education, the argument of this chapter suggests that the case for completely free higher education has not been established from considerations of equal opportunity. There is something anomalous about the present arrangements in which the state pays most of the cost of higher education, but requires a significant contribution from those who wish to avail of it. This is a little like providing most of the cost of a telephone system, but then preventing the most disadvantaged members of society from using it by fixing a high installation charge which they cannot afford. The state currently pays approximately eighty percent of the real cost of any citizens's higher education in Ireland. Most students are expected to provide at least some of the remaining twenty percent from their own resources. This arrangement has the effect of only subsidizing the education of those who can afford to pay part of the cost themselves. Those who are disadvantaged, therefore, help support the system by their taxes but are prevented from sharing its benefits.

The argument in this chapter suggests that the cost of equalizing opportunities for third-level education is probably so high that it cannot hope to be achieved in the near future. The argument also identifies the main objection to the present system: that the status of those who enjoy social and natural advantages in society is further enhanced, at the expense of those who share the cost of the system but are prevented from using it. If education cannot be provided for all, then it should be paid for by those who benefit from it. This can be done in a variety of ways, such as low-interest loans which are repayable when someone is employed, or by a surcharge on earned income which would repay the real cost to the tax-payer of the educational resources made available to an individual. The present scheme in Ireland is unjust. But strict justice does not demand equality of opportunity in either the second or third senses discussed above.

8

Education

The tax-payer, in Ireland, bears the major share of the financial cost of education at every level. Likewise, those who are being educated are, for the most part, the children of tax-payers or are tax-payers themselves who are availing of facilities designed for adult education in its widest sense. Both the Irish Constitution and the churches pay lip service to the educational rights of children, of parents and of the adult individual citizen. Despite all this, parents and tax-payers are rather systematically excluded from any significant influence in education at primary or secondary level.[1] In their place, education at primary and secondary level is mostly controlled by those who are neither parents nor tax-payers' representatives. This anomaly is partly explained by the timidity of state authorities, for almost two centuries, in facing up to the political power and astuteness of the churches. It is also partly explained by the complicity of all those affected by this exclusion in accepting the status quo. It is fundamentally explained by the success of the churches in controlling, not only the relatively meagre educational resources which were available at first and second level in recent times, but also the *beliefs* of the citizens on which their tolerance of church control ultimately rests.

The first two factors are best explained by historians and social scientists.[2] The third factor, the beliefs of citizens, is primarily an ideological question. It raises two issues: (a) identifying the beliefs in question; and (b) the more fundamental issue of the plausibility of such beliefs and their possible justification as an ideological base for a modern democratic society. This chapter is concerned with the ideological question, with those beliefs of citizens which sustain the anomalous state of Irish education.

There is an obvious danger in assuming that all the churches which have an interest in education in Ireland share the same justificatory beliefs about their influence. At the same time, the churches have much

196

more in common, on this point, than they have in common with the counter-thesis; and it would not significantly affect the consideration of their political stance if one conducted a detailed analysis of each church in turn. As in earlier discussions above, I limit the introductory analysis to the beliefs of the Roman Catholic Church about its role in education; partly to shorten the discussion, and partly because it is the church which has most influence in Irish education. In a second section, I briefly examine the constitutional provisions which apply to education, and draw out some implications which appear to be demanded by a literal interpretation of the relevant articles. Finally, in the third section, I contrast the churches' interest in religious and moral indoctrination with the objectives of classic, liberal political theory, especially with the objective of facilitating the development of autonomous individuals who could choose, freely, whatever religious tradition they preferred. On the basis of this contrast, I argue that the aims of democratic theory can best accommodate the religious objectives of the churches by a clear separation of church and state in education, and by tolerant provision for church-controlled religious instruction — in public schools if necessary — at a period after regular school when those who wish may freely take advantage of whatever services the churches wish to offer.

Roman Catholic Educational Policy

The most authoritative recent statement of the Church on education is the *Declaration on Christian Education* of the Second Vatican Council. It is almost redundant to add that the Church's views on education are historically conditioned, and that any adequate interpretation of its views would require a much more comprehensive survey of a variety of statements than could be reasonably anticipated here. In default of such a comprehensive discussion, the Vatican II *Declaration* summarizes a cluster of overlapping claims, without much clear guidance as to which rights or duties yield to others in a situation of conflict. This point is best seen by examining the text. The *Declaration* claims that all persons, Christians, parents, civil society, and the Church, have rights with respect to education.

Every person has a human right to some minimum education:

Since every man of whatever race, condition, and age is endowed with the dignity of a person, he has an inalienable right to an education corresponding to his proper destiny, and suited to his native talents, his sex, his cultural background, and his ancestral heritage.[3]

This 'inalienable right' applies to all; those who are young enough to require moral education are also said to have a right to freedom of conscience in their moral education:

This holy Synod likewise affirms that children and young people have a right to
be encouraged to weigh moral values with an upright conscience, and to embrace
them by *personal choice,* and to know and love God more adequately. Hence, it
earnestly entreats all who exercise government over peoples or preside over the
work of education to see that youth is never deprived of this sacred right (italics
added).[4]

The freedom of conscience which is involved here should be understood
in conjunction with the passage from the *Declaration on Religious
Freedom* which was already mentioned in Chapter 4 above.

However, in spreading religious faith and in introducing religious practices,
everyone ought at all time to refrain from any manner of action which might seem
to carry a hint of coercion or of a kind of persuasion that would be dishonourable
or unworthy, especially when dealing with poor or uneducated people. Such a
manner of action would have to be considered an abuse of one's own right and a
violation of the right of others.[5]

The kind of free adoption of moral or religious values which is central
to this claim is hardly compatible with religious or moral indoctrination
from an early age in primary schools. There can be no real doubt in
anyone's mind that children begin to acquire their religious beliefs, and
the moral values associated with them, at an age when they hardly
understand the words in which many of the beliefs are expressed. Five-
year-olds casually discourse of Heaven and Hell, of God and the
afterlife, in roughly the same way in which they talk of Santa Claus or
the Tooth-Fairy. If the Church thinks it reprehensible to take advantage
of the uneducated and to persuade them of beliefs to which their ig-
norance exposes them, why does it not take a similar view of the indoctrination of children at an age when they could scarcely be said to 'freely'
adopt religious beliefs? There is an implied answer to this question in the
Church's view of its own rights and of the rights of parents.
    Christians are said to be entitled to a Christian education: 'Since every
Christian has become a new creature by rebirth from water and Holy
Spirit, so that he may be called what he truly is, a child of God, he is entitled to a Christian education.'[6] Thus, if we baptize children early
enough in life, they thereby acquire a right to a particular kind of

education. And whereas the 'inalienable right' to education mentioned above was left vague on the question: against whom might one urge one's right?, in this case the answer is clearly: against the Church. The rights of baptized children create corresponding duties in the Church and its representatives.

> Therefore this holy Synod reminds pastors of souls of their acutely serious duty to make every effort to see that all the faithful enjoy a Christian education of this sort, especially young people, who are the hope of the Church. . . . the office of educating belongs by a unique title to the Church, not merely because she deserves recognition as a human society capable of educating, but most of all because she has the responsibility of announcing the way of salvation to all men, . . .[7]

This kind of response to the question about 'free consent' to religious values may appear to be a mere disguise for ideological indoctrination. It looks as if the Church argues: once a child is baptized, he acquires a right to a special kind of education, and we therefore have a serious duty to provide what his rights demand. Hence our obligation to educate the child in a Christian manner. The baptismal intervention, without the child's own consent, gives the Church a duty to educate him in a certain way. And if it has such a duty, then it must also have a right to perform its duties. The rights of the Church, therefore, vis-à-vis the child derive from a sacramental intervention to which the child could not normally consent. How is that any different from taking advantage of the poor or uneducated to persuade them of a creed which they cannot adequately understand? And would it make any difference in the case of uneducated adults if they were baptized first, so that the argument which applied to the children might apply to them also? If they are baptized, they have a right to a Christian education, whether they like it or not!

The obvious way out of this dilemma is to refer to the rights and duties of parents for a justification of the Church's sacramental interventions in the case of children. The consent of parents, it may be claimed, 'supplies' the lack of consent of the child.

> Since parents have conferred life on their children, they have a most solemn obligation to educate their offspring. Hence parents must be acknowledged as the *first and foremost educators* of their children. Their role as educators is so decisive that scarcely anything can compensate for their failure in it. (italics added) . . . Parents, who have the first and the inalienable duty and right to educate their children, should enjoy true freedom in their choice of schools.[8]

Again, this passage should be taken in conjunction with the corresponding claim of the *Declaration on Religious Freedom:*

Since the family is a society of its own original right, it has the right freely to live
its own domestic religious life under the guidance of parents. Parents, moreover,
have the right to determine, in accordance with their own religious beliefs, the
kind of religious education that their children are to receive.[9]

These claims on behalf of parents are difficult to understand and even
more difficult to justify. They only seem plausible from the point of view
of a religious institution which accepts its own beliefs as infallibly true,
and therefore concludes that no significant harm can befall the children
as a result of the 'primary rights' of parents to decide their children's
education. Our perspective on this question is radically changed,
however, if we consider an example of a religious cult which, from our
point of view, we regard as detrimental to the well-being of children.

   Imagine a religious group which has developed its peculiar lifestyle in
a closely-knit community. Assume also that they so control the limited
experience of their children that they have no real opportunity of
challenging their inherited beliefs for want of an alternative with which
to compare them. Finally, assume that some of their beliefs are (in our
view) detrimental to the well-being of their children. For example, one
might imagine beliefs about not availing of contemporary medicine, or
drug-taking in a way which is clearly injurious to one's health. It would
not be unusual for adult members of such a community to claim that
they have an inalienable right to rear their children in the tradition of
their forefathers. Why should anyone, either inside or outside the community, accept their claim to have this right?

   The point of this example is not to undermine all rights-claims of
parents in educational matters. The point is, simply, that the rights which
parents may claim are subject to the more basic rights of the children
themselves. Any other alternative implies connotations of the children
being the 'private property' of parents to which they have exclusive
rights. There is no basis in a contract theory of rights for giving educational rights to parents without reference to the more basic rights of
children. Therefore, the kind of educational decisions made by parents
must be assumed, in some determinate sense, to be in the interests of
children. Any attempt by parents to subvert the children's interests in
keeping with their own religious beliefs, and then to defend their discretion by reference to their rights as parents, should be resisted by

members of any society which acknowledges rights for individuals, including children.

If one impartially applies the same considerations to the Catholic Church's claim about the rights of parents, it is clear that the rights of parents are not absolute. It may be argued that anyone who challenges the educational choice of parents would have to assume the burden of showing that the parents' decision causes some harm to the children. This may be an unenviable challenge in the face of a centuries-old tradition of church-controlled education. Therefore, in the absence of strong evidence to the contrary, the parents' free choice is the crucial link between the Church's aim to educate in a religious manner, and the assumed rights of individuals (even very young individuals) to freedom of conscience. This is clear from the text of the two *Declarations* quoted; each of the passages about the rights of parents continues as follows:

Consequently, public authority which has the obligation to oversee and defend the liberties of citizens, ought to see to it, out of a concern for distributive justice, that public subsidies are allocated in such a way that, when selecting schools for their children, parents are genuinely free to follow their consciences.

Government, in consequence, must acknowledge the right of parents to make a genuinely free choice of schools and of other means of education. The use of this freedom of choice is not to be made a reason for imposing unjust burdens on parents, whether directly or indirectly. Besides, the rights *of parents* are violated if their children are forced to attend lessons or instruction which are not in agreement with their religious beliefs. The same is true if a single system of education, from which all religious formation is excluded, is imposed on all. (Italics added)[10]

The conclusion drawn at the end of the second quotation is only half of what is implied by the preceding argument; it is the half which concerns the Church. The other half, of course, is that it violates parents' rights if a school system is so arranged that those who do *not* share the religious beliefs of the local churches are compelled to send their children to schools which are controlled and managed by churches. Religious freedom is only genuine when it includes the freedom not to be religious. Likewise, freedom of educational choice for parents is only a charade if it means freedom to choose between a limited number of religious schools. This is almost made explicit in the *Declaration on Religious Education*, although the context might imply the more limited thesis about the rights of Christian parents:

For this reason, the Church gives high praise to those civil authorities and civil societies that show regard for the pluralistic character of modern society, and take into account the right of religious liberty, by helping families in such a way that in all schools the education of their children can be carried out according to the moral and religious convictions of each family.[11]

Does this mean that the State should make provision for schools managed by various religious denominations, or does it mean that it should also cater to those who wish to have non-denominational schools? The clear implication of the passage already cited is that Catholic parents should not be financially disadvantaged — as is currently the situation, for example, in the U.S. — by having to support privately financed religious schools. The options remaining include: publicly financed non-denominational schools, in which religious instruction is provided, and financed by, relevant religious groups. This is the option which the Irish Catholic hierarchy has repeatedly rejected as unacceptable.

Before discussing the relative merits of different educational arrangements, it is necessary to conclude the survey of the teaching on education from Vatican II. The educational policy of the Church is based on the child's assumed right to a Christian education; on the parents' limited right to educate children according to their consciences; and finally, on the Church's claim that the parents have an obligation to educate as the Church tells them to educate.

The Church reminds parents of the serious duty which is theirs of taking every opportunity — or of making the opportunity — for their children to be able to enjoy these helps and to pace their development as Christians with their growth as citizens of the world. . . . As for Catholic parents, the Council calls to mind their duty to entrust their children to Catholic schools, when and where this is possible, to support such schools to the extent of their ability, and to work along with them for the welfare of their children.[12]

The theological beliefs of the Church about itself and its mission provides a full circle of consistent beliefs in which the parent, and child, are entrapped by moral obligations. This is a paradigm of successful indoctrination.

One other set of rights and duties is also acknowledged by the Church:

In addition . . . to the rights of parents and of others to whom parents entrust a share in the work of education, certain rights and duties belong to civil society. For this society exists to arrange for the temporal necessities of the common good. Part of its duty is to promote the education of the young in several ways: namely, by overseeing the duties and rights of parents and of others who have a role in education, and by providing them with assistance; by implementing the principle of subsidiarity and completing the task of education, with attention to parental wishes, whenever the efforts of parents or of other groups are insufficient; and, moreover, by building its own schools and institutes, as the common good may demand.[13]

The 'principle of subsidiarity' refers to a principle, endorsed by Pope Pius XI in *Quadragesimo Anno*, to the effect that (in the case of education) the State should not assume the control of education if it can be adequately managed by a less comprehensive agency, such as a local community of parents or of citizens.

The role of the State is also limited by the Church's rejection of a homogeneous system of education imposed on all against their wishes:

[the State] must keep in mind the principle of subsidiarity, so that no kind of school monopoly arises. For such a monopoly would militate against the native rights of the human person, the development and spread of culture itself, the peaceful association of citizens, and the pluralism which exists today in many societies.[14]

It is not clear what would constitute a school monopoly in the Church's eyes. In the *Declaration on Religious Freedom*, the only monopoly which is rejected is one which excludes religious formation: 'the rights of parents are violated . . . if a single system of education, from which all religious formation is excluded, is imposed on all.'[15] The Church's objections to a 'single system' of education, while on the surface opposed to any inflexible homogeneity in school curricula, is in fact primarily aimed at non-religious, state schools. This is consistent with demanding freedom of conscience, and then explaining that concept only in terms of children being denied access to a religious education. Just as religious freedom implies that religion should not be imposed on students, so likewise the objections to a monopoly should equally be applied to a church monopoly of educational resources. In fact, the principle of subsidiarity would be satisfied even if there were only state schools which were organized and managed by local authorities. The Church's real objections are not to a monopoly, but to a state-run monopoly of secular education.

The same kind of qualifications which applied to the Church's theory of religious freedom, in Chapter 4 above, also apply to the Church's claims about education. These are ultimately religious claims, because they depend on religious beliefs and derive their plausibility for those who endorse them from the theological beliefs which are proposed, to be accepted on faith, for members of the Church. They are articulated within a religious tradition in which the borrowed philosophical elements may mask the extent to which, ultimately, these beliefs rest on religious faith. Before they can be accepted, therefore, as a policy for a democratic state, they must be subjected to the same kind of critical analysis which we normally demand for any other comprehensive theory of society. The Church's teaching, precisely because it is based on faith, has no immunity from rational criticism. The president of the U.S. Catholic Bishops Conference puts the same point like this:

. . . religious organizations should be subjected to the same standards of rational, rigorous presentation of their views as any other participant in the public debate. Moreover, religious organizations which address the moral dimensions of public issues are to be judged by the standards of competent moral analysis.[16]

It follows that it is unreasonable for any Christian to simply consult the beliefs of his own church and then demand that these beliefs be implemented in civil society. When challenged, it is not enough to say: we hold these truths, on faith!

Before confronting the larger issue, therefore, of the extent to which a society should respond to the religious demands of any particular church on the question of education, it is equally necessary to consult the tradition of Irish constitutional law and to briefly survey its implications for educational policy.

Education and the Constitution

The Constitution recognizes the educational rights of children, of the family, of the State, and (indirectly) of the Churches. It also goes some of the way towards detailing which of these rights are more fundamental than others.

The rights of the family are acknowledged in Articles 41 and 42. Article 41, section 1 (1°), states:

The State recognises the Family as the natural primary and fundamental unit group of Society, and as a moral institution possessing inalienable and imprescriptible rights, antecedent and superior to all positive law.

Since these fundamental rights of the family are not explicitly mentioned, it is reasonable to interpret Article 42 as an articulation of one such 'antecedent' right, especially in the light of the similar language in which it is expressed. Article 42 reads:

1. The state acknowledges that the primary and natural educator of the child is the Family and guarantees to respect the inalienable right and duty of parents to provide, according to their means, for the religious, and moral, intellectual, physical and social education of their children.

2. Parents shall be free to provide this education in their homes or in private schools or in schools recognised or established by the State.

3. 1° The State shall not oblige parents in violation of their conscience and (in Irish: *nó*) lawful preference to send their children to schools established by the State, or to any particular type of school designated by the State.
   2° The State shall, however, as guardian of the common good, require in view of actual conditions that the children receive a certain minimum education, moral, intellectual and social.

Besides the family, which is obviously given more explicit mention in the Constitution's treatment of education than any other relevant party, children are also recognized as having fundamental rights. Article 42, section 5 directly addresses the role of the State in education and, almost as an afterthought, adds a qualification about the rights of children:

In exceptional cases, where the parents for physical or moral reasons fail in their duty towards their children, the State as guardian of the common good, by appropriate means shall endeavour to supply the place of the parents, but always with due regard for the natural and imprescriptible rights of the child.

The rights of children could just as easily be based on the implicitly guaranteed rights of Article 40, section 3, 1°:

The State guarantees in its laws to respect, and, as far as practicable, by its laws to defend and vindicate the personal rights of the citizen.

The young child is, for purposes of natural rights, as much a person as parents are, and therefore the child enjoys all those natural rights which are implicitly protected by Article 40, section 3. Among the child's rights are a right to a minimal education, understood broadly enough to include the non-academic training which is a pre-requisite for maturation into a competent adult. The educational rights of the child have been recognized and endorsed by a number of court decisions. For example, the Chief Justice, in *G.* v. *An Bord Uchtála*, argued:

The child also has natural rights. Normally these will be safe under the care and protection of the mother. Having been born the child has the right to be fed and to live, to be reared and educated, to have the opportunity of working and of realising his or her full personality and dignity as a human being. These rights of the child and others which I have not enumerated must equally be protected and vindicated by the State. The State, under the provisions of Article 42, section 5 of the Constitution, in exceptional cases is given the duty as guardian of the common good to provide for a child born into a family where the parents for physical or moral reasons fail in their duty towards that child. In the same way, in my view, in special circumstances, in relation to a child born outside the family, the State may have an equal obligation to protect that child even against its mother, if her natural rights are used in such a way as to endanger the health or life of the child or to deprive him of his rights. In my view this obligation stems from the provisions of Article 40, section 3 of the Constitution.[17]

The articulation of children's rights to education depends on further constitutional cases in which the relative importance of conflicting rights are decided by the courts. It is important to notice, however, that children are constitutionally guaranteed, in Article 44, section 2, 4°, the right to attend publicly funded schools without attending religious instruction in such schools. The text of this subsection is quoted below.

Together with the family and children, the state also has a constitutional role in education. Article 42, section 3, 2°, and sections 4 and 5 read:

3. 2° The State shall, however, as guardian of the common good, require in view of actual conditions that the children receive a certain minimum education, moral, intellectual and social.

4. The State shall provide for free primary education and shall endeavour to supplement and give reasonable aid to private and corporate educational initiative, and, when the public good requires it, provide other educational facilities or institutions with due regard, however, for the right of parents, especially in the matter of religious and moral formation.

5. In exceptional cases, where the parents for physical or moral reasons fail in their duty towards their children, the state as guardian of the common good, by appropriate means shall endeavour to supply the place of the parents, but always with due regard for the natural and imprescriptible rights of the child.

Before commenting on the constitutional rights of the state in education, it is appropriate to look at Article 44, in which religious groups are acknowledged as having a right to operate private schools. Article 44, section 2, 4°, 5° and 6° reads:

4° Legislation providing State aid for schools shall not discriminate between schools under the management of different religious denominations, nor be such as to affect prejudicially the right of any child to attend a school receiving public money without attending religious instruction at that school.

5° Every religious denomination shall have the right to manage its own affairs, own, acquire and administer property, movable and immovable, and maintain institutions for religious or charitable purposes.

6° The property of any religious denomination or any educational institution shall not be diverted save for necessary works of public utility and on payment of compensation.

There are two rather different kinds of issue raised by this survey of constitutional provisions: (1) one of them concerns the interpretation of the texts, insofar as this has been already decided by the courts or is likely to be judicially decided in the near future. For such an inquiry, Court decisions provide the evidence, and legal training the appropriate interpretative expertise. This kind of issue is only briefly discussed in this section as a prelude to the subsequent range of issues. (2) The second question is concerned with how Irish educational facilities ought to be structured in a way which is consistent with the Constitution, so as to respect the rights of all the citizens in a less confessional atmosphere than that which has plagued Irish education for close to two centuries. This question will be taken up in conjunction with the earlier discussion of Church policy, under 'Church and State' below.

The educational rights of the Family (Article 41, 1; Article 42, 1), or of parents (Article 42, sections 2-5), raise a number of questions. For example, who is included under the term 'family' or 'parents'? Which rights are protected? And to what extent may these rights yield to the rights of others, such as those of children, the State or the churches? The parents of an illegitimate child, together with the child, do not constitute a family in the sense in which this term is used in the Constitution.[18] However, a married couple and their legitimated child is a family, as is a single parent and child whose legal relationship is based on a prior marriage of the surviving parent to the other parent of the child.[19] Thus, Justice Henchy in *G* v. *An Bord Uchtála*, in reference to Article 42, section 5:

The natural and imprescriptible rights there referred to are those of a child whose parents have married (thereby creating a family in the constitutional sense), and those rights necessarily comprehend the religious and moral, intellectual, physical and social education of the child.[20]

Of course the fact that the rights included in Article 42, 5 are limited to families in a narrow sense does not imply that children who do not belong to such families lose any of the constitutional rights which they would otherwise enjoy.[21]

The educational rights of the family do not extend to a controlling influence on everything which is involved in the development of a child. Thus, in *Ryan* v. *Attorney General*, the fluoridation of drinking water was judged to fall outside the scope of 'education', although it is evidently something which is arranged by State authorities in the interests of the child's health (among others).[22] 'Education', therefore, should be understood as limited to the moral, religious and vocational or academic development of a child, or more generally, to all those factors in the maturation of a child which depend on the co-operation of the child responding, with characteristic human actions, to the influence of others. It does not include any features of the child's development which depend exclusively on unintentional responses of the child. If the State can constitutionally intervene to control many citizens' exclusive source of drinking water, it follows that the State could likewise intervene to facilitate the healthy development of children by means which do not normally fall under the scope of 'education', such as the provision of other compulsory medical services. Whether or not such arrangements are constitutional would obviously depend on what precisely is at issue; whatever it is, it would most probably not fall within the scope of the family's right to 'educate' the child.

The rights of the family are said to be inalienable, imprescriptible, and antecedent to all positive law. Insofar as the constitutional rights of the child can be construed as so-called 'natural' rights, they could be described in exactly the same way. Thus no conclusion follows from the fact that the child's rights are less prominent in the text of the Constitution. The articulation of constitutional law 'in the best interests' of children is a relatively recent development in Ireland.[23] To the extent that the rights of children are expanded, under the scope of Article 40, section 3, the rights of parents must, on occasion, cede to those of their children. Thus Justice Walsh, in *G.* v. *An Bord Uchtála*: 'There is nothing in the Constitution to indicate that in cases of conflict the rights of the parent are

always to be given primacy.'[24] Since the parents' or family's rights are
not absolute, it follows that 'inalienable' and 'imprescriptible' must be
understood relative to the rights of others. Therefore, if parents attempt
to exercise their rights to the detriment of their children, there is no constitutional impediment to a court intervention to protect the latter's
rights.[25]

It follows that the rights of parents cannot be appealed to as if they
were the exclusive and decisive factor in arranging educational facilities
for young citizens. Children also have rights, even if they are not aware
of them, and even if they do not claim their rights in court.[26] Therefore
the courts may constitutionally intervene to protect such rights, against
the express wish of even a majority of parents. There is nothing strange
in this conclusion; a majority of parents in a limited class are as liable to
be wrong about the best interests of their children as, more generally, a
majority of the electorate may be mistaken in supporting legislation
which is unconstitutional.

The 'natural and imprescriptible rights of the child' have to be protected by the courts in the light of current, plausible views about what is
in the best interests of the child.[27] It would be totally implausible for the
courts to argue that children have a natural right to everything which is in
their best interests. Just as the rights of adult citizens are often practically
limited by economic or social factors, so likewise the best interests of
children can only be realized relative to the resources actually available in
a given community. However, in discussing rights in Chapter 6 above, I
argued that there may be agreed lower limits to the negative rights of
citizens. Children are beneficiaries of negative rights just as much as
adults. There is therefore a more serious obligation on relevant parties —
in the first place, the parents; and if they default, the State — to prevent
significant harm to children, than to positively provide everything which
might be plausibly construed as being in their best interests. The courts
have generally favoured the hypothesis that the rights of children are best
protected when they are left in the custody and care of their parents, and
when the parents are allowed a rather extensive discretion in arranging
for their education. This assumption may be defeated by counter-
evidence. In such cases, the State has the constitutional right and duty to
compensate for the parents' default.

The constitutional status of religious education is unclear in the text of
the Constitution. When the family's rights are spelled out in Article 42,
section 1, they extend to 'the religious and moral, intellectual, physical

and social education of their children'. In section 4 of the same article, 'religious and moral formation' is identified as being peculiarly the province of parents, even when their children are attending State organized educational institutions. Finally, Section 3, 1° highlights the 'conscience' of parents as a limit to the State's attempts to educate children in public schools:

The State shall not oblige parents in violation of their conscience and (in Irish: *nó*) lawful preference to send their children to schools established by the State, or to any particular type of schools designated by the State.

One could imagine clear examples of what would directly conflict with this subsection of Article 42. For example, if the Department of Education arranged that all the schools in the State must come under its direct authority and if the Oireachtas then passed a law which purported to oblige all children in the state to attend these schools, that would contravene the guarantee given in the Constitution.[28] The interesting questions arise when one focuses on the other end of the scale, namely: on the limits, if any, to the use of conscience clauses by parents to avail of the guarantee which is given in the Constitution. 'Lawful preference' might be explicated as: 'preference which is consistent with the law'. Since the law is established by the Oireachtas, within constitutional limits, this hardly provides an independent constitutional limit on the educational policies of the State. 'Conscience', however, does seem to provide precisely that; a veto power, given to parents, on whatever educational arrangements might be made by the State. The discussion thus far implies that the rights of parents/family are not absolute, relative to those of the child, and that the claimed rights of parents might be set aside 'in the best interests' of the child. The conscience clause would have to be understood in a similarly relative manner. Otherwise parents would be implicitly granted an absolute veto on the State's educational initiatives on behalf of children, since parents could always plausibly claim that it is against their conscience to allow their children to be educated in a particular way or, indeed, to be educated at all. If the conscience-based policy of a particular family — no matter how authentic or religious it is — could be seen to cause harm to their children (as 'harm' is normally understood by the standards of the community), then the family's conscience would be no more constitutionally defended than similar conscience-based objections to, for example, medical treatment of minor children.

In fact, the argument against the role of conscience is even stronger than that. The State's interest in educating (young) citizens is not based exclusively on its vicarious duties towards defaulting parents. Both sections 3 and 5 of Article 42 indicate that the State is guardian of the common good. While the 'common good' is not a very clear concept, nonetheless it is not empty either. The common good could plausibly be said to require the inculcation of various social virtues and the acquisition of moral standards. These are required, not just for the benefit of individuals, but also for the sake of other members of society. Therefore the State has a positive interest, constitutionally protected, in seeing that the relevant social virtues are acquired by citizens. For this reason, it has a constitutional right to establish minimal requirements for what may count as an adequate education. The State's right to educate, therefore, is based on three different considerations:

a) its duty to vicariously fulfil the duties of parents, when they default;
b) its duty to defend and protect the rights of children, even against the possibly explicit opposition of parents;
c) its claim to require certain social virtues as necessary prerequisites for living in society.

These diverse interests of the State are implicit in the Constitution's injunction on relevant State authorities, to provide for primary education: 'the State shall provide for free primary education . . .'.[29]

The potential conflict between the parents' religious beliefs and the claim of the State to enforce a minimal educational standard has been addressed in a number of recent U.S. Supreme Court decisions, most notably in *Wisconsin* v. *Yoder*.[30] A state law obliged parents to send their minor children to school until they reached their sixteenth birthday. Members of the Amish religion, however, were unwilling to allow their children to attend formal schools beyond the eighth grade because the values which their children acquired at school were contrary to their religious beliefs. The Court decided in favour of the parents, partly because the case only involved two years of schooling:

The conclusion is inescapable that secondary schooling, by exposing the Amish children to worldly influences in terms of attitudes, goals, and values contrary to beliefs, and by substantially interfering with the religious development of the Amish child and his integration into the way of life of the Amish faith community at the crucial adolescent stage of development, contravenes the basic religious tenets and practice of the Amish faith, both as to the parent and the child.

In a concurring opinion, Justice White wrote:

This would be a very different case for me if respondents' claim were that their religion forbade their children from attending any school at any time and from complying in any way with the educational standards set by the State.[31]

In reaching a decision the Court recognized that the religious objections of the parents must be balanced against the state's interest in requiring a minimum of education for young citizens. The fact that Amish parents provided a less formal education during adolescence for their children, and that they would only miss two of the compulsory years at school required by the state of Wisconsin, helped tilt the balance in the parents' favour.

Finally, the Irish Constitution recognizes a definite role for religious institutions in the provision of educational facilities. This implicit recognition is integrated into an Article which is primarily concerned with religious freedom. Article 44, section 2 reads:

Freedom of conscience and the free profession and practice of religion are, subject to public order and morality, guaranteed to every citizen.

Since freedom of conscience is guaranteed to every citizen, the State guarantees not to 'impose any disabilities or make any discrimination on the ground of religious profession, belief or status' (Article 44, 2, 3°). This obviously means both that those who hold religious beliefs, and those who hold none, will be treated equally by the educational arrangements of the State. This subsection applies both to adults and to children. The freedom of conscience of children is made even more explicit in sub-section 4°, which protects the 'right of any child to attend a school receiving public money without attending religious instruction at that school'. It would seem to be the literal meaning and clear implication of this constitutional guarantee that the religious belief, or lack of it, of any child is irrelevant as a factor in determining admission to schools 'receiving public money'. If any school receiving public money tried to determine the religious beliefs of an applicant with a view, for example, to maintaining the religious tradition of the school, it thereby prejudicially affects the constitutional rights of the child. The implications of this are examined in more detail below. The constitutional rights of churches must be noted first.

Churches or religious groups are guaranteed two rights in Article 44: (i) the right to own and operate a private school; and (ii) the right to an

equitable share of any public money which is made available for
denominational schools. The former right is implicit in Article 44, 2,
subsections 5 and 6. Subsection 5 guarantees 'the right to . . . own, acquire and administer property . . . and maintain institutions for
religious or charitable purposes.' While this does not explicitly include
'educational' purposes, the following subsection reads: 'The property of
any religious denomination or any educational institution shall not be
diverted . . .' However, as already mentioned in Chapter 6 above, these
subsections are technically redundant. Those citizens who are 'religious'
have exactly the same property rights under the Constitution as any other
citizen. And since the Constitution also guarantees that no parents shall
be obliged to send their children to State schools, it follows logically that
private groups of citizens, religious or otherwise, have a constitutional
right to found and manage a private school, on condition that it satisfies
those minimal educational standards which are required in the interests
both of the child and of the State. Thus the churches are not recognized
as such, in the Constitution, as having any special role in education, except insofar as they provide a service which is requested by parents or
students. The Irish Constitution is silent on the Catholic Church's claim
that it has a unique, theologically based, role in education.

The other right which is guaranteed to the churches is a hypothetical
one; it only comes into force if and when legislation provides state aid for
private schools. Article 44, section 2, 4°, guarantees that if the State provides public financing for private schools, then it must do so in a way
which does not discriminate between different religious denominations.
The most obvious implication of this guarantee is that the State should
equitably fund a variety of religious schools, if it funds them at all; the
less obvious implication is that the State should equally fund non-
religious schools which are managed by private groups of citizens. Otherwise the State is in breach of Article 44, 2, 3° which reads: 'The State
shall not impose *any* disabilities or make *any* discrimination on the
ground of religious profession, beliefs or status.'[32] This result is consistent with the discussion of pluralism in Chapter 3 above. The universality
of the term 'any' must be understood literally. Those who hold particular
religious beliefs, and those who hold none, must be treated in exactly the
same way by the State. To do otherwise is equivalent to establishing
special rights for religious believers, which is also contrary to Article 44,
2, 2°: 'The State guarantees not to endow any religion.'

The constitutional theory which is reflected in these provisions of the

Constitution is relatively clear on the following points.

(1)   Negatively, that the State will not establish an educational monopoly and compel children to attend schools operated by the State.

(2)   That parents have fundamental rights in determining the education of their minor children; however, it is not explicit on how these rights may have to yield to the rights of children.

(3)   That children have rights which can be understood as natural rights, and therefore they must be protected under Article 40, section 3. The rights of children and of parents are both more fundamental than the rights of the State in education.

(4)   Citizens have a right to religious liberty. This applies explicitly to children. The right to religious liberty protects citizens from a monopoly of secular schools from which all religious instruction is precluded, and equally from the opposite abuse: any coercion of children to attend religious instruction in schools, or any more subtle attempts to determine their religious beliefs.

(5)   Churches, as such, have the same rights as any other organization of citizens; they have no special constitutional role in education.

(6)   The State has a right and duty to determine a minimum level of education for all minor children in the state. It also has a duty to provide for primary education in a manner which respects the rights of children and parents.

(7)   The constitutional rights of citizens are not limited to those which are explicitly mentioned in the text of the Constitution. Therefore, the implications of the Constitution for education remain to be determined, to a large extent, by future court decisions.

(8)   The State may not endow any religion.

Education: Church and State

The policy of the Churches in education is determined by the religious or theological beliefs of the churches about their own mission. Since these theological beliefs are almost indefinitely variable, and since they are not necessarily subject to the standard criteria of rational belief, it would be unacceptable to anyone who is committed to human rights that the education of children be uncritically delivered into the exclusive control of different religious communities or churches. The mere fact that one's belief can be plausibly described as 'religious' does nothing to establish its validity, nor does it grant one immunity from responsibility for the effects on others of one's religion-inspired actions. In any human society in which decisions are fallibly made in the light of the best evidence available, religion cannot be used as an excuse to avoid the critical scrutiny of rational investigation.

The outside observer of Irish educational development, especially at primary and secondary level, is tempted to conclude that the churches want to control education because they wish to determine the religious and moral beliefs of citizens. On closer inspection of the policy of the majority church, it becomes apparent that this conclusion is consistent with the explicit educational policy of that Church. This objective — of ideological control — is realised through indoctrination.

By 'indoctrination' here is meant: causally determining the beliefs of another through non-rational procedures. The qualification 'non-rational' bears the main burden of this explanation, and it would require a much longer philosophical discussion, for its defence, than can be advanced here. However, the point of the distinction between 'rational' and 'non-rational' can be appreciated from a few examples. The paradigm of rational assent is exemplified in those cases where one understands adequately some proposed belief; where one has access to, and understands, the evidence in its favour; where one has been equally informed of whatever significant evidence counts against the belief; and finally, where one understands the connection between the (possibly conflicting) evidence and the proposed belief. In these cases, one tries to match one's degree of commitment, in some belief, to the evidence in its favour. 'Rationality' is therefore primarily concerned with the way in which one acquires one's beliefs, not with their ultimate truth or plausibility. Beliefs are only rationally held to the extent that — given the age, competence, etc. of the believer — the believer has an adequate opportunity of appropriately doubting, testing or questioning proposed beliefs, and then deciding in the light of criteria which can be independently justified as rational.

The opposite to a rational acceptance of beliefs is any procedure which precludes the possibility of doubting, testing, etc., as may seem appropriate. It is to acquire beliefs by by-passing the route which leads from an examination of the relevant evidence to a justified degree of belief. This too brief analysis of 'rational' can easily degenerate into a caricature, if it seems to imply that we must systematically test and evaluate every belief, no matter how trivial, with all the rigour of a convinced sceptic. The caricature is avoided by recognizing that, for many beliefs, indirect evidence will do; when we ask for directions in a strange city, we rationally assume (most of the time!) that we are not being intentionally misled by an unofficial guide.

If the distinction between 'rational' and 'non-rational' assent were adequately analysed, it would be relatively easy to argue that the assent of children to religious beliefs is non-rational. However, one might object that nearly all the beliefs of children are non-rationally acquired, and therefore that one should not isolate religious beliefs for special mention. This is clearly not the case, especially in the case of young teenagers. The beliefs of children about their parents and teachers, about their playmates, and about a great variety of things is determined by their own experience. In those cases in which we think it appropriate to inculcate beliefs which they do not rationally endorse, we also assume that the beliefs are such that they can, in time, be rationally adopted or rejected by the children. We also assume that the interim period of non-rational assent is important enough to justify the recourse (on our part) to paternalistic indoctrination. Religious belief does not fall into either category. It is evidently acquired non-rationally by children; they do not understand what they believe; they do not have access to whatever might count as evidence for or against their religious beliefs; and they do not appreciate the alleged relationship between the evidence and the beliefs in question. Besides, once they mature and their religious beliefs are subjectively entrenched, there is no evidence which could count, definitively, against their beliefs. One can only endorse or abandon them.

Given the special status of theological beliefs, there is an obvious advantage for whoever first indoctrinates the young child. If one could get young children to accept, on faith, the beliefs of some church, then one could hope that at least the majority of them, on maturing, would maintain some kind of residual allegiance to the church into which they were originally initiated. The coincidence of religious beliefs between parents and children, or between children and the society in which they mature, would be inexplicable on any other account.

The indoctrination of religious beliefs is more successful to the extent to which the subjects are protected from alien influences. Such protection might be provided in a number of different ways. One might develop special schools in which religious beliefs are consistently inculcated and integrated into a wider curriculum. Or one might adopt the Amish strategy and refuse to allow young religious believers to be 'contaminated' by the secular beliefs of their peers in society. On establishing and controlling relevant schools, one might help guarantee enrolment by compelling parents, under the threat of serious moral obligation, to send their children to the religious school and to financially support it. The 'theology' of education could be filled in, as is evident in the opening section of this chapter, in terms of the theological rights of children, the moral obligations of parents and children, and the consequent rights of the churches to respond to the educational needs of children and parents. More generally, one might attempt to control not only the school and family environment of children up to the age of majority. One might also attempt to control the wider environment in which both parents and children are likely not to be challenged in their religious beliefs. This could be done by persistent political pressure, both publicly and privately, to censor any opinions, ideas or publications which might jeopardize the controlling interest of the churches. The whole enterprise smacks of theological totalitarianism; and that is exactly what it is.

One's picture of totalitarianism is sometimes coloured by less subtle efforts of some governments to control the beliefs of citizens. However, totalitarianism is not a question of relative subtlety in the way in which the objective is achieved. It is a question of the attempt at total control of citizens, preferably by controlling their beliefs. The objections of the Roman Catholic Church to a State monopoly of schools are well taken on this point; a free society should not endorse such a monopoly in the hands of church or state. It might be objected that what characterizes many totalitarian regimes is the resistance of the population to measures which are imposed against their will, whereas most parents in Ireland are satisfied with the churches' influence in school management. There are two obvious replies to this: (i) many totalitarian governments have succeeded in winning a majority of the electorate to support their measures; and (ii) Irish educational history has not been remarkable for giving parents a genuine alternative to, or even a real influence in, the schools managed by the churches. One chooses freely when given a real alternative to a structure which otherwise only invites endorsement or rejection.

The totalitarian objectives of the churches in Ireland are implemented in their almost total monopoly of primary schools; in their control of teacher-training colleges; in their control of many secondary schools; and in their exclusion of parents — in whose place they vicariously fulfil the primary duty and right of parents to educate — from any real influence in the management of schools. This totalitarianism is a function of a basic value-judgment which explains their paternalistic exclusion of parents from education; namely, the choice of truth (as taught by the churches) rather than the autonomy of potential believers.

The Roman Catholic Church is the best example of this teaching. It puts a premium on children and parents holding the 'correct' beliefs — where 'correct' is understood by reference to the Church's beliefs — rather than on the kind of autonomy or freedom which would characterize the rational appropriation of beliefs; it endorses church-managed education over other alternatives in a situation of genuine choice. Such an attitude betrays an acute understanding of the dynamics of religious belief. It is because the churches realize that belief is ultimately non-rational, and therefore best determined by early indoctrination, that they cannot afford to leave religious belief to the vagaries of adult choice. Most people are born into a religious tradition rather than converted to it. Once this is understood, one must choose between the autonomy of free agents, exercised in the well-informed choices of adults, or the success rate in causing people to hold the beliefs one would wish them to hold, however they come to acquire them initially. The Church objects to adult indoctrination; it castigates as reprehensible any conversion techniques which take advantage of the poor or uneducated. A similar argument can be advanced to support the corresponding conclusion for children: it is based on the citizen's constitutional right to religious liberty.

As already indicated above, the Irish Constitution recognizes the 'natural and imprescriptible rights of the child'. This is explicit in Article 42; it is implicit in the guarantee of natural rights of Article 40, Section 3, at least in the way in which this has been understood by the courts since *Ryan* v. *Attorney General*. The Constitution also acknowledges the 'freedom of conscience' of every citizen, including children. It explicitly protects the rights of children not to attend religious instruction in a school receiving public money. The rights of children are normally claimed, on their behalf, by parents or guardians; however, children may also have rights even against the explicit choice of their parents. If one were to consider what these rights are, one might look to criteria which identify what is central to the concept of a human person, as understood in Western political theory. Freedom of thought, and freedom of conscience are central to this tradition. Therefore, children should enjoy such freedoms to the extent to which they are competent to exercise these rights. This competence hardly arrives in its totality on their eighteenth birthday. The kind of competence involved is gradually acquired in growing up, and the rights which presuppose it for their exercise might therefore be invoked long before reaching the age of legal maturity. It does not follow that, before reaching an age when one's freedom of conscience must be legally respected, parents or guardians might conspire to determine the religious beliefs of a young citizen. The opposite would seem to be implied; namely, that parents, the State and other relevant authorities should protect the developing autonomy of the individual from the overpowering influence of religious indoctrination, in anticipation of freely made religious choices in later life. As K. Henley has argued;

> . . . it makes no sense to say that a child is born, for instance, with religious liberty, but that the child's parents have a protected liberty to coerce the older child to fulfill the religious obligations which the parents choose for him. . . . If we are to say that children are born with liberties, then they are neither mere creatures of the state nor mere creatures of the state and the parents combined.[33]

This is not an argument against religious schools. It is only an argument against a monopoly of religious schools. The constitutional rights of a minor to freedom of conscience can only be protected and defended in an atmosphere in which alternatives to a rigorous religious tradition are made available, especially to young citizens.

Irish courts have already recognized that children have natural or constitutional rights, and they have often been guided in their decisions by constitutional developments in the U.S. If one examines relevant U.S. Court decisions during the last two decades it is immediately apparent that the Courts have squarely confronted the issue of a potential conflict between parents' rights and children's rights.[34] The right of a minor to freedom of thought and freedom of religion is central to this development.

The First Amendment begins as follows: 'Congress shall make no law respecting an establishment of religion, or prohibiting the free exercise thereof.' This is usually understood as involving an Establishment Clause and a Free Exercise Clause; the former is discussed in more detail below, while the implications of the Free Exercise Clause are examined here.

In *Tinker* v. *Des Moines School District* the U.S. Supreme Court ruled:

> First Amendment rights, applied in light of the special circumstances of the school environment, are available to teachers and to students. It can hardly be

argued that either students or teachers shed their constitutional rights to freedom of speech or expression at the schoolhouse gate.

Students in school as well as out of school are 'persons' under our Constitution. They are possessed of fundamental rights which the State must respect, just as they themselves must respect their obligations to the State.[35]

Young students are therefore entitled to First Amendment protection in their religious beliefs, which was also accepted in *Prince* v. *Massachusetts*.[36] However, this protection has usually been accorded to children on the basis of their parents' or guardian's claim to religious freedom in educating children. The question inevitably arises: why should parents (or guardians) have a right to determine the child's religious belief, especially in the case of older children, when the First Amendment guarantees religious freedom for *individuals* against all others? This issue was raised by Mr. Justice Douglas, in a partly dissenting opinion in *Wisconsin* v. *Yoder:*

The Court's analysis assumes that the only interests at stake in the case are those of the Amish parents on the one hand, and those of the State on the other. The difficulty with this approach is that despite the Court's claim, the parents are seeking to vindicate not only their own free exercise claims but also those of their high-school-age children. . . . If the parents in this case are allowed a religious exemption, the inevitable effect is to impose the parents' notions of religious duty upon their children. Where the child is mature enough to express potentially conflicting desires, it would be an invasion of the child's rights to permit such an imposition without canvassing his views.[37]

Justice Douglas appealed to an earlier decision of the Court, *West Virginia Board of Education* v. *Barnette*,[38] in which compulsory saluting of the U.S. flag in school was ruled to be unconstitutional insofar as it attempted to coerce the beliefs of children through an obligatory symbolic action. If every citizen has a constitutionally protected right to religious liberty, it follows that an intentional and systematic attempt to limit this freedom is unconstitutional. There is no need to show that a particular religious indoctrination causes some determinate and independently specifiable harm to a given child; it is rather that *any* indoctrination causes the harm of a denial of fundamental rights.

The mechanism by which this basic right is protected might vary with the age and relative competence of a child. Whereas in many cases depriving a child of fundamental rights, such as freedom of speech or assembly, is less harmful than a similar deprivation of an adult; in the case of religious indoctrination, the opposite is the case. Indoctrination is more effective in inverse proportion to the age and maturity of the subject, as the Chief Justice of the U.S. Supreme Court observed in *Tilton* v. *Richardson*.[39] Hence a greater care needs to be exercised in the case of young citizens than in the case of the more mature. It seems to follow that any systematic religious indoctrination in primary schools is unconstitutional, on this ground alone, whereas a critical exposure to different religious traditions at secondary school level would be less obviously a threat to the rights of the child.

This conclusion would hold, even if a majority of the electorate chose otherwise. This was made explicit in the *Barnette* decision:

The very purpose of a Bill of Rights was to withdraw certain subjects from the vicissitudes of political controversy, to place them beyond the reach of majorities and officials and to establish them as legal principles to be applied by the courts. One's right to . . . freedom of worship . . . and other fundamental rights may not be submitted to vote; they depend on the outcome of no elections.[40]

This brief survey of U.S. cases has obvious and direct application to Ireland. It is simply inconsistent to grant children constitutional rights, and then to arrange a system of education in which one of their most fundamental rights is systematically ignored. Just as the Free exercise Clause of the First Amendment protects U.S. children from any kind of systematic indoctrination of religious or political beliefs in schools (or elsewhere), so likewise the constitutional guarantees of freedom of conscience and religious freedom of the Irish Constitution should protect Irish children from the probable effects of a system of education which leaves them subject, with the parents' consent in most cases, to the systematic indoctrination of the churches.

There is another argument against a virtual monopoly of primary schools in church control. This derives from the constitutional rights of non-believers. There is a subtle but obvious difference between denying rights to citizens, and making it almost impossible for them to exercise their rights. Article 40, section 3, commits the State to actively defending the rights of individuals:

The State guarantees in its laws to respect, and, as far as practicable, by its laws to defend and vindicate the personal rights of the citizen.

The educational rights of children who are non-believers, or of parents who are nominally religious but opposed to church schools, are currently frustrated by a policy of collusion between the churches and the State. One might reply that those children are guaranteed their rights in Article 44, section 2, 4°; however, such a guarantee is useless in a context in which religious schools, supervised by teachers who are trained by religious teacher-training centres, are the only option available to the majority of students in the State. Any child who is different is ostracized in a society in which all his or her peers are at least nominally religious. This may look like a claim that all the schools in the state should be adjusted to suit the preferences of a small percentage of students who are stubbornly holding out against the obvious benefits of religious belief. But this is an attitude that we are coming to question in most other questions; should public transport be adjusted to suit a relatively small percentage of disabled people? Should the laws and courts take such time and effort to protect the constitutional rights of convicts, a small percentage of the population? Should a large share of medical resources be dedicated to the care of the terminally ill, who are only a small percentage of the population? What is at stake is not the number of citizens involved, but whether or not they have rights which are enshrined in the Constitution and then ignored in practice in the educational policies of the State. The rights of non-religious citizens fall into this category.

A third argument against the virtual church monopoly of primary school education derives from Article 44, 2, 2°: 'The State guarantees not to endow any religion.' This article compares with the *Government of Ireland Act*, 1920, section 5, and the *Irish Free State (Agreement) Act*, 1922.[41] The former is more explicit on the distinction between 'establishment' and 'endowment':

In the exercise of their power to make laws under this Act neither the Parliament of Southern Ireland nor the Parliament of Northern Ireland shall make a law so as either directly or indirectly to establish or endow any religion, or prohibit or restrict the free exercise thereof, or give a preference, privilege, or advantage, or impose disability or disadvantage, on account of religious belief . . .

The fundamental objection to the State endowing any religious enterprise is that it thereby chooses to foster and support one religion, or a select number of religions, to the detriment of alternative beliefs. It therefore fails to observe the kind of neutrality with respect to religious belief which is essential to the religious liberty of citizens. This line of argument is made clear by the opinion of Justice Douglas in *Abington School District* v. *Schempp*.[42] In this case, a Pennsylvania law required some Bible reading at the beginning of each school day, from which individual students could be excused on producing a request from their parents. In overturning the Pennsylvania statute, the Court held: 'In the relationship between man and religion, the State is firmly committed to a position of neutrality'.[43] Justice Douglas explained, in a concurring opinion:

Establishment of a religion can be achieved in several ways. . . . The vice of all such arrangements under the Establishment Clause is that the state is lending its assistance to a church's efforts to gain and keep adherents. Under the First Amendment it is strictly a matter for the individual and his church as to what church he will belong to and how much support, in the way of belief, time, activity or money, he will give it.

. . . The most effective way to establish any institution is to finance it; and this truth is reflected in the appeals by church groups for public funds to finance their religious schools.[44]

The neutrality of the state with respect to religion was often reaffirmed by U.S. Courts, for example, in *Epperson* v. *Arkansas:*

Government in our democracy, state and national, must be neutral in matters of religious theory, doctrine, and practice. It may not be hostile to any religion or to the advocacy of no-religion; and it may not aid, foster, or promote one religion or religious theory against another or even against the militant opposite. The First Amendment mandates governmental neutrality between religion and religion and between religion and non-religion.[45]

The state's neutrality is required in the interests of religious liberty. Just as it would infringe the individual's rights if he were coerced to believe, or not believe, against his will, so likewise it infringes the religious liberty of individuals if the state uses its resources to help determine, in any way, the religious or non-religious beliefs of citizens. To respect the individual's liberty requires the state to mind its own business, to allow believers and non-believers alike to determine their own beliefs without any direct or indirect attempt on the part of state officials to influence the individual's free choice. This principle is obvious in the case of those states which actively foster beliefs which *we* think are mistaken. A consistent theory of religious liberty requires that the same principle apply even in the case of those religious beliefs which we may consider to be 'true'.

The Irish Constitution's injunction against state endowment of any religion is hardly compatible with direct and indirect financing for religious schools at primary and secondary level and, at the third level, of a Roman Catholic seminary.[46] The effect of such financing is to help causally determine the religious beliefs of citizens, and thereby to infringe on their constitutionally guaranteed freedom of religious belief. If the churches deny the causal influence of state support of religious indoctrination, then why do they continue to defend it so vehemently? One can only assume that the churches know that state support for religious schools and a virtual church monopoly of primary schools will significantly determine the eventual religious beliefs of a majority of citizens in the state. This, precisely, is what offends the constitutional right to religious liberty. If Soviet schools more or less uniformly indoctrinate their students with a particular political ideology, we are not surprised at the relative uniformity of political belief which results in young adult Soviets; in that case, the Church objects to the secular monopoly of schools.[47] The churches in Ireland assume exactly the same sociological principle as the proponents of ideological homogeneity in any other society. They know that the control of schools will determine the religious beliefs of citizens, in their favour, in a way which is far superior to any preaching or attempts at conversion which are directed to adults.

One might argue, in defence of current state policy, that this is what the majority of parents want. However, this kind of argument does not justify the conclusion which it is meant to support, for the following reasons.

There are few cases in recent years where parents were actually consulted as regards their choice of school. In some cases where they did have such a choice, they opted against a denominational school.

Secondly, constitutional matters are matters of basic principle rather than merely of majority choice. Evidently, one needs a majority of the electorate to endorse the basic principles which are enunciated by a constitution. On the other hand, there are many cases in recent Irish constitutional history in which the electorate, through a majority of their representatives in the Oireachtas, supported legislation which was unconstitutional. One could confessionalize the Constitution even more than it is at present and ratify the endowment of religion; but one can hardly maintain that religion shall *not* be endowed and at the same time systematically channel almost all the finances available for primary education into religious schools which explicitly claim that the teaching of religion is their primary purpose. The Rules for National School (1965), state:

Of all the parts of a school curriculum Religious Instruction is by far the most important, as its subject-matter, God's honour and service, includes the proper use of all man's faculties, and affords the most powerful inducements to their proper use. Religious instruction is, therefore, a fundamental part of the school course, and a religious spirit should inform and vivify the whole work of the school.[48]

Thirdly, the integration of state financing with religious schools is not the official teaching of the Roman Catholic Church. It is, rather, the peculiarly conservative and obstructive stance of the Irish Church. Where political experience has been different, the Church has applied different standards. Thus, Archbishop John Roach, president of the National Catholic Conference of Catholic Bishops in the U.S., openly supports the separation of church and state:

I agree fully with the principle of separation of church and state . . . The Western constitutional tradition embodies the judgment that the state is a part of society, and not to be identified with all of society. Beyond the state is a realm of free political activity where individuals and groups act to give content to the fabric of social life. On the basis of this distinction between state and society, a twofold affirmation can be made about the church's role in society. On the one hand, Catholic theology can and should support and defend the separation of church and state, the principle that religious organizations should expect neither favoritism nor discrimination because they are religious. On the other hand, we should not accept or allow the separation of church and state to be used to separate the church from society.[49]

As already indicated, and as is more than evident from the relevant U.S. cases cited, this argument is not directed against the right of the churches to own, operate and manage schools at every level. It is an argument in favour of *neutrality*, on the part of civil authorities, with respect to religion. This kind of neutrality is demanded in deference to the religious liberty of individuals. It precludes the State from directly or indirectly affecting the religious beliefs of citizens. It prevents the State from choosing between different religions, or choosing to foster religion rather than no religion. It is based, ultimately, on the fundamental assumption that with respect to freedom of thought and freedom of religion, the state must mind its own business. This kind of assumption is always clear to us as long as the ideology being fostered by state authorities is one with which we disagree; however, as soon as it comes to our own preferred religious beliefs, we change principle and then argue that the state may justifiably help foster *our* beliefs because they are 'true'.[50] Our belief in the truth of our religious beliefs is no more secure a basis for a change in principle, than the equally strong belief of others in the truth of their own ideology. Everyone argues from the assumed truth of his own religious or ideological beliefs.

Therefore the only consistent principle, which is already clear in the Irish Constitution, is for the State to remain strictly neutral with respect to religious belief. This means that it should neither hinder nor encourage it; it should not discriminate in any way between citizens on the basis of their religious beliefs or their lack of such beliefs. If this principle is impartially applied to the early education of school-age children, it implies that the civil authorities should be strictly neutral with respect to religious teaching. It should not finance any religious indoctrination. Instead, it should actively defend the liberties of young citizens against all those who might, in good faith or otherwise, conspire to determine the religious beliefs of individuals in the hope of realizing what, according to their own theological beliefs, is the salvation of individual 'souls'.

9

Theory and Ideology

The word 'theory' has unfortunately acquired connotations of unfounded speculation. It is often used to contrast theory and facts, or theory and practice, as if the second member of each contrasting pair were sufficiently independent of theoretical contamination that it could be understood without even an implicit reliance on theory. This is not the central concept of theory in modern science, nor is it an appropriate understanding of theory in moral and political discourse. In science and politics, both facts and practice are theory-laden.

Since the concept of a scientific theory has been the subject of intensive work in recent philosophy of science, it provides a reliable starting-point for understanding the role of theory in any coherent set of beliefs. Obviously, the use of the term 'theory' may change significantly from one context to another, and the unwary or unwise are likely to transpose it uncritically between contexts in which it serves quite different functions. Despite this caveat, it still seems like a good idea to get a relatively clear idea of how a theory operates in science, and then to examine other contexts in the hope of applying the scientific concept of theory, at least by analogy. The first section of this chapter discusses the extent to which 'facts' and 'theory' are interdependent in science, and also the extent to which theories are not completely determined by the facts which support them as confirming evidence.

This standard account of scientific theory is then applied to ethics and politics to explore the theoretical character of moral/political judgments, and to examine the extent to which moral/political theories are even less determined by relevant facts than their scientific counterparts. The flexible relationship between facts and theories of value provides an opening for ideological indoctrination.

Once the concept of ideology is explained as a value-determined world view, this provides the framework for a critique of church teaching and

theology as ideological articulations of the fundamental beliefs of a
religious group. To characterize church teaching as ideological is not
equivalent to rejecting it, nor does it exclude alternative world-views, by
implication, from the possibility of ideological explanation. The conclusion to be drawn, rather, is that we should more honestly face the choice
between competing ideologies, and that this choice can only be rationally
made, if at all, by allowing the alternatives to be presented to each individual as an autonomous subject of human choice. This is anticipating
the conclusion; the argument begins with a discussion of scientific
theory.

Scientific Theory

Standard accounts of scientific knowledge assume a distinction between an objective physical reality about which we talk, and the talking
or writing which we use to describe or explain the objective reality. A second distinction is usually made within the scope of our talking about objective reality; this distinction is the source of misunderstanding the term
'theory'. We imagine that we can separate all the things we say about
reality into two groups: one of them reports facts, while the other merely
speculates about the facts. The latter is then somewhat pejoratively
called a theory. Of course everyone agrees that even our reports of so-
called 'facts' are themselves pieces of a language, and therefore are only
facts to the extent to which they have already been transformed into the
conceptual framework of a given language community. Yet, despite the
obviousness of this admission, we still tend to think that such facts, even
if they are linguistic, bear a peculiarly direct relationship to the realities
which they purport to describe. In a metaphorical sense, they seem to be
close enough to the realities they describe that they almost slide across
the basic distinction made above, between objective reality and our talking about reality. They should not be allowed this licence, of course, for
reasons which will become clear in a moment; 'facts' must stay where
they belong, namely, among our linguistic utterances about the world.

The main reason for keeping facts in their proper, linguistic place is
to protect them from masquerading as eternal truths. There is nothing
final or definitive about how we describe the world in English. There is
nothing eternally true or perenially valid about the basic concepts we use
to divide up our experience of reality. We could change our basic concepts, for example, by learning a language which is conceptually very different from English, and we would then interpret our experience in such

a way that we would be recognizing different facts. Any significant conceptual shift in our language entails a corresponding shift in our store of facts about the world.

The recognition of the conceptual relativity of facts undermines the plausibility of any lingering positivist assumptions, in philosophy of science, that there is a set of observation sentences available which remain 'true' no matter what changes may take place in our theories. Our ordinary language for describing the world of experience is itself a theory of sorts.[1] It involves a set of concepts which are found, by experience, to be a useful means of interpreting our experience and communicating with each other; it also involves a whole range of assumptions (or hypotheses) about how the world is. The use of certain concepts and the (tentative) endorsement of a set of hypotheses go together. It only seems as if you can have one without the other because the hypotheses in question are seldom explicit and usually accepted.

In fact, a viable account of scientific knowledge makes the status of 'facts' even more theoretical than this. Not only are factual claims implicitly supported by general assumptions about reality; they are also contaminated by the theories in which they are integrated as supporting evidence.[2] So that what might initially look like 'objective facts' are nothing of the sort. We can speak about an objective reality, of course, but our talking or thinking about reality will have to be properly classified as precisely that: *our* talking or thinking. This is not to suggest that all our talking is equally speculative, as if a report about the colour of a bus and a claim about quarks were on exactly the same theoretical level. The point is rather this; all of our talking about reality is irreducibly dependent on the concepts in terms of which we have learned to describe or explain our experience of reality. Within this language some claims are more immediately related to experience than others, and we think of these as facts. Other claims are indirectly related to experience, and we classify those as theories to explain the facts. Our interpretation of the so-called facts often changes in conjunction with a change in theory. Thus in many well-known scientific revolutions both the facts and the theory changed at the same time. This is not the trivial claim that we sometimes have to reject, as untrue, something which we formerly believed. Rather, we sometimes have to completely reconceptualize a particular experience of reality. In that case, a whole set of facts disappears and is replaced by a new set. For example, this was the kind of radical shift demanded by the change from Aristotelian science to modern science in the seventeenth century. The history of scientific theories, therefore, can be understood as a series of more or less radical shifts in the ways in which we have conceptualized, and explained, our experience of physical reality.[3] Within this evolving enterprise it is only possible to speak about 'facts' relative to a particular slice of the overall history; for a certain time some concepts were accepted as adequate to describe our experience of reality and some reports of experience, expressed in those concepts, were taken as true. Different theories competed as explanations of the commonly agreed facts. However, it is also true that the advent of new theories often required the rejection, not only of previously accepted facts, but of the very concepts in which such alleged facts were expressed.

The relativity of facts to the conceptual framework within which they are expressed is sometimes rejected because of a fear of relativism. This is a mistake. In the first place, our fears about relativism or our commitment to the formulae of an earlier age is not a reasonable basis for closing our eyes to the lessons of the history of science. Secondly, the relativity of facts to theories is not equivalent to denying the existence of an objective reality. The history of science is the history of variations within *our* conception of reality.

Another strategy for side-stepping the implications of the history of science for our understanding of facts and theory is to put some distance between science and 'ordinary language'. Thus, one might concede that the theory-relativity of facts within science has been established, but still claim that our non-scientific descriptions of reality are not contaminated by that kind of theory dependence. However, this only amounts to repeating the mistake already made within the history of science about the privileged status of facts. The 'ordinary language' of today represents those elements of earlier theories which have been baptized as common sense. There is no way to talk about experience, either in so-called ordinary language or in science, without relying on some set of concepts in which to express our beliefs. Whatever set of concepts we use is a theory of sorts which can be replaced by an alternative theory. We have no guarantee of the eternal validity of the way in which we currently conceptualize reality, even in ordinary language. Paradoxically perhaps, the point at which the available evidence most strongly supports our current understanding of the universe is not at the level of ordinary language at all, but at the theoretical level of scientific hypotheses, such as the periodic table of the elements.

One other point about scientific theories should be mentioned at this stage, since it will be put to work in the subsequent discussion of ideology. Scientific theories are *underdetermined* by the facts which they are designed to explain. That means that there is never enough evidence available to definitively decide between competing theories, so that we might simply rest our research and conclude that we have reached the 'truth'. Any set of so-called facts is compatible with a number of competing theories. Therefore the decision to adopt one theory rather than another cannot be explained solely in terms of the evidence in its favour. Other considerations come into play, such as relative simplicity, mathematical tractability, and even social or historical reasons, which help determine theory choice for a given community of scientists. The relatively flexible 'fit' between theory and facts can be exploited in a number of different directions. In the case of political theory, it leaves open the possibility of ideological indoctrination.

Moral and Political Theory
One can make similar distinctions in the case of ethics and politics to those which obtain in physical science. Corresponding to an objective physical reality are those types of human behaviour which are morally characterized as good or bad. Corresponding to our multi-level language of description and explanation in science are the moral evaluations of actions and the comprehensive, general accounts which attempt to explain the coherence of our moral evaluations. If one focuses on our talk about human actions, rather than on the actions themselves, then we notice a similar interdependence, within moral language, between moral descriptions (moral facts) and moral theories. Before we can make any sense of the hundreds of distinctions between good or evil actions which we spontaneously make, we must recognize the extent to which we have mastered a rather sophisticated theory of action which is presupposed in our application of moral categories. For example, we assume a distinction between human actions and the non-voluntary acts of man; within the group of more or less voluntary actions, we further distinguish between intentional and unintentional actions. We have a whole battery of concepts available to sort out the degrees of voluntariness, and corresponding degrees of responsibility, which we attribute to actions. While all this conceptual framework is being learned, we also learn how to apply moral categories in order to distinguish good and evil actions. When the whole language has been learned, we can say: 'killing that person under those

circumstances was immoral'. This is a first-level moral description of an action, corresponding to: 'there is acid in that glass beaker'. Implicit in the apparent obviousness of the moral description is a learned theory of action, and a learned set of moral categories together with the rules for their appropriate application.

Moral theories are usually understood, by analogy with scientific theories, as coming into play at that point at which we are already making many moral descriptions. The role of the theory is to give a coherent explanation of the multiplicity of our moral descriptions of actions.

Just as in the case of scientific theories, however, it is essential to recognize that even our unreflective moral descriptions are themselves theory-laden. They depend on a theory of human action (for such distinctions as intentional versus unintentional), and on a series of moral norms which are implicitly learned in acquiring our initial training in moral evaluation. As Alasdair MacIntyre has argued, the extent to which our moral judgments or descriptions are coherent depends to a great extent on the coherence of the many remnants of earlier moral theories which we have learned 'at our mother's knee'.[4] In other words, our standard moral descriptions probably involve various bits and pieces of different theories borrowed from disparate sources such as: Aristotelian anthropology, Christian theological ethics, pagan taboos or Victorian views on sex. The disparity between the original sources becomes evident when we try to construct a coherent account which integrates all our usual moral descriptions.

Moral evaluation, therefore, is unavoidably a theoretical enterprise. Any moral evaluation presupposes a theory of human action to identify actions which are susceptible of moral evaluation; secondly, the moral categories which are then applied derive from a theory, or a number of different theories, of how we ought to live or ought not to live. The extent to which we operate within the scope of various theories need not be consciously recognized by those who engage in moral evaluation, no more than the theoretical character of the ordinary language we use to describe reality is explicitly recognized as such.

We learn our first language from the unsystematic training of those around us. In a similar way, we imbibe the moral categories and descriptions of the culture in which we are reared from the unsystematic (and later systematic) training of those who guide our early behaviour. In both cases, of learning our native language and learning the moral values of a society, we are being trained in a theory: in one case, a theory of what is the case, in the other a theory of how we ought to live. Having acquired a relatively unsystematic version of the community's moral theory, we are then in a position to question it and to try to give a plausible account of why we endorse it'to the extent that we do. This is where explicit theory comes in. Just as we speak a language long before we ever master the details of syntactic theory (if ever), so likewise we acquire a good working knowledge of some set of moral values long before we ever try to give a coherent explanation of how they fit together.

One of the characteristic features of scientific theories is that they are open to correction on the basis of experience. The process by which this is realized is very much more complicated than any Popperian account of science might suggest. Whatever the complex mechanics of the art, however, there is an undeniable sense in which scientific theories must face the tribunal of experience;[5] there must be some kind of 'fit', even if it is flexible, between our experience and our theoretical account of reality. The situation with moral/political theories is even more fluid, for our moral/political theories are meant to tally with our behaviour, not with the way the world is. The extreme flexibility of the 'fit', in this case, is such that theory can dictate behaviour and thereby guarantee that it is never challenged by reference to human experience. There are no independent criteria which must be reckoned with in testing the viability of a moral/political theory; no matter what the implications for action and no matter what the consequences, we can always consolidate our views by changing other beliefs and by modifying our actions to provide a coherent programme for action.

This means that the restricted underdetermination of theories in science is matched by theoretical anarchy in the case of ethics and politics. This should be taken literally. Even if a particular policy causes extreme pain to others or even to oneself; or if it risks the annihilation of a culture or of a nation; literally nothing can definitively disconfirm a political or moral view. And no progress is made in this direction by resorting to the concept of rationality. It simply does not work to say that a policy or theory is unreasonable, because one's concept of what is reasonable is often more subject to persuasive redefinition than one's commitment to a political or moral ideal.

The net result of these considerations is to highlight the extent to which moral/political views are theories which are almost beyond the pale of rational control. They are theories in the same sense in which scientific theories are conceptual models of reality; yet they are not subject to the usual empirical contraints on scientific theory. The extreme flexibility of their relationship to lived experience provides a foothold for ideological indoctrination.

Ideology

The term 'ideology' is used in a great variety of ways.[6] Karl Mannhein captures the relevant sense for this discussion in *Ideology and Utopia:*

The concept 'ideology' reflects the one discovery which emerged from political conflict, namely, that ruling groups can in their thinking become so intensively interest-bound to a situation that they are simply no longer able to see certain facts which would undermine their sense of domination. There is implicit in the word 'ideology' the insight that in certain situations the collective unconscious of certain groups obscures the real condition of society both to itself and to others and thereby stabilizes it.[7]

Some of the implications of this definition deserve a more extended commentary.

The first point to notice is that there is an obvious difference between someone being mistaken or lying, and being in some sense deluded by an ideology. We usually understand a non-veridical belief relative to some general background assumptions which are shared both by those who hold the belief and by those who claim it is defective. For example, disagreements about the distance between two towns only make sense if the contending parties agree on how to measure the relevant distance: in miles or kilometres, along the surface of the earth, by road or 'as the crow flies', and so on. Once the background assumptions are agreed, there is a relatively simple sense in which one person can claim that another is either mistaken or is lying. One of the characteristic feature of ideological disagreements, however, is the failure to agree on relevant background assumptions.

The least contentious example of such background disagreement is one which corresponds exactly to the kind of conceptual changes one finds in the history of science. The concepts used to express moral or political claims change over time. In some cases the same words are retained but their meaning is so different that the extent of the change is hidden by the apparent continuity in terminology. Any attempt to cross boundaries between contrasting conceptual frameworks, in ethics or politics, will therefore develop into an ideological debate to the extent that different parties are essentially speaking different languages. The extent to which one language can be translated into the other, and even the more basic question about what would count as an acceptable or accurate translation, is linked to some other features of ideological debate, especially the value-ladenness of moral/political language.

As already pointed out in the case of physical science, it is no longer novel to claim that the very concepts we use to describe or interpret our experience of the physical world are themselves theory-laden. That means that knowing what the concepts mean or knowing how to apply them depends on the theory within which we are operating; theory and concepts are inter-dependent. The same applies in ethics and politics. The apparently neutral terms by which we categorize our moral or political experience can only be understood in terms of some basic value-judgments we probably make spontaneously and unselfconsciously. If one assumes that the basic values of a community or a society at a certain point in time constitute a reasonably coherent set of fundamental assumptions, then the kind of incommensurability which obtains in comparing scientific theories has an exact analogue in ethics and politics; conflicting systems or networks of value-judgments undermine the assumption of common criteria on which the possibility of a comparative evaluation of moral/political views depends. This systematic disparity in basic values is a second feature of ideological disagreement.

Thirdly, to describe someone's beliefs as ideological usually has pejorative connotations of false consciousness or of distorted belief. The terms 'false' and 'distortion' seem to imply that there is some absolute perspective available to the critic of another's beliefs, from which he can diagnose these beliefs as mistaken or distorted. This kind of attitude is especially characteristic of Englightenment critiques of religion from the perspective of modern science. However, if the belief of any distinctive group or class can be partly explained in terms of their unconsciously motivating interests, then the same applies even to those who are criticising them. Therefore, a consistent theory of ideological thought should develop into a comprehensive sociology of knowledge, including even a sociology of scientific knowledge.[8] This suggests that we should interpret the distorting effect of ideologies, not from some absolute perspective outside history, but from the perspective of competing systems relative to which the distorting effect of a particular ideology is more clearly thrown into relief.

Of course the lack of an absolute viewpoint does not effectively preclude an examination of the validity of competing ideologies. To take the most obvious example of this: if those who are politically and economically dominated in a society challenge the ideological web of beliefs of their masters, they need hardly assume a transcendental perspective in order to reject their unjust condition. In such a situation, they would correctly describe the beliefs of the ruling class as ideological, in the sense that they provide a system of values which justifies the behaviour of the ruling class and thereby camouflages the perceived injustice of the situation from those who are responsible for its perpetuation. Ideological discussions take place between competing sets of beliefs; they neither need, nor could they reasonably assume, some more absolute point of view from which the competing claims to validity of different ideologies could be 'objectively' decided.

It is time to put together the points made by Mannheim about ideology and the earlier discussion of the pervasive role of theories in ethics and in science. One of the standard results of recognizing the dominant role of theory in science is that one must often discount apparently disconfirming evidence; one can only salvage one's theory by closing one's eyes to what looks initially like evidence which would disconfirm it. There is nothing odd or irrational about this, and the history of science is replete with examples where experimenters correctly (in retrospect) disregarded various pieces of evidence. A second point to notice is that, as already mentioned, our understanding of reality is not fully determined by empirical evidence alone; it is also determined in part by our basic values. Given the extreme flexibility of values, and assuming that people try to put together a coherent understanding of man and his place in the universe, we have all the makings of a significant influence from our values on the view of man which we eventually adopt. If these values or interests are strong enough, they can resist challenge from so-called 'rational' criticism, and at the same time significantly distort our understanding of what might otherwise seem to be patently clear and uncontentious. This identifies some of the characteristic marks of an ideology: it is a comprehensive understanding of man and his place in nature; it is a theory which is significantly influenced by the fundamental values or interests of those who endorse it; and from the perspective of others who often suffer from its implementation in policy decisions, it distorts the understanding of its adherents in roughly the way in which theories characteristically blind their supporters to the relevance or significance of refractory bits of evidence.

The holistic picture which this suggests — of values, theory and understanding coherently related — and the assumed dominance of the values or interests in the whole package, make it very difficult to successfully challenge an ideology. One is inclined to say that ideologies are inherited or propagated rather than that individuals are convinced of them for independent reasons. One of the ways in which they are propagated is by indoctrination.

The processes by which ideologies are indoctrinated might be caricatured by pictures of corrupt conspirators intentionally misleading a gullible public by tricking them into believing something which they clearly ought to question. This is presumably a caricature, at least in most interesting cases of ideological debate. The actual processes by which people are led to hold the beliefs they do are much more varied, sophisticated and poorly understood. Even a consistent sociology of knowledge might not be able to explain the causal mechanism by which the interests of a class of people, for example, determine their economic or political beliefs; however, it is helpful if one can recognize the coincidence of interests and corresponding beliefs, even if we have no plausible account of any causal relationship between them. Given the extreme flexibility (or underdetermination) of moral or political beliefs, it is hardly surprising if a class of people endorses political or economic beliefs which are consistent with their class interests. The propagation of the appropriate beliefs can take place, therefore, by exactly the same relatively innocent means by which any set of beliefs is propagated. The question of indoctrination only looms large at the point at which those beliefs are challenged from another perspective and the believers resort to various defensive manoeuvres.

The discussion up to this point relied on the assumption that one can draw a distinction between more or less uncritically held beliefs, and some systematic theory which is generated to account for one's beliefs. This is equally true of factual beliefs and of moral or political judgments. Thus, if the beliefs of a given class are challenged, one of the defensive measures open to them is to invoke the help of their resident wise men to rationally justify their beliefs and thereby provide the beliefs with a moral force which makes them worth defending. From the point of view of a competing ideology, this may appear to be nothing more than a rationalization, so that the ultimate explanation of both the original belief and its newly-acquired 'rational' defense is still class interests. The rational defence may, in turn, justify a series of other defensive measures which are apparently aimed at preserving the 'truth' of the belief system;

but again, these are ultimately motivated by class interests.

As already mentioned above, indoctrination is understood here as a mechanism for getting someone to endorse a belief by short-circuiting the kind of challenges which are appropriate to the kind of belief involved. One might wonder at the moral acceptability of any such procedure; however, that too can be taken care of within the ideologist's theory. He can compare the relative merits of indoctrination and its opposite. On the plus side, he counts the defensive value to his own interests of fending off any serious challenge; he might also include here the value to others, paternalistically imposed, of having the 'truth', especially in the light of their natural penchant for recognizing false prophets or their gullibility in being misled by propaganda. On the negative side is the disregard of others' freedom or autonomy, but this can be rated as a small price to pay for all the 'benefits' which result. These kinds of consideration yield the conclusion: get the 'truth' across first at almost any cost; worry later about the procedures used! Once people are converted to the 'truth' they will probably recognize its worth and be grateful for our concern in their regard; and if we get them to accept the truth, as we see it, there is a very good chance that they will continue to subscribe to our beliefs, especially if we discourage them from exposure to alien ideologies.

If one puts together the various pieces of the analysis up to this point, the picture which emerges includes the following elements:

(a) The language or set of concepts in which any group either conceives or expresses its moral and political values is irreducibly a theory of how they ought to live their lives. This theory is unsystematically imbibed in learning a language of moral or political evaluation; it is more systematically and reflectively evident in our attempts to construct a comprehensive account which provides a coherent explanation and justification of our sundry value judgments.

(b) Unlike scientific theories, our moral/political theories are extremely flexibly related to our experience of living; the looseness of fit between theory and lived experience allows for a greater latitude for persuasive arguments in this area than might succeed in the sciences.

(c) If one understands an ideology as a comprehensive theory of man and how he ought to live, where the values espoused by adherents tend to warp their picture of reality to accommodate the primacy of their basic value-judgments; and if one keeps in mind the extent to which moral/political values, as a relatively free-wheeling theory, are open to persuasive argument; it follows that any ideology will prosper in proportion to the evangelical zeal of its proponents (among other factors). Indoctrination plays a key role at this juncture.

(d) The kinds of claim which are usually made about the relationship between the interests and ideology of any group, if they are at all plausible, may be equally applied in every case. This means that recognizing the ideological basis of one's beliefs is an essential part of understanding them; and this kind of recognition can only be achieved to the extent that one is open to challenge from alternative ideological positions. The absence of some absolute perspective, or at least of one which participants in an ideological discussion would accept, implies that all ideological discussion takes place as a dialogue between competing sets of beliefs. In scientific work, there is no transcendental point from which one can examine the absolute merits of any given theory; we can only examine the merits of a theory relative to the competing merits of an alternative, and relative to our current interpretation (itself theory-laden) of the 'facts'. Likewise, the evaluation of any proposed ideology is best undertaken from the perspective of its competitors. The rejection of competition, in principle, is therefore one of the key signs of ideological commitment.

Ideological Hegemony

Anyone familiar with standard ways of replying to comprehensive theories will question the status and the plausibility of any ideological analysis of beliefs. Thus, if someone suggests an ideological explanation of a church's teaching on education or the exclusion of women from the ministry, those who defend the church's teaching are likely to reply: what exactly is the status of the ideological explanation? And what evidence is available for thinking that it might be true? More basically, can the objection itself be explained in terms of the objector's commitment to some other, equally insecure, ideology?

In answer to the first question: any ideological analysis of the beliefs of a society or group, such as a church, would have to be understood as an empirical hypothesis. That means that it is a proposal which is constructed to explain a set of empirically based 'facts'. To the extent that it fits these facts into a coherent picture, then the hypothesis is more or less plausible; to the extent that it fails to do this, or insofar as alternative accounts can equally well explain the available data, then the hypothesis must await further work to help decide in its favour or otherwise.[9]

There are a number of features of the churches' role in politics which make it plausible to suggest that their teaching should be classified as ideological. Two in particular deserve special mention: the apparent attempt to exercise power over people; and the churches' attempts to control the exposure of their members to alien systems of thought. Both seem to be motivated by the same basic desire to consolidate the results of religious indoctrination.

The drive towards political power of the Christian churches is evident both in the history of their involvement with different states and in their own self-understanding as a human institution. The historical account hardly needs repeating here; it is already well known, and survives in this century in the establishment of different churches or, in the case of the Roman Catholic Church, in the treaties it has signed with various 'Catholic' states. The changing historical fortunes of the churches are reflected in their changed conception of themselves. In some cases this is liturgical and symbolic, as in the recognition of Christ as King; in others, it is primarily juridical and political, as in the Catholic Church's conception of itself as a 'perfect society'.

The concept of a perfect society was developed by reference to the concept of law. While many associations or societies, such as an historical or literary society, could pass statutes or draw up rules which apply to their members, they could not pass a 'law'. The legislation and enforcement of laws is technically reserved for a society which is as comprehensive, in its authority over members, as a modern state. The Church's theory of perfect societies was the language in which it asserted its legislative authority over both members and potential members. However the concept of 'law' might be further refined, therefore, the Church assumes that any such analysis could be appropriately transposed to fit its conception of itself.

Since modern states are the obvious contemporary paradigms of legislative authorities, and since the Church wished to define its independence of civil authority, it developed the theory of two kinds of 'perfect' or legislative society: one dealing primarily with the 'outer forum', the other with the 'inner forum' of conscience. The outer forum deals principally with how fast one drives a car, where one may build a house, how often one votes, and so on; the inner forum specializes in what one ought to believe about God, man, the afterlife and morality. It is the domain of religious belief and moral conscience. Since the inner life of man is obviously more important than his outer life, and since the authority of the state only derives, ultimately, from the authority of God, it is clear that one perfect society is more important than the other! The beliefs one acquires in the Church and the moral obligations which derive from them are more important than the purely secular laws of civil society; in a conflict between two obligations, one must follow one's conscience and defy the state.

The difficulties with this division of a citizen's loyalties into outer and inner are obvious. There is no effective way in which one can limit one's religious and moral duties to inner free acts of compliance with the laws of God and the Church; likewise, there is no non-arbitrary way in which one can limit a citizen's obligations to the society in which he lives by reference to traffic regulations or planning permissions for houses. The chapters on Religious Freedom and on Morality and the Law above both testify to the unavoidable intermingling of moral, political and legal obligations. The obvious implication of the Church's conception of itself as the dominant perfect society — perhaps vaguely anticipated by those who endorsed the theory initially — is that one's primary political and moral allegiance must be to the Church. This is the exact counterpart to the atheistic totalitarian state's attitude to the Church: one's primary allegiance is to the state, and all controversial or disputed questions are resolved according to the state's criteria. If, having satisfied all the state's requirements, one persists in organizing private religious meetings to discuss various issues which are irrelevant to the state's perception of its dominant interests — such as a transcendent God or the afterlife — then that kind of religious behaviour might be tolerated. The Church's mirror image of the same thesis is: the Church determines what one ought to believe, what kind of legislation is conducive to the common good, and so on. Once all these primary interests have been satisfied, then it is acceptable for church members to associate in civil society and to pass laws which regulate a great variety of matters which are irrelevant to the Church's perception of its role in society. The illusory separation of inner and outer forum is a disguised theory of ideological hegemony.

The second index of ideological commitment is the church's attempt to control the beliefs of its members. This should not be understood naively as if those who made the relevant decisions in the church hierarchy were malevolent dictators who were addicted to controlling the thought of others. They have a theory to explain why some control is necessary, and why it is ultimately in the best interests of those who are controlled to benefit from the paternalistic intervention of an elite band of censors. The history of censorship in the Church is as well known as its involvement in politics. The use of a list of banned books (the 'Index') to prevent members of the Church from even reading competitors to the Church's theories was the most direct method by which this policy was implemented; the less direct methods involve lobbying in favour of censorship in any state (such as Ireland) which seems amenable to Church persuasion.

The theory which supports these strategies is complex. It relies in part on the claim that man is in need of redemption; without redemption he is corrupt in some fundamental way which theological controversy for close to two thousand years has failed to clarify. Secondly, most people are not only morally corrupt but also relatively unsophisticated in ideological matters. Perhaps their dim-wittedness is also partly explained by 'Original Sin' — the 'clouding of the intellect' — or perhaps it is just a natural condition which many people suffer from. Whichever version one adopts, the combination of dim wit and a penchant for immorality conspire to put the majority of the faithful at risk if exposed to the guiles of false philosophies. Since what is at stake is nothing less than one's eternal salvation, it seems not unreasonable that one should be protected from dangers with which one cannot cope by those who are more adept at recognizing the danger of 'false' philosphies.[10]

The protection of the faithful from the guile of false prophets is therefore a central task of the Catholic hierarchy. It is not enough to simply point out that the Church's teaching is inconsistent with someone else's theory; it is better if the faithful never read the writings of competitors, and if they are never exposed to the teaching of dissidents. And there is a theory to defend even this move. As the Popes have often pointed out in this century, the choice of a way of life and the endorsement of its attendant theory is not simply a matter of 'reason'. Rational analysis can only go so far (i.e., not far enough). To belong to the Church is ultimately a matter of faith, and faith (by definition) is not subject to mere rational considerations. Therefore, if someone is going to have the faith required, he cannot change his allegiance whenever his 'reason' seems to point him in a different direction. This is obviously what is liable to happen if he allows himself to read and study the competing merits of different ideologies.

The analogy with the defensive manoeuvres of totalitarian states is obvious. If the citizens of a totalitarian state are exposed to the 'lies' or 'guiles' of foreign propaganda they are liable to be duped by it — for reasons which are secular equivalents of the moral weakness and intellectual diminishment caused by Original Sin. Therefore it is in their own best interests that those who are better informed should shield them from the adverse effects of alien ideologies. As in the case of the Church hierarchy, it is not necessary to assume that those who defend such a theory of civil intolerance are merely hiding their political objectives behind the trappings of a theory which they do not genuinely believe. Rather, even those in the secular hierarchy who implement a policy of censorship may be true believers of the theory which supports it.

The characterization of an ideology which was suggested above explains why the churches are keen on protecting the allegiance of their members; it equally well explains why the members could only hope to be emancipated from the restrictions of widespread censorship by experiencing the merits or demerits of alternative systems of belief. It is because ideological commitment is ultimately beyond the scope of empirical testing, in any wide sense of that term, that the allegiance of members can only be consolidated by some kind of philosophical protectionism. Likewise, for the same reason, those who are already committed to a particular ideological position can only appreciate the relativity of their own position from the perspective of an alternative viewpoint.

Whether or not it is plausible to classify a particular religion as an ideology must remain a matter of judgment which is only partly decided by empirical evidence. If the concept of an ideology has any explanatory force at all, then it seems to be the case that one can establish a striking correspondence between those features of any belief system which deserves the name 'ideology' and equivalent features of the Christian tradition. Of course this does not necessarily imply that Christianity is 'false' in any usual sense of that term; rather, it provides a convenient explanatory framework in which many features of Christianity can be readily understood. Thus, apart from the political machinations of the churches and their efforts to control their members, which are the more obvious features amenable to an ideological interpretation, it also throws into relief the status and role of theology.

The word 'ideology' ambiguously denotes two rather different stages in the development of a group's set of beliefs, which correspond to the two levels of theory construction in science. At the primary level, it refers to their world-view insofar as this is unreflectively accepted, for the most part, and implemented in the daily lives of its members. When this is challenged, the local wise men are called in and asked to produce a justification or rational defense of the lived ideology of members; in other words, they are supposed to provide a theory. This is a second sense of the term 'ideology'. In this case it denotes the speculative, explanatory hypotheses which are constructed in order to give a coherent account of the ideological beliefs of the group. Christian theology is an ideology in this latter sense. The theology of any particular Christian tradition, of any church, is completely determined by the faith of its members. The starting point of any theological construction must be the faith of the church. If a theologian loses sight of these restrictions and defers instead to historical, empirical or philosophical argument, then his church is likely to respond: 'that may seem correct to you, but it does not accurately reflect our beliefs. For that reason alone, it is heretical.' There is no way out of this circle of theological interpretation, because fidelity to an historical tradition of religious belief is the definitive touchstone of orthodoxy.[11] For this reason, Christian theology can be understood as an ideological construction or theory which is constrained within the limits of what a particular community of believers is willing to accept as an authentic reflection of its beliefs.

It is clear that the epistemological status of a theology — i.e. its status as some kind of knowledge — corresponds closely to the status of a political theory which is intentionally constructed to reflect the ideological beliefs of a given political community. The analogy is more exact if the political community is closed to 'alien' influences, and if they have some formal mechanism for dealing with ideological dissidents. For example, if I write something which criticizes the government or which challenges some of the basic political beliefs of the society in which I live, an investigative committee might be established to examine my criticism. It might announce its decision as follows: 'we have examined what you wrote and we find it does not reflect our beliefs. For that reason alone, it is anathema.' There is no suggestion that the dissident's beliefs might be a viable alternative to the locally endorsed ideology; and there is no other reason given for condemning it except that it fails to match the entrenched beliefs of a given political group. Of course the judgment might be couched in the apparently objective language of 'doing harm to the members of society'. Those who know the 'truth' might say: 'these opinions are dangerous and are likely to harm the members of our society.' However, it seems clear that the principal danger feared is the likelihood of people changing their beliefs. The language of causing harm is a substitute for a rejection of ideological dissent.

Ideological Dialogue

Christian theology and more generally christian faith has been classified in the previous pages as an ideology in order to highlight certain of its features which might otherwise seem to be protected from criticism. The same kind of challenge might be made to any closed system of thought which defines orthodoxy exclusively by reference to its own beliefs, and which attempts to conserve the allegiance of its members by insulating them from the experiences which might raise questions in their minds about the ultimate basis of their commitment. This is especially true in the case of moral or political theories.

In the discussion of moral theory in Chapter 1 above, I assumed the possibility of broad agreement about certain basic goods which most human beings would recognize as such. Even if this were granted, it still appeared as if we could never avoid a fair amount of disagreement in first principles, where these were understood as general strategies for realizing basic goods. It was even more likely that we should anticipate further disagreement when attempting to apply these general principles to particular cases. One of the reasons for what might otherwise look like intellectual dithering should now be clear: the possibility of an ideological interpretation of any moral/political theory. The kinds of things which human beings value is a matter of fact; it is true that most people value being fed and clothed, being free, and so on. However, the possibility of an ideological explanation of these so-called facts raises a question about the relative primacy of different values, and of the extent to which an indoctrination of values can alter one's perspective on what might otherwise seem like value-free facts. This is a major question which can hardly be adequately dealt with in a few pages.

The only point being made at this stage is that the *least* honest way of meeting this challenge is to insulate oneself against the efficacy of criticism from outside one's own set of beliefs. This can be done in a great variety of ways, and most of them have been tried both by churches and totalitarian states. We could burn dissidents in public, or we could more discreetly refer them for psychiatric treatment. The second alternative is hardly an effective therapy if it is based, in A. MacIntyre's words, 'on a theory that is certainly no better confirmed — and perhaps not as well confirmed — as witchcraft or astrology.'[1] Instead of some kind of behaviour modification (if burning can be included under that heading), we might tackle the problem 'theoretically'. That means that we could invent an account of the certainty of our own preferred theory so that those who disagree with us have no further difficulties in recognizing the 'truth'. In other words, we would provide both the 'truth' and a guarantee of its validity, such as the Church's doctrine on infallibility. However, as was already pointed out, those who do not believe in the Church's teaching would include the theological theory of infallibility among the beliefs which they reject.

Any attempt to control the beliefs of another individual is a crude exercise of power which directly overrides the other's autonomy as a person. Once we recognize the value-ladenness and theoretical character of our beliefs, including religious, moral or political beliefs, there is no longer any justification for imposing our views on others, or for discreetly arranging that those whom we wish to 'protect' will not be exposed to views which might undermine their allegiance to our ideology. If we recognise the autonomy of the human person, then we must respect his right to seek the truth as best he can and to endorse those values or religious views which he prefers. If, on the other hand, we try to control his beliefs and to constrain his choice of ideology within limits which we determine, then we effectively deny the autonomy of the human person.

Notes

INTRODUCTION

1 *The Works of the Right Honourable Edmund Burke,* 16 vols. (London: Rivington, 1815), vol. 5, p. 173.

2 Evidently, individual autonomy is not an absolute value, so that anyone who hopes to defend it as a central value in contemporary political theory must leave room for the many qualifications which competing values require. Cf. Robert A. Dahl, *Dilemmas of Pluralist Democracy: Autonomy vs. Control* (New Haven and London: Yale University Press, 1982); Joel Feinberg, *Rights, Justice, and the Bounds of Liberty* (Princeton University Press, 1980), Chapter 1.

3 See, for example, I. Kant, *Groundwork of the Metaphysic of Morals,* trans. by H.J. Paton (New York: Harper & Row, 1964).

4 Cf. D. Clarke, 'The Role of Natural Law in Irish Constitutional Law,' *The Irish Jurist,* XVII (1982), 187-220, for a discussion of the use of natural law arguments in recent Irish jurisprudence.

5 *Submission to the New Ireland Forum from the Irish Episcopal Conference,* January 1984 (Dublin: Veritas, 1984), p. 19. The sentence quoted was originally written by Rev. C. Byrne, O.P., and is quoted in support of the argument in Section 3 of the Bishops' submission.

6 'The State is no more entitled to require or forbid something simply because it is required or forbidden by the Catholic Church than it is entitled to require or forbid something simply because it is required or forbidden by any other Church.' *Submission to The New Ireland Forum from the Irish Episcopal Conference, January, 1984,* p. 18.

7 *Ibid.,* p. 18. The italics have been added.

8 *Ibid.,* p. 19.

9 By 'population control' here I mean measures taken to either increase or decrease the population. In his judgment in *McGee* v. *Attorney General,* [1974] I.R. 284, Mr. Justice Walsh accepted that it may be justifiable, in certain circumstances, for the state to control the population by making contraceptives unavailable. It may also be justifiable for the state to encourage smaller families. 'This is not to say that the State, when the common good requires it, may not actively encourage married couples either to have large families or smaller families' (pp. 311-312). Cf. also p. 308.

CHAPTER I: MORAL CONVENTIONS

1 For recent discussion of objectivity in morals, see J.L. Mackie, *Ethics: Inventing Right and Wrong* (Penguin Books, 1977), pp. 15-49; Jack Meiland and Michael Krausz, eds., *Relativism: Cognitive and Moral* (University of Notre Dame, 1982), pp. 149-225.

2 See, for example, Basil Mitchell, *Law, Morality, and Religion in a Secular Society* (Oxford University Press, 1967), p. 93: 'Suppose that we believe that questions of morality are objective in the sense that, if two people disagree about them at least one of them must be mistaken . . .'

3 See D. Hume, *A Treatise of Human Nature*, ed. L.A. Selby-Bigge (Oxford, 1888), pp. 469-70. Neither the distinction between fact and value, nor between reason and cause, are meant to be insurmountable dichotomies; they are more like labels which indicate important distinctions which are not necessarily sharp.

4 Hume's distinction is sometimes expressed in naive empiricist terms which suggest that science is exclusively factual, while morals or politics are irremediably non-factual and evaluative. Current philosophy of science, by contrast, emphasizes the extent to which scientific theories are not determined by empirical evidence alone, and also the extent to which they are based on general value-judgments which are implicitly shared by members of a scientific community. Thus, scientific theories may be said to be value-based. However, this approach to science does nothing to minimize the implications of Hume's thesis; instead, it merely widens the scope of its application to include the sciences too. Hume's point is that there is a significant distinction between factual claims and evaluative claims, even if these both operate in science; and that any time we hope to make a value-judgment, we cannot adequately justify such a claim without at least an implicit reliance on some other value-judgment. Value judgments are not reducible to factual claims.

5 For a contract view of moral justification, see John Rawls, *A Theory of Justice* (Oxford: Clarendon Press, 1971); G. Harman, *The Nature of Morality* (Oxford University Press, 1977).

6 I. Kant, *Foundations of the Metaphysics of Morals*. Trans. by L.W. Beck (Indianapolis, 1969).

7 The example of a gunman with power but no authority is developed by H.L.A. Hart, in *The Concept of Law* (Oxford: Clarendon Press, 1959), pp. 80-81.

8 Cf. Philippa Foot, 'Morality as a System of Hypothetical Imperatives', in *Virtues and Vices* (Oxford: Blackwell, 1978), pp. 157-73.

9 By a two-valued logic is meant the assumption that every statement must be either true or false, and that no other possibilities are available. Thus, any moral claim must be true or false; if two claims conflict, at least one of them must be false.

CHAPTER 2: NATURAL LAW

1 Leo Strauss, *Natural Right and History* (University of Chicago Press, 1953), p. 2 and p. 5.

2 Cf. below, Chapter 9.

3 For a survey of some natural law theories, see A.P. d'Entrèves, *Natural Law*, 2nd ed. (London, Hutchinson, 1970); Richard Tuck, *Natural Rights Theories* (Cambridge University Press, 1979); B. Crowe, *The Changing Profile of the Natural Law* (Hague: Nijhoff, 1977).

4 This is Strauss' mistake above; for a more recent example of the same fallacy, see Michael Adams, 'Censorship of Publications,' in D. M. Clarke, ed. *Morality and the Law* (Mercier Press, 1982), pp. 71-79.

5 This is a rather crude account of axiomatic methods. The rules of inference by which one argues from one step to the next in a proof must also be included in the assumptions of such a system. It should also be noted that in contemporary axiomatic theory, the axioms of a system are not said to be true except in the innocuous sense of being conditionally accepted in order to see what can be proved on such assumptions.

6 *Summa Theologiae*, Ia IIae, question 94, article 2.

7 *Ibid.* For recent discussion of the self-evidence of first principles, see Jacques Maritain, *The Rights of Man and Natural Law* (London, 1944), p. 36: 'The only practical knowledge all men have naturally and infallibly in common is that we must do good and avoid evil;' cf. John Finnis, *Natural Law and Natural Rights* (Clarendon Press, 1980), chapter 3.

8 Cf. Maritain, *op. cit.* p. 36: 'Natural law is the ensemble of things to do and not to do which follow from the first principle in *necessary* fashion, and *from the simple fact that man is man*, nothing else being taken into account.' Other things, surely, must be taken into account, and therefore the relevant inferences are no longer 'necessary'.

9 For the distinction between 'true' theories and mere hypotheses in the history of science, see Pierre Duhem, *To Save the Phenomena* (Chicago University Press, 1969).

10 With the possible exception of supernatural actions.

11 The fallacy involved is usually called the naturalistic fallacy. For a discussion of the mistake involved in this kind of reasoning, see William Frankena, 'The Naturalistic Fallacy', in J. Hospers and W. Sellars, eds. *Readings in Ethical Theory* (Appleton-Century-Crofts, 1952), and W.D. Hudson, *The Is/Ought Question* (London: Macmillan, 1969).

12 Maritain, *The Rights of Man*, pp. 34-35.

13 Cf. the discussion by Ralph McInerny, 'The Principles of Natural Law', *American Journal of Jurisprudence,* 25 (1980), 1-19, and the reply by G. Grisez and J. Finnis, 'The Basic Principle of Natural Law: A Reply to Ralph McInerny', *American Journal of Jurisprudence*, 26 (1981), 21-31.

14 [1980] I.R. 32. I have discussed many of the cases where natural law has played a role in Irish judicial decisions in 'The Role of Natural Law in Irish Constitutional Law', *The Irish Jurist*, XVII (1982), 187-220.

15 *Lumen Gentium* (Dogmatic Constitution on the Church), section 79.

16 Section 29. Cf. section 2: 'It is well known how highly the Church regards human reason, for it falls to reason . . . to express properly the law which the Creator has imprinted in the hearts of men.'

17 English translation, National Catholic Welfare Conference, U.S.A., pp. 36-37.

18 Paragraph 34.

19 *Casti Connubii*, Pope Pius XI, English trans. p. 37; Cf. p. 44: 'For the preservation of the moral order . . . religious authority must enter to enlighten the mind . . . Such an authority is found nowhere save in the Church instituted by Christ the Lord.'

20 Paragraph 4.

21 Paragraphs 43, 45.

22 *Quadragesimo Anno*, paragraph 53.

23 *Humanae Vitae*, paragraph 10.

24 *Ibid.*, paragraph 16.
25 *Casti Connubii*, Eng. trans. pp. 19, 20, 21, 25.
26 Paragraphs 10, 11, 13, 17.
27 *Casti Connubii*, Eng. trans. p. 24.
28 *Humanae Vitae*, Section 14.

CHAPTER 3: TOLERANCE AND PLURALISM

1 Geoffrey Harrison, 'Relativism and Tolerance', *Ethics*, 86 (1976), 122-35.
2 Cf. Peter Singer, *Practical Ethics* (Cambridge University Press, 1979), pp. 150-151.
3 There may be a difference between the official teaching of the highest church
   authorities on some of these issues, and the kind of unsophisticated version of church
   teaching which filters down to the people in local communities. See, for example, the
   preaching of the church against the dangers of dance halls in Ireland, in J.H. Whyte,
   Church and State in Modern Ireland, 1923-1979, 2nd ed. (Gill and Macmillan, 1980),
   chapter 2.
4 *On Liberty*, Chapter 2.
5 R.P. Wolff, in R.P. Wolff, B. Moore and H. Marcuse, *A Critique of Pure Tolerance*
   (Boston: Beacon Press, 1965), comments: 'It is absurd to decide on rational grounds
   that one will accept non-rational authority!' (p. 35).
6 Cf. Michael Davis, 'The Budget of Tolerance', *Ethics*, 89 (1979), 165-78.
7 See Wolff, *op. cit.*, pp. 40-51.
8 Whyte's history of church-state relations in Ireland provides ample evidence of the
   kind of church interference which is intended here.
9 The metaphor of logical space refers to the problem of explaining how one can consistently hold a moral principle and yet not implement it in a particular action. If all
   principles required unconditional implementation there would be no room in which to
   balance the demands of some principles with the conflicting demands of others. The
   possibility of tolerance presupposes that there are situations in which we ought not act
   on the basis of some moral principles in deference to the demands of others.
10 In Marcuse, *op. cit.*, pp. 82 and 90.
11 The classic statement of this thesis is found in John Locke, *A Letter Concerning
   Toleration (1689)*, edited by James Tully (Indianapolis: Hackett, 1983).
12 'One crucial characteristic of a free society is the absence of a single overriding
   "national purpose". The attempts, never completely successful, to impose such a purpose are the stigma of the modern totalitarian state.' Barrington Moore, *A Critique of
   Pure Tolerance*, p. 71. Cf. Chapter 6 below for a discussion of 'the common good'.
13 As already indicated in the Introduction above, this point was underlined by the *Submission to The New Ireland Forum from the Irish Episcopal Conference*, January,
   1984. However, the Bishops raise this question in a context where they seem to defend
   the influence of majority opinion (even if religious opinion) on legal systems. They
   seem to want to strike a balance between legal systems which endorse religious traditions too indiscriminately, and those which do so in a more discriminating way. They
   favour the latter. They want the Irish legal system to support Catholic teaching, not
   because it is Catholic teaching, but because it is the truth.
14 Cf. John Rawls, *A Theory of Justice* (Oxford: Clarendon Press, 1971), pp. 205-221.

CHAPTER 4: RELIGIOUS FREEDOM AND THE ROMAN CATHOLIC CHURCH

1   The most obvious examples of this are in the Trinitarian invocation at the beginning of the Constitution, and in Article 44, sec. 2, subs. 4, in which the state is committed implicitly to public aid for religious schools.

2   For purely stylistic reasons, I use the phrase 'the Church' as an abbreviation for 'the Roman Catholic Church', without prejudice to the claims of other churches to be churches in exactly the same sense. What is at stake in this chapter are the beliefs of the Roman Catholic Church about religious liberty, as the church of which most Irish citizens are members.

3   Cf. the 1973 Statement of the Irish Episcopal Conference, p. 1; and the statement issued after the Irish Catholic Bishops' Conference, June 14-16, 1976. In both statements the bishops explain that they are not claiming that the state should enforce Catholic moral views by legislation, simply because they are the moral views of the Church; at the same time, they maintain their right to advise members of their church on such issues, in virtue of their right to preach and teach. The recent discussion on the Eighth Amendment to the Constitution exemplifies the explicit rejection of a political role by the Hierarchy, combined with equally explicit guidance as to how Catholics ought to vote. The Bishops wrote: 'We recognise the right of each person to vote according to conscience.' However, the final paragraph of their statement reads as follows: 'While some conscientiously hold a different opinion, we are convinced that a clear majority in favour of the Amendment will greatly contribute to the continued protection of unborn life in the laws of our country. This could have a significant impact in a world where abortion is often taken for granted. A decisive 'Yes' to the Amendment will, we believe, in the words of Pope John Paul II in Limerick, constitute a "witness before Europe and before the whole world to the dignity and sacredness of all human life, from conception until death".' *A Statement from the Irish Episcopal Conference*, 22 August, 1983.

4   See Chapter 6 in which this is further discussed.

5   Cf. Frederick Schauer, *Free Speech: A Philosophical Inquiry* (Cambridge University Press, 1982).

6   This is also discussed in more detail in Chapter 9 below.

7   I have translated the quoted sections from the Latin text published by the Vatican, *Constitutiones, Decreta, Declarationes* (Vatican Press: Rome, 1966). In each case, I give the section number and page number to facilitate consultation with various English translations.

8   See above, Chapter 2, for the Church's attitude towards natural law theory.

9   This argument is developed by Eric D'Arcy, *Conscience and its Right to Freedom* (London and New York: Sheed and Ward, 1961).

10 'In error' here means in error relative to some commonly accepted moral framework.

11 This is repeated in *Lumen Gentium* (The Dogmatic Constitution on the Church), paragraph 14. Cf. Pope Pius XII, Encyclical letter *Humani Generis* (1950), paragraph 27.

12 Cf. *Lumen Gentium* (The Dogmatic Constitution on the Church), paragraph 25.

13 In the subsequent section, p. 519, the *Declaration* claims that religious freedom is not compromised if one church is given a special constitutional status in a state.

14   After writing this paragraph I was pleased to find similar reservations expressed by Philip S. Denenfeld, 'The Conciliar Declaration and the American Declaration', in John C. Murray, ed., *Religious Liberty: an End and a Beginning* (London: Macmillan, 1966), 120-132.

15   The issues concerning religious education are discussed in detail in Chapter 8 below. They are only raised at this point to help interpret the unclear doctrine of the *Declaration on Religious Freedom*.

16   *Lumen Gentium* (The Dogmatic Constitution on the Church), paragraph 25.

17   Cf. the extraordinary teaching of St. Thomas Aquinas, *Summa Theologiae*, IIaIIae, Q. 64, article 2, according to which it may be justifiable to put a heretic to death to defend the common good!

CHAPTER 5: PRIVATE MORALS AND PUBLIC POLICY

1   For a selection of recent cases which reject legal positivism in Irish jurisprudence, see James O'Reilly and Mary Redmond, *Cases and Materials on the Irish Constitution* (Dublin, 1980); see also D.M. Clarke, 'Emergency Legislation, Fundamental Rights, and Article 28.3.3 of the Irish Constitution', *Irish Jurist*, XII (1977), 217.

2   H.L.A. Hart addresses these arguments in *Law, Liberty, and Morality* (London: Oxford University Press, 1963).

3   Lord Devlin defends this line of argument, in Patrick Devlin, *The Enforcement of Morals* (London: Oxford University Press, 1965).

4   The Irish Catholic Hierarchy seems to support the opposite opinion, in its written submission to the New Ireland Forum, January, 1984: 'To require in the name of pluralism that public policy tolerate or even facilitate forms of public morality of which the majority of the citizens could not approve may sometimes be reasonable in the interests of the common good of harmony between all the citizens; *but where the offence to the moral principles of the majority of the citizens would be disproportionately serious it is not unreasonable to require sacrifice of minorities in the interests of the common good.*' (Dublin: Veritas Publications, 1984), p. 18. Italics added.

5   C.L. Ten examines this argument in Chapter 2 of *Mill on Liberty* (Oxford: Clarendon Press, 1980), pp. 10-51.

6   *Summa Theologiae*, IIa IIae, Question 11, article 3.

7   Cf. Joel Feinberg, 'Harmless "Immoralities" and Offensive Nuisances', in N.S. Care and T.K. Trelogan, eds., *Issues in Law and Morality* (Cleveland and London, 1973).

8   For a discussion of some of the issues raised by paternalism, see Gerald Dworkin, 'Paternalism', in R. Wasserstrom, ed., *Morality and the Law* (Belmont, California, 1971), and J. Feinberg, 'Legal Paternalism', in *Rights, Justice and the Bounds of Liberty* (Princeton University Press, 1980).

9   Cf. J. G. Murphy, 'Incompetence and Paternalism', *Archiv für Rechts und Sozialphilosophie*, LX (1974) 465-486; W. Gaylin and Ruth Macklin, *Who Speaks for the Child? The Problems of Proxy Consent* (Plenum Press, 1982).

10   I. Berlin, in his famous essay *Two Concepts of Liberty*, (Oxford: Clarendon Press, 1958) clarifies the dangers of defining 'true freedom' in terms of 'freedom to do what one ought to do', where what one ought to do is decided by someone other than the agent and the result may be a form of tyranny redescribed as paternalistic concern.

11   John Stuart Mill, *On Liberty* (Penguin Books, 1974), p. 68.

12   Justice Brian Walsh in his judgment in the *McGee* case, considered the possibility that the common good might require either larger or smaller families, and that the State might justifiably interfere in family life to encourage one or the other outcome. 'This is not to say that the State, when the common good requires it, may not actively encourage married couples either to have larger families or smaller families. If it is a question of having smaller families then, whether it be a decision of the husband and wife or the intervention of the State, the means employed to achieve this objective would have to be examined. What may be permissible to the husband and wife is not necessarily permissible to the State.' *McGee* v. *Attorney General*, [1974] I.R., 284 at 311-312.

13   Statement of the Irish Episcopal Conference, 1973, page 1.

14   Pope Pius XI, *Casti Connubii*, Eng. trans. p. 45.

15   Pope Pius VI, *Humanae Vitae*, Eng. trans. paragraph 23, p. 17.

16   1973 Statement, quoted above. This should be taken in conjunction with an earlier paragraph in the same statement: 'The question at issue is not whether artificial contraception is morally right or wrong. The clear teaching of the Catholic Church is that it is morally wrong. No change in State law can make the use of contraceptives morally right since what is wrong in itself remains wrong, regardless of what State law says.' Notice the crucial transition in the final sentence between what is morally wrong in the Church's eyes and what is morally wrong, without qualification. It is this transition, implicit in church teaching, which makes it almost impossible for church leaders to recognize that they are discreetly enforcing their own religious views on others, because they collapse the distinction between 'immoral' and 'immoral by church teaching'.

17   Statement from the Irish [Catholic] Bishops' Conference on proposed Legislation dealing with Family Planning and Contraception, 1978, page 1.

18   General Observations by the Irish Catholic Bishops' Conference on the Attorney General's Discussion paper on the Law of Nullity in Ireland, March, 1977, page 2.

19   *Ibid.*

20   Cf. A Statement from the Irish Episcopal Conference, 22 August 1983, concerning the proposed Eighth Amendment to the Constitution. 'The Church has a duty to proclaim the moral law. When, for example, it declares abortion in all circumstances to be morally wrong, it does so with the authority given it by its Founder, Jesus Christ.' This could be translated as saying: 'we *believe* that Jesus Christ gave us authority to teach morality, and we *believe* that abortion is always immoral.' Both beliefs are based exclusively on religious faith.

CHAPTER 6: HUMAN RIGHTS AND THE COMMON GOOD

1   For a survey of recent developments, see Louis Henkin, *The Rights of Man Today* (Colorado: Westview Press, 1978).

2   Constitution Article 29, section 6; *Application of Michael Woods to the Supreme Court*, [1970] I.R., 161; *In re Ó Laighléis* [1960] I.R., 124-5; the *Fourth Amendment of the Constitution Act, 1972*, provides among other things that 'No provision of this Constitution . . . prevents laws enacted, or measures adopted by the Communities, or institutions thereof, from having the force of law in the State'. It is not clear if this amendment changes the legal status of the European Convention in Ireland.

254 Notes to Pages 137-139

3   For example, the *United Nations Declaration* includes such disparate rights as: 'Article 5. No one shall be subjected to torture or to cruel, inhuman or degrading treatment or punishment', and 'Article 24. Everyone has the right . . . to periodic holidays with pay.' Although the right to work has been recognized as a basic constitutional right in Ireland, the right to holidays with pay has not. See *Tierney* v. *Amalgamated Society of Woodworkers*, [1972] I.R., 330.

4   The Irish version of Article 40 is more definite about the obligations of the State not to interfere with the personal rights of the individual and to defend them as much as possible. According to Article 25, section 5, sub-section 4, the Irish version is decisive in cases of alternative interpretations of the Constitution. For Article 40, the Irish text reads: 'Ráthaíonn an Stát gan cur isteach lena dlíthe ar chearta pearsanta aon saoránaigh, agus ráthaíonn fós na cearta sin a chosaint is a shuíomh lena dhlíthe sa mhéid gur féidir é.'

5   *Ryan* v. *Attorney General*, [1965] I.R., 294, at p. 312. On appeal to the Supreme Court it was held that the personal rights of the citizen 'are not exhausted by the enumeration of 'life, person, good name, and property rights' in Section 3, 2°' (*ibid.*, p. 344-5).

6   For a recent summary of the variety of rights which are now constitutionally recognized in Ireland, see Justice Declan Costello, 'Aspects of a juridically developed jurisprudence of human rights in Ireland', in Alan D. Falconer, ed., *Understanding Human Rights* (Dublin: Irish School of Ecumenics, 1980).

7   This interpretative procedure was defended *In the matter of a reference by the President of the Criminal Law (Jurisdiction) Bill, 1975* to the Supreme Court. 'The correct meaning of any constitutional document may be ascertained by construing it with regard to the historical circumstances in which it came into existence . . . the Constitution contains more than legal rules: it reflects, in part, aspirations and aims and expresses the political theories on which the People acted when they enacted the Constitution.' [1977] I.R. 129.

8   The concept of a human person is somewhat imprecise, just as most other concepts are. We characteristically apply the concept to someone who at least shows signs of conscious life similar to the normal adult. We extend the concept, by implication, to those who share many other human qualities with the normal adult but have permanently lost what we regard as a minimal use of reason, and to those (like young babies) who have not yet reached the stage of being full-fledged persons in the usual sense. How we further define the concept of 'person' is merely a clarification of how we use the English language; we could no more resolve moral problems about how we ought to treat doubtfully human creatures by excluding them from the class of persons by definition, than we could justify any immoral act by redescribing it in morally acceptable language. See D. Dooley-Clarke and D.M. Clarke, 'Definitions and Ethical Decisions', *Journal of Medical Ethics*, 3 (1977), 186-8.

9   Nor does one need to claim human rights in order to have them, as M. Cranston suggests. See *What are Human Rights?* (London: Bodley, 1973), p. 81. 'A right presupposes a claim; if a claim is not made, the question of a right does not arise.' Cf. *The State (Healy)* v. *Donoghue*, [1976] I.R. 325, at p. 361: 'A *right* to legal aid would be a very empty right if it depended for its implementation on a young, uneducated, illiterate defendant who may not be aware of his right and of the possible serious consequences to him of a failure to have legal aid.' One may define the concept of a right so that it presupposes the possibility of its being claimed; but any definition which includes the fact of its being claimed in the concept of a right is inappropriate to the discussion of basic human rights.

10   A.I. Melden, *Rights and Persons*, p. 185.

11   Cf. Stuart M. Brown, Jr., 'Inalienable Rights', *Philosophical Review*, LXIV (1955), 192-211.

12   See Richard Wollheim, 'Equality', *Proc. Aristotelian Society*, New Series, VI (1955-56), 282.

13   For the distinction between negative and positive rights, see Ronald Dworkin, *Taking Rights Seriously* (London: Duckworth, 1977), pp. 188-89.

14   Article 26; Article 34, section 3 and section 4.

15   For example, *Ryan* v. *Attorney General* [1965] I.R. 294.

16   Cf. Melden, *Rights and Persons*, p. 167.

17   See H.L.A. Hart, 'Are There Any Natural Rights?' *Philosophical Review*, LXIV (1955), 175-191.

18   Cf. *G.* v. *An Bord Uchtála* [1980] I.R. 32 at p. 55 in which the waiver of 'natural rights' by those who enjoy them is considered.

19   Article 43, section 1, sub-section 1.

20   Declan Costello, 'The Natural Law and the Irish Constitution', *Studies* (Winter, 1956), 403-414. In arguing for the distinction of the two kinds of rights Mr. Costello mentions that 'property rights are not included under the heading of 'personal rights' . . .', p. 405. While there is a separate article for property rights, they are also mentioned in Article 40, section 3, sub-section 2, as one of man's personal rights.

21   Article 42, section 5; Article 44, section 2, sub-section 4. See also *In re F. an Infant* (High Court), [1966] I.R., 295, at p. 301; *The State (Nicolaou)* v. *An Bord Uchtála* [1966] I.R. 567, at pp. 643-4.

22   [1947] I.R. 77. For a contrary view, see John Kelly, *Fundamental Rights in the Irish Law and Constitution* (2nd ed., Dublin: Figgis, 1967), p. 166, and Melden, *Rights and Persons,* pp. 167-8.

23   Both sections 4, 1° and 5 of Article 40 guarantee that the right to freedom and to the inviolability of one's home shall not be limited 'save in accordance with law'. By this phrase these sections set minimum conditions for limiting individual rights. The immunity from challenge in the courts which is provided for emergency laws by Article 28 is a more serious 'legal' limitation on rights than anything implied in Article 40, sections 4, 1° and 5.

24   Article 42, section 3, sub-section 2 and Article 42, section 5. There are eleven references to the 'common good' in the text of the Constitution. The ways in which this term might be plausibly understood in Irish constitutional law are explored in D.M. Clarke, 'The Concept of the Common Good in Irish Constitutional Law', *Northern Ireland Legal Quarterly* (Winter, 1979), 319-342.

25   Article 43, 1, 2° reads: 'The State accordingly guarantees to pass no law attempting to abolish the right of private ownership or the general right to transfer, bequeath, and inherit property.'

26   [1940] I.R. 470 at p. 481.

27   [1950] I.R. 67 at p. 83.

28   [1965] I.R. 217; [1974] I.R. 284 at p. 310; [1976] I.R. 325. The quotation from the last mentioned case is from p. 335.

29 Cf. *Quinn's Supermarket* v. *The Attorney-General* [1972] I.R. 15; *McGee* v. *Attorney General* [1974] I.R. 284 at p. 317 (per Walsh J.): 'The Constitution recognises and reflects a firm conviction that the people of this State are a religious people and that . . . while we are a religious people we also live in a pluralist society from the religious point of view. In my view, the subsequent deletion of sub-ss. 2 and 3 of s. 1 of article 44 by the fifth amendment to the Constitution has done nothing to alter this acknowledgment that, religiously speaking, the society we live in is a pluralist one.'

30 Mr. E. de Valera, *Dáil Debates*, vols. 67-68, p. 1635.

31 Joseph Collins, 'Law and the Common Good', *Irish Theological Quarterly*, XXIV (1957), p. 133.

32 *Ibid.*, p. 207.

33 *Ibid.*, p. 213.

34 [1977] I.R. 159, at p. 174. It should be noted that Article 28, 3, 3° grants immunity from court challenge to a law, and not to a bill. This leaves open the possibility that proposed emergency legislation could be declared to be unconstitutional, by the Supreme Court, if it is referred to the Court by the President under Article 26. The Court may declare, in those circumstances, that a bill is unconstitutional because it infringes on various rights which are already guaranteed by the Constitution. However, once a bill is passed into law, it enjoys immunity from further challenge because of Article 28.

35 [1977] I.R. 159, at p. 171-2, 176.

36 [1950] I.R. at page 67: 'We do not feel called upon to enter upon an inquiry as to the foundation of natural rights or as to their nature or extent. . . . It is sufficient for us to say that this State, by its Constitution, acknowledges that the right to private property is such a right, and that this right is antecedent to all positive law. This, in our opinion, means that man by virtue, and as an attribute, of his human personality is so entitled to such a right that no positive law is competent to deprive him of it, . . .'

37 [1974] I.R. 294, at p. 310 and p. 318.

38 I have argued that the Constitution is logically inconsistent in 'Fundamental Rights, Emergency Legislation, and Article 28.3.3 of the Constitution', *Irish Jurist*, XII (1977), 217-33.

39 The significance for human rights of emergency legislation is considerably underestimated by Robert F. Heuston, in 'Personal Rights under the Irish Constitution', *Univ. of British Columbia Law Review*, XI (1977), 294-314. On p. 298 he says simply: 'No more will be said about these decisions. This is not to minimise their significance. In one sense they are very important: if the men of violence win, there will be no Constitution and no Court. But in another and deeper sense the decisions are marginal to the Court's main achievements in the area of constitutional jurisprudence . . .'

40 See the decision of the Supreme Court on the *Emergency Powers Bill, 1976* [1977] I.R. 159, at 173.

41 The Irish version of Article 40, section 4, sub-section 6 has 'le linn eisíthe nó ceannairce faoi arm', where Article 28, 3, 3° has 'in aimsir chogaidh nó ceannairce faoi arm'.

CHAPTER 7: EQUALITY OF OPPORTUNITY

1   For a discussion of equality in Irish constitutional law, see M. Forde, 'Equality and the Constitution', *The Irish Jurist*, XVII (1982), 294-339.

2   For a detailed development of this thesis, see Alan H. Goldman, *Justice and Reverse Discrimination* (Princeton University Press, 1979), Chapter 2.

3   Cf. J.S. Coleman, 'The Concept of Equality of Educational Opportunity', *Harvard Educational Review*, 38 (1968). For a systematic analysis of the relative influence of various inequalities on students' performance and job prospects, see Christopher Jencks, *Inequality: A Reassessment of the Effect of Family and Schooling in America* (New York: Basic Books, 1972). A recent Irish study of equality of opportunity in education provided results which did not significantly differ from those of earlier U.S. studies. See Vincent Greaney and Thomas Kellaghan, *Equality of Opportunity in Irish Schools* (Dublin: Educational Company, 1984).

4   Cf. Onora O'Neill, 'Opportunities, Equalities and Education', *Theory and Decision*, 7 (1976), 275-296.

5   Robert Nozick, *Anarchy, State and Utopia* (Basic Books, 1974).

6   This point is developed at length by John Rawls, in *A Theory of Justice*.

7   Cf. for example, Frank Field, *Inequality in Britain* (Fontana, 1981); Milton Fisk, *Ethics and Society: A Marxist Interpretation of Value* (Sussex: Harvester Press, 1980).

8   Dale Tussing, *Irish Educational Expenditures — Past, Present and Future* (Dublin: Economic and Social Research Institute, 1978); A.C. Barlow, *The Financing of Third-Level Education* (Dublin: Economic and Social Research Institute, 1981).

9   A similar argument is developed by A. Goldman, *op. cit.*, pp. 44-45.

10 While it is objectionable in the sense explained that the financial status of parents might hinder the educational progress of children, it does not follow that the state should provide free higher education for those who qualify on educational criteria. The reason for this is that state financing is equivalent to some members of the population financing the educational advantages of others who are likely to benefit for the rest of their lives from such advantage. Cf. C. Jencks, *op. cit.*, pp. 259-260: 'If we assume that higher education, like concerts and football games, will be used unequally, we must decide how to finance it. A system that makes students dependent on money from home, which many cannot get, is clearly unacceptable. But a system which finances higher education out of general tax revenues and then allows individual students to use their education for private gain also seems unacceptable. It is hard to see why, for example, an auto worker should pay taxes to send his cousin to law school and should then have to pay his cousin fat fees to obtain legal services . . . . In a society where individuals are free to retain most of the economic benefits of their education for themselves, it seems reasonable to ask them to pay most of the costs. The equitable way to do this, in our judgment, would be to provide every student with free tuition and a living stipend, and then impose an income surcharge on those who had had these benefits.'

11 Cf. Jencks, *op. cit.*, p. 255: 'None of the evidence we have reviewed suggests that school reform can be expected to bring about significant social changes outside the schools. More specifically, the evidence suggests that equalizing educational opportunity would do very little to make adults more equal. . . . the experience of the past 25 years suggests that even fairly substantial reductions in the range of educational attainments do not appreciably reduce economic inequality among adults.'

CHAPTER 8: EDUCATION

1   There are some obvious exceptions to the general rule, such as Model Schools, and
    schools under the control of VECs; the general point remains valid, however.

2   For a recent history of Irish education, see John Coolahan, *Irish Education: History
    and Structure* (Dublin: Institute of Public Administration, 1981); E. Brian Titley,
    Church, State, and the Control of Schooling in Ireland 1900-1944 (Dublin: Gill and
    Macmillan, 1983).

3   All references to the *Declaration on Christian Education* are to the standard English
    translation in Walter M. Abbott, ed., *The Documents of Vatican II* (New York, 1966);
    p. 639.

4   *Ibid.,* p. 639-40.

5   *Ibid.,* p. 682.

6   *Ibid.,* p. 640.

7   *Ibid.*. pp. 641, 642.

8   *Ibid.,* pp. 641, 644.

9   *Ibid.,* p. 683.

10 *Ibid.,* pp. 644, 683. Notice that the text only speaks of the rights of parents, and there
    is no recognition that the rights of children might be violated in the same cir-
    cumstances. At pp. 639-40, however, children and young people were said to have a
    right to religious liberty.

11 *Ibid.,* p. 645.

12 *Ibid.,* pp. 645, 647.

13 *Ibid.,* pp. 641-2.

14 *Ibid.,* p. 644.

15 *Ibid.,* p. 683.

16 *Origins: NC Documentary Service,* 11 (Dec. 3, 1981), p. 392.

17 [1980] I.R. 32, at pp. 55-6.

18 *The State (Nicolaou)* v. *An Bord Uchtála* [1966] I.R. 567, at pp. 643-4.

19 *In re F an Infant* [1966] I.R. 295.

20 [1980] I.R. 32, at p. 86.

21 Their rights are then protected under Article 40, Section 3.

22 [1965] I.R. 294.

23 This tends to happen in custody or adoption cases, but not exclusively; in *The State
    (M)* v. *The Attorney General* [1979] I.R. 73, Justice Finlay held that a minor had a
    right to travel and therefore had a right to a passport. Cf. James O'Reilly, 'Custody
    Disputes in the Irish Republic: The Uncertain Search for the Child's Welfare', *The
    Irish Jurist,* XII (1977), 37-65.

24 [1980] I.R. 32 at p. 78.

25 *In re Frost, Infants* [1947] I.R. 3, at p. 28, the Chief Justice gave the following judgment on behalf of the Supreme Court: 'I cannot, however, accept . . . the proposition that the rights of parents . . . are absolute rights, the exercise of which cannot, in any circumstances, be controlled by the Court. That a child has natural and imprescriptible rights is recognised by the Constitution (Art. 42.5), and if Mr. Ryan's . . . proposition were accepted, it would follow that the Court would be powerless to protect those rights should they be ignored by the parents. I am satisfied that the Court has jurisdiction to control the exercise of parental rights, but in exercising that jurisdiction it must not act upon any principle which is repugnant to the Constitution.'

26 Cf. *The State (Healy)* v. *Donoghue* [1976] I.R. 325, at p. 361 (per Griffin, J.): 'A right to legal aid would be a very empty right if it depended for its implementation on a young, uneducated, illiterate defendant who may not be aware of his right and of the possible serious consequences to him of a failure to have legal aid.'

27 Cf. J. Goldstein, A. Freud, A.J. Solnit, *Beyond the Best Interests of the Child* (N.Y.: Free Press, 1979), and *Before the Best Interests of the Child* (N.Y.: Free Press, 1979); Willard Gaylin and Ruth Macklin, *Who Speaks for the Child: The Problems of Proxy Consent* (N.Y. and London: Plenum Books, 1982).

28 *Pierce* v. *Society of Sisters*, 268 US 510 (1925) is the classic example of this. The state of Oregon passed a law which compelled all children, between the ages of 8 and 16, to attend state-managed schools. This law was judged unconstitutional. Mr. Justice McReynolds gave the opinion of the U.S. Supreme Court: 'The fundamental theory of liberty upon which all governments in this Union repose excludes any general power of the State to standardize its children by forcing them to accept instruction from public teachers only. The child is not the mere creature of the State; those who nurture him and direct his destiny have the right, coupled with the high duty, to recognize and prepare him for additional obligations' (at p. 535).

29 In *Crowley* v. *Ireland*, the Supreme Court decided that the obligations of the state were adequately performed when it provided *for* primary education, even if it did not actually succeed in providing education in a given location for children of school-going age. See the discussion in W.N. Osborough, 'Education in the Irish Law and Constitution', *The Irish Jurist*, XIII (1978), 145.

30 406 U.S. 205 (1972). See also *Prince* v. *Massachusetts*, 321 U.S. 158 (1944); in this case a state statute which prohibited minors under the age of twelve from selling publications or other merchandise on the public streets was challenged by Jehovah's Witnesses, because it precluded their minor children from selling religious publications. The court agreed that such street selling was a religious exercise on their part, but it still upheld the right of the State of Massachusetts to control the public behaviour of minor children.

31 406 U.S. 205 (1972), 218; *ibid.*, p. 238.

32 Italics added. In *J. McG and W. McG* v. *An Bord Uchtála,* Justice Pringle ruled tht religious discrimination against adoptive parents was unconstitutional. ILTR (1975), 109, p. 62.

33 Kenneth Henley, 'The Authority to Educate', in O. O'Neill and W. Ruddick, eds., *Having Children* (N.Y.: Oxford University Press, 1979), 254-64, at pp. 260, 261.

34 This issue has arisen especially in relation to the right to privacy of minors in respect of abortion without their parent's consent, and their right to contraceptives and information about contraceptives. See, for example, *Carey* v. *Population Services International*, 431 U.S. 678 (1977); *Moore* v. *East Cleveland*, 431 U.S. 494 (1977); *Planned Parenthood of Central Missouri* v. *Danforth*, 428 U.S. 52 (1976); *Bellotti* v. *Baird*, 428

U.S. 132 (1976). For a survey of recent decisions, see John H. Garvey, 'Child, Parent, State, and the Due Process Clause: An Essay on the Supreme Court's Recent Work', *Southern California Law Review*, 51 (1978), 769-822; Michael S. Wald, 'Children's Rights — A Framework for Analysis', *UCD Law Review*, 12 (1979), 255-282; Lee E. Teitelbaum, 'The Meanings of Rights of Children', *New Mexico Law Review*, 10 (1979-80), 235-53; 'Developments in the Law — The Constitution and the Family', *Harvard Law Review*, 93 (1980), 1156; Howard Cohen, *Equal Rights for Children* (New Jersey: Littlefield, Adam, 1980).

35 393 U.S. 503, and 506, 511.

36 321 U.S. 158 (1944).

37 406 U.S. 205 (1972) and pp. 241, 242.

38 319 U.S. 624 (1943).

39 403 U.S. 672 (1971).

40 319 U.S. 624 (1943) and p. 638.

41 Paragraph 16 of the schedule reads: 'Neither the Parliament of the Irish Free State nor the Parliament of Northern Ireland shall make any law so as either directly or indirectly to endow any religion or prohibit or restrict the free exercise thereof or give any preference or impose any disability on account of religious belief or religious status or affect prejudicially the right of any child to attend a school receiving public money without attending the religious instruction at the school or make any discrimination as respects State and between schools under the management of different religious denominations or divert from any religious denomination or any educational institution any of its property except for public utility purposes and on payment of compensation.' For a discussion of the application of these principles to education in Northern Ireland, see Edgar Graham, 'Religion and Education', *Northern Ireland Legal Quarterly*, 33 (1982), 20-51.

42 374 U.S. 203 (1963).

43 *Ibid.*, p. 226.

44 *Ibid.*, pp. 277, 228, 229.

45 393 U.S. 97 (1968), at pp. 103-4.

46 In *McGrath and Ó Ruairc* v. *Trustees of Maynooth College* (November 1, 1979, unreported), the Supreme Court unanimously held that Maynooth is, legally, a Roman Catholic seminary. O'Higgins, C.J. held: 'The essence of Maynooth is that it is a religious seminary and only the Oireachtas acting within the Constitution can permit it to be otherwise. . . . I take the view that Maynooth is, always was and remains a seminary.' This raises a question about the constitutionality of endowing a religion by providing public funds for an educational institution which is exclusively managed by Roman Catholic bishops under statutes drawn up by the same body. Griffin, J. adverted to this point in his judgment: 'Whether it is constitutionally permissible for the College while remaining essentially the seminary of a particular religion, to be financed as it is by the State, and whether in any event its statutes need to be revised to meet its changed academic status and composition, are questions that lie outside the scope of this litigation.' There is no question but that Maynooth can be managed as a seminary by the Catholic bishops, and that they have the constitutional right to establish statutes which reflect the beliefs of the Church. But it seems as if one cannot have it constitutionally both ways: completely independent of state control as a religious seminary, and financed by the State as a recognized college of the National University.

47 See above, p. 201, where the *Declaration on Christian Education* only objects to a secular monopoly of schools.

48 *Rules for National Schools under the Department of Education* (Dublin: Government Publications, 1965); Rule 68, p. 38.

49 Archbishop John Roach, *loc. cit.*, 390-391.

50 Cf. John Locke, *A Letter Concerning Toleration*, pp. 32-33, where he rebukes those who only favour tolerance as long as they are in a minority, but as soon as they have a majority in a society, they enlist the support of civil authorities in favour of their version of orthodox religious belief. If the state should not indoctrinate young citizens, then it should not do so in favour of Roman Catholicism. In Locke's words, 'every church is orthodox to itself'. Since the state is not competent to decide between competing religious claims, the only consistent principle is to refrain from entanglement with religious controversies.

CHAPTER 9: THEORY AND IDEOLOGY

1 This thesis is almost the orthodox account in contemporary philosophy. See for example, Mary Hesse, *The Structure of Scientific Inference* (London: Macmillan, 1974), and W.V.O. Quine, *Word and Object* (M.I.T. Press, 1960), and *Ontological Relativity and Other Essays* (N.Y.: Columbia University Press, 1969).

2 For the theory-dependence of scientific facts, see N. Hanson, *Patterns of Discovery* (Cambridge University Press, 1958), and Paul K. Feyerabend, *Philosophical Papers*, 2 vols. (Cambridge University Press, 1981).

3 Cf. Thomas S. Kuhn, *The Structure of Scientific Revolutions*, 2nd ed. (University of Chicago Press, 1970), and G. Gutting, ed., *Paradigms and Revolutions* (University of Notre Dame Press, 1980).

4 Alasdair MacIntyre, *After Virtue* (University of Notre Dame Press, 1981).

5 A simplified version of 'Popperian' methodology would imply that scientific theories can be refuted by individual items of evidence which apparently contradict them. For a less strict description of the role of disconfirming evidence, see W.V. Quine and J.S. Ullian, *The Web of Belief*, 2nd ed. (N.Y.: Random House, 1978), and S.G. Harding, ed., *Can Theories be Refuted?* (Hague: Reidel, 1976).

6 Among recent attempts to analyse the concept of ideology see Karl Mannhein, *Ideology and Utopia* (New York: Harcourt, Brace, 1936); John Plamenatz, *Ideology* (New York: Praeger, 1970); Jorge Larrain, *The Concept of Ideology* (London: Hutchinson, 1979). The relevance of 'ideology' to Christian belief is examined by Nicholas Lash, in *A Matter of Hope: A Theologian's Reflections on the Thought of Karl Marx* (University of Notre Dame Press, 1982), Ch. 11, 'Ideology', pp. 125-134.

7 Mannhein, *op. cit.*, p. 36.

8 Cf. J. Habermas, *Knowledge and Human Interests* (Boston: Beacon Press, 1971), and David Bloor, *Knowledge and Social Imagery* (London: Routledge & Kegan Paul, 1976).

9 The difficult question of what counts as an explanation is avoided here. A mere redescription of a set of events in a new, fancy language is not an explanation, as Molière made clear with his example of 'sleep-inducing powers'. In standard scientific examples, to explain something is to give an account of the mechanism which causes it;

however, to explain a text is to interpret it, not to give an account of how it was written. Ideological explanations are more like the former than the latter.

10   Cf. Mannhein, *op. cit.*, p. 77: 'In our contemporary social and intellectual plight, it is nothing less than shocking to discover that those persons who claim to have discovered an absolute are usually the same people who also pretend to be superior to the rest.'

11   Cf. Catholic bishops' Submission to the New Ireland Forum, pp. 15-16: 'It will not do for a theologian to justify his position by invoking a principle of theological pluralism . . . it is for the larger community of the believers of the denomination *through its proper organs of authority* to decide whether these theological views come within the range of the acceptable in their effort to understand and explain the Faith, or whether, in fact, they go beyond just limits, and, if accepted, would ultimately prove destructive of the Church or denomination in question.' (Italics added) Authority decides what may or may not be believed.

12   A. MacIntyre, *Against the Self-Images of the Age* (New York: Shocken Books, 1971).

Bibliography

Abbott, Walter M., ed. *The Documents of Vatican II*. New York: Guild Press, 1966.

Adams, Michael. 'Censorship of Publications', in D.M. Clarke, ed., *Morality and the Law*, pp. 71-9.

Adams, Paul, *et al*. *Children's Rights*. New York: Praeger, 1971.

Barlow, A.C. *The Financing of Third-Level Education*. Dublin: Economic and Social Research Institute, 1981.

Berlin, I. *Two Concepts of Liberty*. Oxford: Clarendon Press, 1958.

Bier, William C. *Conscience: It's Freedom and Limitations*. New York: Fordham University Press, 1971.

Bird, Otto. *The Idea of Justice*. New York: Praeger, 1967.

Bloor, David. *Knowledge and Social Imagery*. London: Routledge and Kegan Paul, 1976.

Brest, Paul. 'The Fundamental Rights Controversy: The Essential Contradictions of Normative Constitutional Scholarship', *Yale Law Journal*, 90 (1981), 1063-1109.

Brown, Stuart M., Jr. 'Inalienable Rights', *Philosophical Review*, LXIV (1955), 192-211.

Brown, Terence. *Ireland: A Social and Cultural History, 1922-79*. Fontana, 1981.

Burke, Edmund. *The Works of the Right Honourable Edmund Burke*. 16 vols. London: Rivington, 1815.

Chubb, Basil. *The Constitution and Constitutional Change in Ireland*. Dublin: Institute of Public Administration, 1978.

Clarke, Desmond M. 'Natural Law and the Dynamics of the Will', *Philosophical Studies*, XXVII (1980), 40-54.

————. 'Emergency Legislation, Fundamental Rights, and Article 28.3.3° of the Irish Constitution', *The Irish Jurist*, XII (1977), 217-33.

————. 'The Concept of the Common Good in Irish Constitutional Law', *Northern Ireland Legal Quarterly*, 30 (Winter, 1979), 319-42.

————. 'The Role of Natural Law in Irish Constitutional Law', *The Irish Jurist*, XVII (1982), 187-220.

————. ed. *Morality and the Law*. Cork: Mercier Press, 1982.

————, and Dooley-Clarke, D. 'Definitions and Ethical Decisions', *Journal of Medical Ethics*, 3 (1977), 186-88.

Cohen, Howard. *Equal Rights for Children*. New Jersey: Rowman & Little-field, 1980.

Cohen, M., Nagel, J. and Scanlon, T., eds. *Equality and Preferential Treatment*. New Jersey: Princeton University Press, 1977.

Coleman, J. S. 'The Concept of Equality of Educational Opportunity', *Harvard Educational Review*, 38 (1968), 7-22.

Collins, Joseph. 'Law and the Common Good', *Irish Theological Quarterly*, XXIV (1957).

Coolahan, John. *Irish Education: History and Structure*. Dublin: Institute of Public Administration, 1981.

Cooper, David E. *Illusions of Equality*. London: Routledge and Kegan Paul, 1980.

Costello, Declan. 'The Natural Law and the Irish Constitution', *Studies* (Winter, 1956), 403-14.

_____. 'Aspects of a Juridically Developed Jurisprudence of Human Rights in Ireland', in *Understanding Human Rights: An Interdisciplinary and Inter-faith Study*, ed. Alan D. Falconer. Dublin: Irish School of Ecumenics, 1980.

Cranston, M. *What Are Human Rights?* London: Bodley, 1973.

Crowe, M.B. *The Changing Profile of the Natural Law*. Hague: Nijhoff, 1977.

Dahl, Robert A. *Dilemmas of Pluralist Democracy: Autonomy vs. Control*. New Haven and London: Yale University Press, 1982.

D'Arcy, Eric. *Conscience and its Right to Freedom*. London: Sheed and Ward, 1961.

Davis, Michael. 'The Budget of Tolerance', *Ethics*, 89 (1979), 165-78.

Denenfeld, Philip S. 'The Conciliar Declaration and the American Declara-tion', in John C. Murray, ed., *Religious Liberty: An End and a Beginning,* pp. 120-32.

d'Entrèves, A.P. *Natural Law*. 2nd ed. London: Hutchinson, 1979.

Devlin, Patrick. *The Enforcement of Morals*. London: Oxford University Press, 1965.

Duhen, Pierre. *To Save the Phenomena*. Chicago University Press, 1969.

Dworkin, Gerald. 'Paternalism', in R. Wasserstrom, ed. *Morality and the Law*. Belmont, California: Wadsworth, 1971.

Dworkin, Ronald. *Taking Rights Seriously*. London: Duckworth, 1977.

_____. 'What is Equality? Part I: Equality of Welfare; Part II: Equality of Resources'. *Philosophy & Public Affairs*, 10 (1981), 185-246; 283-245.

Ely, John Hart. *Democracy and Distrust*. Harvard University Press, 1980.

Eysenck, H.J. *Race, Intelligence and Education*. London: Temple Smith, 1971.

Farsan, Richard. *Birthrights*. New York: Macmillan, 1974.

Feinberg, Joel. *Rights, Justice, and the Bounds of Liberty*. Princeton Univer-sity Press, 1980.

Feyerabend, Paul K. *Philosophical Papers*. 2 vols. Cambridge University Press, 1981.

Field, Frank. *Inequality in Britain*. London: Fontana, 1981.

Finnis, John. *Natural Law and Natural Rights*. Oxford: Clarendon Press, 1980.

_____ and Grisez, G. 'The Basic Principles of Natural Law: A Reply to Ralph McInerny', *American Journal of Jurisprudence*, 20 (1981), 21-31.

Fisk, Milton. *Ethics and Society*. Sussex: Harvester Press, 1980.

Fiss, Owen M. 'The Forms of Justice', *Harvard Law Review*, 93 (1979), 1-58.

Flew, Anthony. *Sociology, Equality and Education*. London: Macmillan, 1976.

Foot, Philippa. 'Morality as a System of Hypothetical Imperatives', in *Virtues and Vices*. Oxford: Blackwell, 1978, pp. 157-73.

Forde, M. 'Equality and the Constitution', *The Irish Jurist*, XVII (1982), 295-339.

Frankena, William. 'The Naturalistic Fallacy', in J. Hospers and W. Sellars, eds., *Readings in Ethical Theory*. New York: Appleton-Century-Crofts, 1952.

Gaffney, Edward McGlynn, Jr., ed. *Private Schools and the Public Good: Policy Alternatives for the Eighties*. Indiana: University of Notre Dame Press, 1981.

Garvey, John H. 'Child, Parent, State, and the Due Process Clause: An Essay on the Supreme Court's Recent Work', *Southern California Law Review*, 51 (1978), 769-822.

Gaylin, Willard. 'The Competence of Children: No Longer All or Nothing', *Hastings Center Report*, 12 (April, 1982), 33-38.

_____, and Macklin, Ruth. *Who Speaks for the Child? The Problems of Proxy Consent*. New York and London: Plenum Press, 1982.

Goldman, Alan H. *Justice and Reverse Discrimination*. New Jersey: Princeton University Press, 1979.

Goldstein, Joseph; Freud, Anna; Solnit, A.J. *Beyond the Best Interests of the Child*, 2nd ed. New York: Free Press, 1979.

_____. *Before the Best Interests of the Child*. New York: Free Press, 1979.

Graham, Edgar. 'Religion and Education', *Northern Ireland Legal Quarterly*, 33 (1982), 20-51.

Greaney, Vincent and Kellaghan, Thomas. *Equality of Opportunity in Irish Schools*. Dublin: The Educational Company, 1984.

Grey, Thomas C. 'Do We Have an Unwritten Constitution?' *Stanford Law Review*, 27 (1975), 703-718.

Gutting, Gary, ed. *Paradigms and Revolutions*. Indiana: University of Notre Dame Press, 1980.

Habermas, J. *Knowledge and Human Interests*. Boston: Beacon Press, 1971.

Harman, Gilbert. *The Nature of Morality*. Oxford University Press, 1977.

Harding, S.G., ed. *Can Theories be Refuted?* The Hague: Reidel, 1976.

Harrison, Geoffrey. 'Relativism and Tolerance', *Ethics*, 86 (1986), 122-135.

Hart, H.L.A. 'Are there any Natural Rights?' *Philosophical Review*, LXIV (1955), 175-91.

————. *The Concept of Law.* Oxford: Clarendon Press, 1959.

————. *Law, Liberty and Morality.* Oxford University Press, 1963.

Hasler, August Bernhard. *How the Pope Became Infallible.* Translated by Peter Heinegg. New York: Doubleday and Co., 1981.

Henkin, Louis. *The Rights of Man Today.* Boulder, Colorado: Westview Press, 1978.

Henley, Kenneth. 'The Authority to Educate', in O'Neill and Ruddick, eds. *Having Children*, 254-64.

Hesse, Mary. *The Structure of Scientific Inference.* London: Macmillan, 1974.

Heuston, Robert F. 'Personal Rights under the Irish Constitution', *University of British Columbia Law Review*, XI (1977), 294-314.

Hudson, W.D. *The Is/Ought Question.* London: Macmillan, 1969.

Hume, David. *A Treatise of Human Nature.* Ed. by L.A. Selby-Bigge. Oxford, 1888.

Husak, Douglas N. 'Paternalism and Autonomy', *Philosophy and Public Affairs*, 10 (1981), 27-46.

Jencks, Christopher. *Inequality: A Reassessment of the Effect of Family and Schooling in America.* New York: Basic Books, 1972.

Jensen, A.R. *Genetics and Education.* Edinburgh: Constable, 1972.

Kant, I. *Foundations of the Metaphysics of Morals.* Trans. L.W. Beck. Indianapolis: Bobbs-Merrill, 1969.

Kelly, John. *Fundamental Rights in the Irish Law and Constitution*, 2nd ed. Dublin: Figgis, 1967.

————. *The Irish Constitution.* Dublin: Jurist, 1980.

Kirp, David L. *Just Schools.* University of California Press, 1982.

Kohlberg, Lawrence. 'Indoctrination versus Relativity in Value Education', *Zygon*, 6 (1971), 285-310.

Kuhn, Thomas S. *The Structure of Scientific Revolutions.* 2nd ed. Chicago: University of Chicago Press, 1970.

Larrain, Jorge. *The Concept of Ideology.* London: Hutchinson, 1979.

Lash, Nicholas. *A Matter of Hope: A Theologian's Reflections on the Thought of Karl Marx.* Indiana: University of Notre Dame Press, 1982.

Leff, A.A. 'Unspeakable Ethics, Unnatural Law', *Duke Law Journal*, (1979), 1229-49.

Locke, John. *Two Treatises of Government.* Ed. by Peter Laslett. 2nd ed. Cambridge University Press, 1970.

————. *A Letter Concerning Toleration.* Ed. by James H. Tully. Indianapolis: Hackett, 1983.

McCarney, Joe. *The Real World of Ideology.* Sussex: Harvester Press, 1980.
McDonagh, Enda. *Church and Politics.* Indiana: University of Notre Dame Press, 1980.
McInerny, Ralph. 'The Principles of Natural Law', *American Journal of Jurisprudence*, 25 (1980), 1-19.
MacIntyre, Alasdair. *Against the Self-Images of the Age.* New York: Schocken Books, 1971.
————. *After Virtue.* London: Duckworth, 1981.
Mackie, John L. *Ethics: Inventing Right and Wrong.* Penguin, 1977.
Mannhein, Karl. *Ideology and Utopia.* New York: Harcourt, Brace, 1936.
Manning, D.J., ed. *The Form of Ideology.* London: Allen & Unwin, 1980.
Maritain, Jacques. *The Rights of Man and Natural Law.* London: Centenary Press, 1944.
————. *The Person and the Common Good.* Indiana: University of Notre Dame Press, 1966.
Meiland, Jack W. and Krauz, M., eds. *Relativism: Cognitive and Moral.* Indiana: University of Notre Dame Press, 1982.
Melden, A.I. *Rights and Persons.* Berkeley: University of California Press, 1977.
Mill, J.S. *Three Essays on Religion.* London: Longmans, Green, Reader and Dyer, 1874.
————. *On Liberty.* Penguin, 1974.
Milder, Murray, Jr. *The Illusion of Equality: The Effect of Education on Opportunity, Inequality, and Social Conflict.* London: Jossey-Bass, Inc., 1972.
Mitchell, Basil. *Law, Morality and Religion in a Secular Society.* Oxford University Press, 1967.
Murphy, J.G. 'Incompetence and Paternalism', *Archiv für Rechts— und Sozialphilosophie*, 60 (1974), 465-86.
Murphy, Walter F. 'An Ordering of Constitutional Values', *Southern California Law Review,* 53 (1980), 703-760.
Murray, John Courtney, ed. *Religious Liberty: An End and a Beginning.* London: Collier-Macmillan, 1966.

Newman, Jay. 'The Idea of Religious Tolerance'. *American Philosophical Quarterly,* 15 (1978), 187-195.
————. *Foundations of Religious Tolerance.* Toronto: University of Toronto Press, 1982.
Noonan, John T., Jr. 'Natural Law, The Teaching of the Church and the Regulation of the Rhythm of Human Fecundity', *American Journal of Jurisprudence*, 25 (1980), 16-37.
Nozick, Robert. *Anarchy, State and Utopia.* Oxford: Blackwell, 1974.

O'Boyle, Michael P. 'Emergency Situations and the Protection of Human Rights; A Model Derogation Provision for a Northern Ireland Bill of Rights', *Northern Ireland Legal Quarterly*, 28 (1977), 160-187.

Ó Buachalla, Séamus. 'Education as an Issue in the First and Second Dáil', *Administration*, 25 (1977), 57-75.

O'Neill, Onora. 'Opportunities, Equalities and Education', *Theory and Decision*, 7 (1976), 275-95.

O'Neill, O., and Ruddick, W., eds. *Having Children*. Oxford University Press, 1979.

O'Reilly, James and Redmond, Mary, eds. *Cases and Materials on the Irish Constitution*. Dublin: Incorporated Law Society, 1980.

O'Reilly, James. 'Custody Disputes in the Irish Republic: The Uncertain Search for the Child's Welfare', *The Irish Jurist*, XII (1977), 37-65.

Osborough, W.N. 'Education in the Irish Law and Constitution', *The Irish Jurist*, XIII (1978), 145-180.

————. 'Irish Law and the Rights of the National Schoolteacher, Parts I and II', *The Irish Jurist*, XIV (1979), 36-60; 304-328.

Pennock, J. Roland, and Chapman, J.W., eds. *Human Rights* (Nomos XXIII). New York: New York University Press, 1981.

Pius XI, Pope. *Sixteen Encyclicals of His Holiness Pope Pius XI*. Washington: National Catholic Welfare Conference, n.d.

Plamenatz, John. *Ideology*. New York: Praeger, 1970.

Quine, W.V.O. *Word and Object*. Cambridge, Mass.: M.I.T. Press, 1960.

————. *Ontological Relativity and other Essays*. New York: Columbia University Press, 1969.

Quine, W.V.O. and Ullian, J.S. *The Web of Belief*. 2nd ed. New York: Random House, 1978.

Rawls, John. *A Theory of Justice*. Oxford: Clarendon Press, 1971.

Rees, John. *Equality*. London: Macmillan, 1971.

Ross, Jaries F. 'A Natural Rights Basis for Substantive Due Process of Law', *Universal Human Rights*, 2 (1980), 61-79.

Schauer, Frederick. *Free Speech: A Philosophical Inquiry*. Cambridge University Press, 1982.

Singer, Peter. *Practical Ethics*. Cambridge University Press, 1979.

Stanlis, Peter J. *Edmund Burke and the Natural Law*. Ann Arbor, Mich.: University of Michigan Press, 1958.

Strauss, L. *Natural Right and History*. University of Chicago Press, 1953.

Strike, Kenneth L. *Educational Policy and the Just Society*. Urbana: University of Illinois Press, 1982.

Teitelbaum, Lee E. 'The Meanings of Rights of Children', *New Mexico Law Review*, 10 (1979-80), 235-253.

Ten, C.L. *Mill on Liberty*. Oxford: Clarendon Press, 1980.

Titley, E. Brian. *Church, State, and the Control of Schooling in Ireland 1900-1944*. Dublin: Gill and Macmillan, 1983.

Tuck, Richard. *Natural Rights Theories*. Cambridge University Press, 1979.

Tussing, Dale. *Irish Educational Expenditures — Past, Present and Future*. Dublin: Economic and Social Research Institute, 1978.

Twining, W.L. and P.E. 'Benthan on Torture', *Northern Ireland Legal Quarterly*, 24 (1973), 305-456.

Van Eikema Hommes, H.J. *Major Trends in the History of Legal Philosophy*. Amsterdam: North-Holland, 1979.

Vardin, Patrick A.; Brody, Y.N., eds. *Children's Rights: Contemporary Perspectives*. New York: Teacher's College Press, 1979.

Vatican II. *Constitutiones, Decreta, Declarationes*. Rome: Vatican Press, 1966.

Wald, Michael S. 'Children's Rights — A Framework for Analysis', *UCD Law Review*, 12 (1979), 255-82.

Wasserstrom, R., ed. *Morality and the Law*. Belmont, California: Wadsworth, 1971.

Weale, Albert. *Equality and Social Policy*. London: Routledge and Kegan Paul, 1978.

Whyte, J.H. *Church and State in Modern Ireland, 1933-1979,* 2nd ed. Dublin: Gill and Macmillan, 1980.

Wilkerson, Albert E. *The Rights of Children*. Philadelphia: Temple University Press, 1973.

Williams, Bernard. 'The Idea of Equality', in *Problems of the Self* (Cambridge University Press, 1973).

Wollheim, Richard. 'Equality', *Proceedings of the Aristotelian Society*, New Series, VI (1955-56), 282.

Wolff, R.P., *et al. A Critique of Pure Tolerance*. Boston: Beacon Press, 1965.

Wolff, R.P. *In Defence of Anarchism*. New York: Harper & Row, 1970.

Wringe, C.A. *Children's Rights: A Philosophical Study*. London: Routledge and Kegan Paul, 1981.

Index

Abbot, W. M., 258n3
Abington School District v. *Schempp*, 223
Adams, M., 248n4 (Ch. 1)
amendments of the Constitution; fourth, 253n2; fifth, 107, 256n29; eighth, 253n20
Application of Michael Woods, 253n2
Aquinas, St. Thomas, 49, 51, 52, 58, 59, 67, 120, 249n6, 252n17, 252n6
Aristotelian science, 50-52, 58
Aristotle, 50, 51, 52, 58
authority, 39-40, 102, 106
autonomy, 11-14, 17, 20, 61, 85-6, 126-127, 131, 144, 147, 185, 218, 246
axioms, 51, 249n5

Barlow, A. C. 257n8
Bellotti v. *Baird*, 259n34
Berlin, I., 252n10
Bloor, D., 261n8
Brown, S. M. Jr., 255n11
Buckley v. *A-G.*, 154, 164
Burke, E., 11, 247n1 (Intro.)
Byrne, C., 247n5

Care, N. S., 252n7
Carey v. *Population Services International*, 259n34
Casti Connubii, 61, 64, 133, 249n19, 250n25, 250n27, 253n14
certainty, vs. truth, 103-4
children's rights, 205-6, 208-9, 219-20
Clarke, D. M., 247n4, 248n4 (Ch. 2), 254n8, 255n24, 256n38
Cohen, H., 260n34
Coolahan, J., 258n2

Coleman, J. S., 257n3
Collins, J., 256n31
common good, 18, 86, 211, 136-69 *passim*; definition of, 149-62
competence, 124, 127-8, 129, 175
conceptual change, 229-30, 234-5
contraception, 57, 63-66
convention, 29-30
Copernicus, N., 52
Costello, D., 145, 254n6, 255n20
Cranston, M., 254n9
Crowe, B., 248n3 (Ch. 2)
Crowley v. *Ireland*, 259n29

Dahl, R. A., 247n2
D'Arcy, E., 251n9
Davis, M., 250n6
Declaration on Christian Education, 197-204 *passim*, 261n147
Declaration on Religious Freedom, 91, 95-111 *passim*, 198, 200, 203, 261n13, 252n15
Denenfeld, P. S., 252n14
denominational schools, 108
d'Entrèves, A. P., 248n3 (Ch. 2)
desert, 184
de Valera, E., 256n30
Devlin, P., 252n3
Directive Principles of Social Justice, 152-3
Dooley-Clarke, D., 254n8
Duhem, P., 249n9
Dworkin, G., 252n8
Dworkin, R., 255n13

education, 18, 19, 107-108, 196-226 *passim*; in the Constitution, 204-214

271